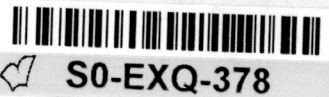

Data archives
for the social sciences:
purposes, operations
and problems

David Nasatir
Director, International Data
Library and Reference Service
Survey Research Center
University of California, Berkeley

Unesco

Recognizing that the formation of international archives of investigations conducted in the social sciences has become essential for the development of research and of international co-operation in research, the Director-General of the United Nations Educational, Scientific and Cultural Organization (Unesco) was authorized under resolution 3.221, adopted by the General Conference of Unesco at its fifteenth (1968) session, to study the conditions required for the establishment within an international centre of card indexes of archives of investigations carried out in the domain of the social sciences.

Dr. David Nasatir of the International Data Library and Reference Service, Survey Research Center, University of California at Berkeley, was contracted to carry out the feasibility study. The conclusions of his study and the recommendations for the establishment of an International Federation of the Directors of Social Science Data Banks are contained in the last chapter of this study report.

Social science data, existing in a format that can be manipulated by computing machinery, can be used for many purposes in addition to those for which they were initially collected. Scholars and government planners should have ready and equal access to such material and these groups will be best served if they are informed regarding the characteristics of the materials available to them and the means for their proper utilization. Several barriers prevent the realization of this goal. Foremost among them is the absence of a central organization that will co-ordinate the activities of diverse independent efforts; establish standards for processing, documenting, and storing data; work toward developing procedures for servicing the needs of users; disseminate information pertaining to the operations and contents of social science data archives; provide a common meeting ground for professionals engaged in the management and development of these archives; and help to secure funds to accomplish these tasks. The study report is concerned with overcoming the barriers to realizing the fullest utilization of machine readable social science data.

TABLE OF CONTENTS

Chapter 1

AN OVERVIEW OF THE ARCHIVE MOVEMENT

THE DATA EXPLOSION

The social scientist of today is faced with a surfeit of data. Every hour of every day the production of data from academic, commercial and governmental sources continues at an increasing pace. Most of this information is seen only in its organized form - that is, reports, analyses, and interpretations of data as it appears in books, monographs, articles, reports and similar productions of what is sometimes called "hard copy". It is to the tables and charts, the graphs and correlations, percentages and statistical analyses that the reader turns as he studies the ways in which the author of the particular study has rearranged, summarized and interpreted the data at hand.

Traditionally, the rôle of the scholar, scientist and analyst has been to study the work of others and accept or modify conclusions based upon the data presented. In some cases the research worker goes on to rearrange published data, to summarize it or analyse it in some new fashion and to publish some new analysis of it. More and more, however, data is produced which is never published and never appears in "hard copy". The amount of data gathered for the 1970 census of the United States, for example, is so vast that a complete analysis and interpretation - even a complete publication of all of this material - is not even contemplated. Similarly, as an ordinary by-product of the workings of governments and industry, a tremendous flow of raw data is regularly produced for which there is little or no possibility of organization and publication in a traditional form. Even where data is gathered to answer a specific question or describe a particular situation, it is increasingly the case that far more data is gathered than will actually be utilized. This is also characteristic of work in a great variety of scholarly disciplines. More data is gathered by scholars attempting to reconstruct genealogies of fourteenth century Florentine families, or in the attempt to determine the mobility rates of immigrant groups in nineteenth century Philadelphia, for example, than can ever be exploited by the historical researcher himself - by his own admission. Thus the generally recognized explosion of information reflected in the increasing flow of journals and articles, of books and other publications, is only a very weak indicator of the real explosion in the production of social science data.

The data itself, without interpretation or analysis, is being produced in ever increasing amounts and stored on punched cards, paper tapes, magnetic tapes, magnetic discs, microfilm, and a variety of mechanical devices which facilitate its rapid retrieval, rearrangement, processing and summarization. Unlike the traditional published format, raw data in a form suitable for direct input to and manipulation by modern computing machinery facilitates analysis and reanalysis by permitting its reorganization and summarization time and time again at a minimum of cost and a maximum of speed according to the interest and skills of the individual analyst. Where analysts differ in their needs, the same information may be organized, summarized, analysed, and criticized from a variety of perspectives with equal facility. Machine readability of data facilitates its retrieval and reanalysis in a way that publication in traditional form does not.

In addition to traditional sources of statistics such as government and industry, the past four decades have also produced a continuously growing amount of data on an extraordinary variety of topics due to steadily growing interest in public opinion polling and market research. The success of these techniques has led to a steady increase in the number of firms engaged in this type of research and in the amount of data produced by them. The great impetus to this development was given, of course, by the refinement of scientific sampling theory and its application to the social sciences combined with the availability of automatic data processing equipment to permit the handling of the vast amount of information produced by polling procedures. Also, in the post-World War II era, an increasing amount of money and equipment became available for social science research and for social scientists, not only for the scientific and commercial interests but also in response to an ever more pressing quest for data to satisfy the needs of government and the requirements of rational planning. The result has been a torrent of data from these sources which in many cases has paralysed and immobilized researchers and decision-makers rather than assisting them in their quest for knowledge. This paradox arises from the recognition that the desired data may already exist - somewhere, but is not readily available.

THE UTILITY OF DATA FOR SECONDARY ANALYSIS

Data gathered for specific purposes may also be of additional utility for a great variety of other purposes - not all of which may have been anticipated by the original data gathered. One of the most important of such uses is to provide a basis for comparative analysis. Independent studies of the same population often provide a basis for testing the validity of findings generate on rather specialized samples. In this way, more general propositions may be formulated on the basis of a variety of data sets rather than narrow propositions based only on a single one - as is usually done. In a similar manner, propositions derived from general theories can be tested with data from a variety of independent sources and providing, thereby, more rigorous tests and stronger assurances in the robustness of the final conclusions. Kenneth M. Walker's work on political socialization provides a good example of this kind of research (Revista Latinoamericana de Sociología, Vol. 65, No. 2, p. 200), as does that done by Glaucio A.D. Soares on political attitudes of intellectuals (Revista Latinoamericana de Sociología, Vol. 66, No. 1, p. 43). In both instances the authors utilized data collected in several countries independently by other research workers - for other purposes - to generate and to test hypotheses.

Independent studies of the same population have been used by secondary analysis to gain some estimate of biases in the data, and the reanalysis of existing data also permits the employment of new analytic models and techniques as well as the generation of entirely new theoretical perspectives. Contemporary reanalysis of early opinion polling and census data is now being carried out with the employment of statistical models undeveloped at the time the data was initially gathered and performing computations that simply were not possible prior to the availability of modern computing machinery.

Robert Alford has shown (Party and Society) how the relationship of the same variables can be studied in different populations to permit the elaboration of analyses, testing the robustness of relationships, and examining the generality of the conclusions. Thus secondary and comparative analyses

of this type often may utilize data from many different sources in ways never anticipated by the initial new data gatherers. In a similar fashion, new levels of theorizing and analysis are now permitted by the facility to mix different units of analysis. Census data and survey data may be combined, aggregate and individual data synthesized to provide new insights into historical periods, social processes and contextual effects. The facility with which such data manipulation can now be accomplished has given a considerable impetus to the development of new social science theories as well as the analysis of more complicated social phenomena.

In addition to the analytical uses of already existing data, the archiving of data provides a new opportunity for systematic review of existing work from a historical perspective. It is now possible to examine election polls from a 30-year period, for example, so that studies initially designed as single, cross-sectional, independent samples become transformed into historical time series.

The richness of new data resources are now being used in teaching students the intricacies of data analysis. A common complaint of professors everywhere has been that time and resources rarely permit students to gather data of sufficient magnitude and quality to permit their instruction in even the most elementary of analytical techniques. By utilizing materials already available, however, it is possible to introduce students to the most advanced and sophisticated kind of data processing and statistical, analytical techniques, while working with sophisticated and stimulating data.

The existence of already collected machine readable data has finally made it possible for scholars to focus upon a single problem and to bring together general different studies of various kinds and various types for their analyses. The resulting integrated data base, permits testing of many complex hypotheses not one of which was ever anticipated by the initial researchers and gatherers of the data.

DIFFICULTIES OF THE INDIVIDUAL RESPONSE TO THE DATA EXPLOSION

There have been many and varied attempts to deal with this explosion of data. The first were those of concerned individuals and scholars who wished to bring together materials necessary for their own work. They quickly discovered, however, that they were confronted with tremendous costs and many difficulties in obtaining the materials and in dealing with the data once it had been acquired. In order to acquire the materials, a great deal of time and energy must be spent in simply determining their location. This involves scanning the appropriate literature to discover possible leads and then trying to communicate with the authors of the appropriate articles or books - if, in fact, those authors can be located. Or it may mean finding some appropriate person within a ministry or firm which may have been responsible for the initial production of the materials. In many cases this involves a considerable effort to try and discover where the materials might actually be stored - if they still exist at all. Many commercial firms and government agencies (as well as individual scholars) have not been particularly sensitive to the variety of possible uses which might be made of their data by others. Consequently they have not taken particular pains to store the data in any form that would facilitate its re-use.

Even when the location of the materials can be determined, it is often necessary for the interested researcher to travel directly to the source of the materials in order to receive an actual copy as local suppliers often do not have adequate facilities (reproducing machines) to produce copies easily for other users. Extensive travel may also be necessary in order to convince potential suppliers of the legitimacy of the secondary analyst and of the purposes to which the data will be put. It has often been necessary for scholars to spend a great deal of time developing a close personal contact with the potential supplier of each set of data actually acquired.

Once acquired, however, materials are usually not in a form that lend themselves readily to immediate utilization by someone else. Ambiguities in coding, local conventions in data formating and a general lack of appropriate documentation all conspire to make secondary analysis difficult. Data must therefore be prepared using skilled local specialists to translate existing documentation, if that is necessary, recreate the necessary documentation in considerable detail where possible, verify the nature of codes that have actually been employed and, generally "clean" the data to remove erroneous punches, identify ambiguous ones and change the data format where necessary in order to make it more suitable for local computer installations. Such procedures are usually prohibitively costly to permit their employment by any individual scholar.

A heavy burden often faced by the individual scholar trying to respond to the data explosion is simply a lack of sufficient expertise in a variety of unrelated fields. In order to prepare data for local processing, for example, even when the data arrives in machine readable form, the services of one or more assistants who have skills in both the substantive area of the proposed investigation and those necessary to deal with computers and computing itself are usually required. Such people are costly and hard to find. As a consequence it is usually necessary to retain them on a continuing basis. It is difficult and inefficient to train a new assistant to work on each study that is acquired. Note that in addition to the standard needs for data processing associated with the secondary analysis of materials it is also necessary to have people capable of "cleaning"

data and translating documentary materials - often from languages or frequently encountered in the research workers own environment - into a language more widely spoken, read and understood. Clearly, it takes highly specialized personnel for these tasks as well as others associated with the acquisition, preparation, storage and retrieval of data for secondary analysis.

As the amount of information actually available for reanalysis grows, it becomes increasingly important to devote energies to indexing and documenting the materials at hand. This often requires a further reliance on computers due to the magnitude and complexity of the task. This in turn requires keypunching of the initial data documentation. Once a considerable investment has been made to acquire materials and to make them useful for secondary analysis, their very possession often becomes a real burden to the research worker initially acquiring them as others begin to make inquiries of him and requests for the finished or processed data.

ARCHIVE GOALS

While the archives are manifestly organized for the obvious purpose of gathering together and preserving data which might otherwise be lost, thereby making it possible to prevent duplication and waste in data gathering which would take place if existing data sources were simply ignored, they are also organized to create integrated collections of data. They bring together materials from different perspectives on the same topic bringing together materials which may have been gathered by different individuals or for different purposes but which provide in their combination a new and much greater resource and synthesizing materials collected on the same topic at different periods of time. Archives have been used in efforts to create social indicators that will measure the state of the polity and a society over time - the level of political discontent, for example, or changing civic attitudes, observing the responses of the populus to health programmes, monitoring the impact of educational processes. But the consequences of these efforts are important organizationally as well as scientifically. In most instances, for example, the creation of an archive also creates a collection of specialized people. Specialists focus on specific topics or disciplines within the complex of the archive setting by utilizing the resource of the data archive. The interaction between problem-oriented research workers and technical people concerned with making the data accessible provides a research context of much greater potential than is normally found in the case of the individual researcher working in relative isolation. Perhaps, then, the most important purpose of data archives is not gathering data but facilitating research.

THE FORMATION OF DATA ARCHIVES

The obvious advantages of archives combined with problems outlined above confronting the individual researcher, have led to several independent attempts to create more general archives of machine readable data in the social sciences organizations, that would facilitate the work of many scholars and policy-makers. Occasionally, individual scholars have mustered sufficient resources to create personal archives. That is, studies required for a scholar's own work would be brought together and, by dint of his own efforts (as well as those of a research assistant or two) would form the nucleus of a collection tailored specifically for his own needs. Of course this is a solution available only to those researchers with considerable resources and is hardly designed to maximize the returns on the initial investment. Nevertheless, some of these private collections have evolved into more public facilities; particularly as the cost of their maintenance became so great as to require the support of external funds.

A more promising approach to the creation of archives of machine readable social science materials has emerged from attempts to adapt already existing information service organizations to serve the data needs of local clientèle. Thus as long ago as 1957, York Lucci and Stein Rokkan proposed a library centre of survey research data in a project sponsored by the School of Library Service at Columbia University. Yet few libraries have actually developed any awareness of machine readable social science data - not to mention a capacity for dealing with it directly. The relative unresponsiveness of such organizations to deal with what might appear to be a logical and reasonable extension of their traditional services is intriguing. A brief examination (based on an original paper by Howard White of the Graduate School of Library Science at the University of California, Berkeley) of barriers to successful efforts along this line is instructive for anyone interested in the problems of establishing social science data archives. The shortage of properly trained personnel and the absence of training programmes, as will be noted in the following paragraphs, constitutes, perhaps, the most difficult barrier to the development of library associated data archives. Inherent in the librarian's difficulties can be seen some of the obstacles to the creation of social science data archives in general.

The management of data archives, whether in the social sciences or in other academic fields, is a subject at the frontier of librarianship as far as training is concerned. Librarians in America and in the United Kingdom are only now becoming adjusted to the computer as an aid in performing some of their traditional work, such as circulation control and cataloguing. These are, needless to say, book-related jobs, and even the introduction of "information science" into library school curricula has had a strong documentary thrust, involving,

e.g., automatic classification or automatic indexing of scientific papers. The growth of data archives, as mentioned before, has come about as a by-product of the growth in censuses and sample surveys. While the finished studies - documents - emerging from such projects have been accepted by librarians as their responsibility, the raw data have always been left to the social scientists in control of the projects to manage as they saw fit. Usually the data were recorded on cards or tapes - media not traditionally in the library purview - and the idea of running a service in which the cards or tapes were used for new studies (secondary analysis) has recommended itself chiefly to teachers in the social sciences, rather than to librarians. It is an idea that librarians would find immediately intelligible, since it parallels work of their own, but it cannot be said to have been presented in such a way that librarians would see it as an opportunity, and not merely a new headache.

"Social science data archives", Clifton Brock writes, "have developed entirely outside the scope of library systems; apparently no data archive is operated by or in conjunction with a library."[1] Reflecting the separation between the two activities, his report on bibliographical services in political science deals first with a "literature sector", in which he discusses printed materials found in research libraries, and then with a "data sector". In the latter part he summarizes events in the history of the data archive movement (through ca. 1966), the notable fact being that the scholars, organizations, and publications he names are wholly outside the world of conventional librarianship. There is scant reason to believe that the gap has been closed as of 1971. A check of Library Literature, for instance, shows that, although the headings "Archives, Social Science" and "Data Archives" have been established, this major indexing service for librarians has scarcely used them during the past five years, despite the outpouring of articles on the subject. The reviews (totaling 150 pages) of the literature of sociology and political science in A Reader's Guide to the Social Sciences,[2] an otherwise impressive new handbook for librarians, make no mention of data archives. In so far as reports of social science data archives have penetrated the "information science press" (e.g., bulletins such as Information Retrieval and Library Automation) or the publications dealing with national informational policies, they are likely to be found in the collections of schools of librarianship. But it is doubtful whether these reports have entered librarians' professional reading and discussion to any extent, and the schools seem to lag still farther behind. Although tapes are mentioned when the new "non-book" media are discussed for librarians, only music and foreign language tapes seem to have reached textbook status.[3]

In short, the lines of cleavage that appeared five years ago, when Jack Ferguson attempted a typology of social science information sources, probably still hold. [4] Ferguson's study was an off-shoot of the survey conducted by the National Science Foundation and Columbia University's Bureau of Applied Social Research to gather material for A Directory of Information Resources in the United States: Social Sciences. He divided information sources along four dimensions: (1) whether their input was literature or data; (2) whether their output was literature or data; (3) whether in processing the input they merely collected it or transformed it; and (4) whether their organizational goal was to initiate research or to facilitate research. A figure is reproduced from Ferguson overleaf, showing his examples of the various types of sources. The library gets literature as input, processes it into an organized collection, and releases it as output, in order to facilitate research. The data bank or archive carries out a parallel activity; inputting data, processing it into a collection, and outputting it, again to facilitate research. However, the basic division between literature and data remains. Ferguson may have intended ideal types, but actual libraries and data archives in the social sciences seem to follow his scheme; there is very little evidence that the two kinds of organizations are converging.

Who's pursuing whom?

One may wonder why the two should converge if they deal with basically different materials. After all, we see few mergers between libraries and museums, even though their operations are often comparable. The British Museum, which also houses the national library of the United Kingdom, has been described as organizationally anachronistic. Are libraries seeking alliances with data archives, or is it the other way about?

The initiatives toward mergers have come almost exclusively from data archive advocates, who seem to see libraries as a financially secure and relatively stable base of operations. Their arguments have stressed the kindred nature of data management and the management of literature. Thus a political scientist, Ithiel de Sola Pool, has argued:

The storing of basic data in retrievable and manipulable form is, indeed, a library function. The library is an archive of that type of information that is of interest to many members of the university community and that is too bulky or expensive for each to retain or own.
If this is a function of the library in the university, then clearly data archives also belong in the library. Records of /survey and census data/ are of great interest to large numbers of members of the academic community, yet are too mammoth and too expensive for any member of the community to obtain them for himself. They therefore belong in the library where all can share them. [5]

His essay, which appeared as an appendix to the 1965 report on the Massachusetts Institute of Tech-

nology's (M. I. T.) information transfer experiments (INTREX), was well placed to be seen by the more technologically advanced librarians, particularly those veering toward information science, but it appears to have had little influence. An argument along similar lines was presented by Ralph L. Bisco, Executive Director of the Council of Social Science Data Archives, in a 1967 speech at the dedication ceremony for the Graduate Research Library, University of Florida. [6] Asking, "Why should university libraries undertake data services when social science data archives are already providing them?" Bisco gave a five-point answer. In brief:

The library's acquisitions staff could obtain cards or tapes from distant archives, even when an archive existed on campus to serve the local faculty.
It would be a natural extension of the library's reference service to move from seeking statistics in printed sources to seeking them as machine output, tailored to user demands.
The library may become a storage and service agency for all sorts of machine readable texts produced by the publishing industry, and therefore may find survey and census data merely another routine type of material.
The library could increase its range of informational resources for teaching and research if it took on data services.
The library's conventionally trained personnel could learn data-base management and development from the archivists, while the latter profited from the librarians' knowledge of such matters as indexing.

In the same year as Bisco's speech, however, a group of his colleagues took a much more pessimistic view of the situation in a study made for the National Academy of Sciences. [7] They frankly pointed out that proposed liaisons between data archives and academic libraries were motivated by the weak financial position of the archives. They were not even sanguine about "general university support" of archives over the long run, and looked to some sort of federal financing as the only long-term solution. The group, whose chairman was Philip E. Converse of the University of Michigan's Survey Research Center, drafted what is still probably the best brief description of why the academic libraries have not been receptive to the data archive movement:
Some years ago it appeared plausible that maintenance of repositories of behavioural science research data would gradually be brought under the umbrella of the conventional research library in matters of personnel and financing, after the initial innovative phase. Such a possibility is not, of course, to be ruled out completely for the future, but it is already clear that such a future remains distant.
Most data facilities for research are growing up outside conventional library institutions. Few research libraries are adequately subsidized or staffed even to keep up with current advances in bibliographic automation. Pressures to fulfil a

PRODUCTION TYPOLOGY FOR INFORMATION SOURCES

COLLECT

Output

Input	Literature	Data
Literature	Library	
Data		--Museum --"Data Bank" --Archives

TRANSFORM

Output

Input	Literature	Data
Literature	--State-of-the art reviewing --Abstracting and translating services	--Content analysis center
Data	--Research organization	--Statistics organization

ORGANIZATIONAL TYPOLOGY FOR INFORMATION SOURCES

INITIATE RESEARCH

Processing

Input	Collects	Transforms
Literature		Content analysis center
Data		Research organization

FACILITATE RESEARCH

Processing

Input	Collects	Transforms
Literature	Library	--State-of-the art reviewing --Abstracting and translating services
Data	--Public Museum --"Data Bank" --Archives	

new set of rôles in the maintenance of archives of machine readable behaviour science data are understandably greeted with indifference, if not horror, by research librarians. At his formative stage conventional libraries appear overwhelmed by information revolutions on other fronts. The differentiation between "book libraries" and "data libraries" is likely to persist for some time, and may even harden permanently. [8]

The report in which these paragraphs appear was written at a time when the Council of Social Science Data Archives was functioning, and the writers placed their hopes in it and in the United States Government for improved data services. In light of the international character of the data archive movement, it is interesting that, in their recommendations section, they mention international organizations (e.g. Unesco) only where improvements in conventional documentation are concerned, not when they discuss their hopes for data services. Perhaps they were wise. It would seem that tape librarianship, only barely established in the United States and Western Europe, is even more of a novelty in other places.

How are they trained?

If tape librarianship is emerging as an occupation, how is it that it has made so little impact on the library school curricula? The answer is hard to come by. Many library schools are now offering courses in "information science", library automation, non-book media and technologies, industrial librarianship, and information services for scientists. It is relatively easy to find what various schools offer on paper, but not to find what they actually teach. There have been conferences on the training of "science information specialists", sponsored by the National Science Foundation; the proceedings do not appear to be oriented toward the social sciences, nor do they take up the problems of running a data library. [9] (Although they are filled with descriptions of courses that might prepare persons superbly well for such a job, one observes struggles to define basic terms and a good deal of attention to propaedeutics.) It remains difficult to find out the backgrounds of the persons who are actually running tape libraries. Rowena Swanson of the Air Force Office of Scientific Research, who has made some effort to be informed on the training of information specialists, has this to say:

There are no less than three distinctly different sets of people, with vastly different academic backgrounds, involved in information work today at least in the U.S.A. Most professional librarians hold bachelor's degrees in the arts or humanities; they qualify as librarians after one year of subsequent study in a library school. Individuals for whom there is no generally accepted occupational title range from subject specialists with Ph.D.'s to high school graduates. (The title "information specialist" or "information scientist" is often used for those at the mature end of the spectrum.) Computer personnel range from senior computer scientists to clever programmer "dropouts". [10]

When persons who have talked to a good many practising librarians make general assessments of their competence vis-à-vis the computer, we usually find that the "arts or humanities" background referred to above has not served them well:

The education and training of professional librarians and other library personnel has ill-prepared them to appreciate or assimilate the capabilities and promise of the new technology. At the same time, persons skilled in the computing art and in other aspects of the changing technology are rarely equipped to deal with the specific and complex requirements of library operations. [11]

The latter point should be borne in mind when the temptation arises to belittle librarians for their deficiencies. Persons without library training or experience who have made computer science their platform for re-doing librarianship have been brought up short many times; for instance:

It seemed almost ludicrous for computer scientists and engineers to be discussing automation in libraries when they did not have the slightest acquaintance with elementary bibliographic apparatus. Indeed, the lack of training and exposure to such systems may account for the large number of absurd "solutions" offered by hardware-oriented engineers who were not conscious that one might retrieve information in one minute by use of a printed index that would require hours on the most sophisticated computer available. [12]

The real difficulty seems to lie in the infrequency with which almost all non-librarians (even if they are knowledgeable in social science techniques involving the computer) consult librarians on projects of mutual interest. Thus York Lucci, in what is probably the earliest major formulation of a proposal for a social science data archive, gives considerable attention to the problems of cataloguing the material, appears to grasp the almost chaotic state of the art in this particular field, but believes the technical kinks can be worked out by one librarian employed on a half-time basis. [13] Such naïveté would be terrifying if it were not so typical. An English librarian, commenting on the deficient indexing of Kendall and Doig's Bibliography of Statistical Literature (an inventory not too different from the sort data archivists might compile) is very forthright:

The point here is not that Professor Kendall should have left the whole task to librarians, but that if their participation had been sought in the early stages of his project, a means might have been found of meeting a very much wider range of needs than does the present work, with only a little more effort than has gone into it now. The economical application of bibliographical techniques for specific functions is something central to the practice of librarianship, and there was a clear chance here for a contribution. (14)

Librarians were not altogether left out of the deliberations of the Council of Social Science Data Archives; Bisco, in the speech mentioned earlier, names two (Herbert Ahn and William Jones) who were members of the information retrieval committee. (15) And in looking over the staff lists of various social science data archives in the United States, one sees persons who are designated "librarian", but of course there is no way of telling what their training or their contribution is without direct inquiries.

The thin end

There is one development, observable now, that might serve to transform at least a few exceptionally advanced libraries into repositories of machine readable records. At the same time it might confront conventionally trained librarians, in an unprecedented way, with the implications of data management as a new professional field. That is the Census Bureau's interest in letting libraries manage the summary tapes of the 1970 census. A member of the Bureau's Data Access and Use Laboratory writes:

The convenience of such a set-up where users could go directly to a local library and borrow tapes and printouts or acquire them outright is obvious. To turn this possibility into reality, the Lab is approaching a number of libraries. The Lab decided to contact first some 12 libraries which seem most likely to be interested and capable of becoming part of the 1970 census summary tape distribution network. These libraries, nine of which are university-affiliated and three are State libraries, are government depository libraries and hence presumably familiar with census materials and aware of the importance of census data in meeting the nation's information needs. They are also participants in the Library of Congress' Project MARC and presumably equipped with the necessary facilities, experience, and interest in managing data on computer tape. (16)

This is the one area in which the data archive movement is converging with academic libraries. The coming together of the two still seems highly problematical. It is true that sociologists and political scientists have long been aware of the potential of new cross-tabulations from Census Bureau tapes as evidence in research. It is also true that businessmen have on occasion derived fresh marketing data from the tapes. But whether a new public will turn to libraries with computer capability for novel manipulations of the data remains to be seen. If the census tapes form the thin end of the wedge, a large number of sample survey data tapes now held in archives may follow. Along with them will come the problems of cataloguing tapes variable responses (and the accompanying documentation) that up to now the library profession has hardly encountered, let alone solved.

A final problem must be mentioned. For data archive work involving studies not made in a major European language, linguistic competence as well as a knowledge of tape librarianship is desirable. Librarians with the language skills to organize collections in the various "area studies", or from the developing countries, are probably even rarer than librarians with training in computer science. Since competence in non-Western languages is rare among professionals with library school training (even assuming they know something about managing computer tapes), students with the requisite language skills would seem to be worth training as data archivists in major language capitals, just as many are now trained to be librarians there. (17) In saying this, I am assuming that library schools, information science departments, or perhaps social science institutes will develop courses in data library management that do not now exist. Failing that, on-the-job training with governmental or even private agencies having tape libraries would remain a possibility.

A third distinct approach to the problem of creating an archive of machine readable social science materials has been to look beyond the library and create a special organization uniquely suited to serving a local clientele. Thus the Center for International Studies Data Bank at the Massachusetts Institute of Technology was especially created to serve the needs of scholars at that institution interested in the utilization of a common data base for a variety of purposes.

A fourth mode for the creation of data archives has been to concentrate on data suppliers and, for example, to establish a special bureau to serve the particular clientele of organizations devoted to the production of data. Thus the Data Access and Use Laboratory of the United States Census responds to the requests of users throughout the world for information from their holdings. They take primary responsibility for the preservation of the data files in their organization and for promoting the widespread use of these particular materials.

A fifth type of data archive root has been the creation of a unique organization to serve a very general clientele; the International Data Library and Reference Service of the University of California is a good example. This organization initially formed to serve the needs of a local scholar, was transformed with the assistance of the National Science Foundation. In its revitalized form it was designed to facilitate the access of scholars throughout the world to social science materials (in machine readable form) gathered in Asia and Latin America. Thus a variety of substantive materials covering a broad geographical range attracts the interest of a great diversity of scholars.

A sixth type has been the creation of a special organization to serve a very special clientele - such as government planning bureaux. The creation of the Columbia University School of Public Health and Administrative Medicine Research Archives, for example, has been particularly responsive to the needs of medical researchers at Columbia.

In every attempt to deal with the problem of archiving machine readable social science data, several problems seem to emerge again and again. Each organization, for example, has had to face the dilemma of acquiring relatively specific materials as opposed to the problem of developing a policy to include more broadly related materials.

In the case of some institutions, the consequences of an early policy decision on this matter has been the cause of later success or failure. A decision to acquire, uncritically, the entire production of several commercial polling sources, or to peruse all data on a topic without regard for methodological quality has, in some cases, inundated the archive with data and overcome its resources. Such decisions often make it extremely difficult for the archive to respond to specific needs expressed by potential users and may lead to the creation of mammoth - but unused - collections of data.

FUNDING STRATEGIES

In order to obtain funds for archives and for the acquisition of data to be included in them, three different techniques have commonly been employed. The first is to obtain basic institutional support, either from a host institution such as a university or from an external agency such as a government or foundation. Sometimes these are shared, as in the case of the Berkeley Data Library which was supported, in the main, by the National Science Foundation but also obtained additional benefits accruing from its position within the University of California. The second technique has been to charge to users directly for the marginal cost incurred in responding to user requests. This technique has been employed by many archives. Notable among them has been the Roper Center which has been able to carry out almost all of its operations by charging to the user the marginal costs of the services performed for him. The third common funding technique has been to form together groups of users, either individuals or institutions, to underwrite the activities of an archive in order to serve them all. The most notable example of this type, of course, has been the Inter-University Consortium for Political Research at the University of Michigan. Most archives, however, utilize some mixture of these three sources of funding. As a consequence, they also represent a mixture in terms of their degree of specialization, the amount of data collection they undertake, and their responsiveness to changing user needs. Different funding strategies however, often have serious consequences for the relative flexibility of an archive as reflected in the cost to which it can respond to widely divergent requests from individuals for data and documentation of very different sorts.

LOCATION OF ARCHIVES

Most of the existing archives were founded at centres of social science research, that is, universities. This is particularly true of those created by demands from users at those universities who, in their own work, order data from many and diverse sources. In instances where an archive has been created by the needs of a data producer, they have been located within the producing agency most frequently. There are as yet very few examples of archives which stand apart either from the great centres of academic research or commercial and governmental bureaux which are the great producers of social science data.

All archives, regardless of their location, have many requirements in common. These requirements are met in different ways depending upon whether the archive is part of a larger organization or must stand alone. Each solution has important consequences for the nature of the archive's development - particularly with respect to its flexibility. Where resources are available from a host institution, very often personnel and equipment can be used on a part-time basis as the archive's needs require. Thus the archive need not keep a full-time staff of translators, for example, as this type of resource can be easily obtained, as needed, from the large pool of multilingual resources available at a host institution like a university. Similarly, although it may be desirable, perhaps, to have some computer programmers permanently attached to the staff of an archive, large-scale programme development can be undertaken by contracting this work out to a staff of specialists if they are available in a large host institution. Not only programmers, of course, but staff such as professional key-punch operators, secretarial help, and data processing and computing machinery operators, can be contracted for special purposes, not to mention a similar arrangement with machinery itself. This leads to a staffing pattern of a small number of highly-skilled administrative personnel and consequent ease in reorganization when necessary.

When archives must supply all the resources for themselves, they usually tend toward a low capital, labour-intensive style of development. That is, they tend to acquire unit record rather than computing machinery and utilize a small number of very skilled multipurpose, rather than many highly-specialized personnel. The consequence of this decision, typically, is a slower and more limited ability of the organization to respond to shifting user needs. After investing in one type of equipment, for example, they may be only able to provide data in punch card format or only punched according to one set of character conventions, or only utilizing one type of card. Perhaps due to staff limitations, they can only provide documentation as copies of the original - without translation and without checking against the data. Once expertise (technical or substantive) has been laboriously obtained, the archive will be slow, indeed, to shift its emphasis as a response to user demands and will, instead, seek ways to justify what it does do well and gain funding on that basis. Some of the pressures for establishing a specialized staff - if an archive is not located within a rich social science-oriented data processing environment can be sensed by considering more closely the actual forms in which data may arrive at an archive and the demands placed upon the staff.

Raw data in a machine readable and manipulatable format is the usual form of input to the data archive. It may arrive on punched cards, on magnetic tape or sometimes, under special circumstances, on specially coded microfilm or other such devices. In a few instances, the data may arrive in more conventional format and must be made machine readable. In any event, it is necessary for the archive to prepare coherent data sets which are adequately documented and from which it is possible, where necessary, to prepare subsets or work decks suited to the peculiar needs of an individual researcher. The documentation required for utilization of machine readable data is, of course, a crucial factor. Central to the entire procedure is the "codebook" that relates the holes in a punched card or the peculiar concentrations of magnetic oxides on a computer tape to the social science information this bit of information is intended to represent. It is the codebook that says a punch in the first row of the fourth column of the second card indicates that the respondent is a male where a punch in the second row of that same column would indicate a female; or that the figures appearing between columns 5 and 8 of the fifteenth card of a data set indicate the total population of a voting district.

The decisions regarding the appropriate form for storing the knowledge about how the social science information is represented, that is for the construction of codebooks, has an important impact on the total system of data archive operations. They will influence the nature of the types of information retrieval system that may be employed and thus will also affect the capacity of an archive to exchange data rapidly, efficiently, and economically with other archives as well as its capacity to locate, retrieve and process data that is required for archive users.

These considerations, of course, are of interest to an archive staff since the staff is frequently called upon to do more than simply retrieve all of the data in the archive that might be of possible interest to a specific user. They may be asked to perform certain kinds of special analyses as well, and they may even be asked to answer questions about the problems of conducting research in different settings, presuming that they have learned something about the problems in the efforts to document acquired data sets sufficiently for later use. One must also take into account how much space such an operation will actually require. Is stor-

age itself so expensive that it is necessary to worry about the reduction of data to a storage format that occupies less physical space? If that is to be done, then, are the techniques used for storing data (on magnetic tapes, for example) safe from deterioration from changes in temperature or humidity, dust, rodents, etc.? What efforts are then required to maintain the data once it has been acquired and placed into this new format? What steps are necessary to prevent deterioration simply by natural causes, what provisions must be made for altering or modifying the data as new information comes to light, and what about insuring the safety of the data where some of it may, temporarily at least, be considered proprietory.

Data itself may cover many content areas. There may be surveys on attitudes, beliefs, or behaviour, and studies may deal with topics as varied as religion, economics, and politics. It may be aggregate data dealing with voter turn-out or the percentage of voters casting their ballots for different candidates in different elections. It is clearly necessary for an archive to have information about the data which is not necessarily contained in the data itself. Examples of such considerations are the scope of the sample and sampling methods employed, the general contents of every study in more theoretical terms, and its accessibility; restrictions on its use, if any, and whether restrictions or not, it is physically accessible and currently a form that would permit its utilization by researchers.

Data may come into the archive on punched cards, magnetic tape or any other form suitable for input to the computer. They may be from surveys, polls, censuses, content analyses, voting records or vital records, and may deal with individual units such as persons or manufacturing establishments, or aggregate units such as precincts, counties, cantons or countries. Data may consist of newspaper editorials or responses to objective tests converted to a format readable by a computer and may consist of materials that were initially gathered for an immense variety of different purposes, such as tax records, shipping manifests, or national censuses. There may be summaries of the data as well as the data itself and there may be entire integrated collections of data having multipurpose and historical utility. The great heterogeneity in both content and the form of data creates continuous pressures on archives to specialize somewhat in their operations.

Archives are usually in no position to place size limitations on their holdings, although storage may be a real problem. They may try to place restrictions on the substantive areas of the data acquired, however, and establish minimum standards for the methodological quality of only data to be included in the archive. The most wide reaching restriction and the one most generally employed to rationalize the acquisition problem, however, is that which requires data to be in a form that is both machine readable and computer manipulable.

By restricting their concerns to this very small fraction of social science data many problems are resolved - although a tremendous amount of potentially irreplaceable data is inevitably and irretrievably lost by this decision. This is particularly true of information gathered in previous periods - prior to the widespread adoption of mechanical and electronic aids to data processing. By resisting the pressures to acquire these materials, archives have forced the user community to establish their own priorities more clearly - i.e. a user must decide that the material is of sufficient importance to justify its transformation to machine readable form. Even then, in many cases, further conversion must be made by an archive serving a computer-oriented clientele. Conventions adopted by scholars working with unit record machinery (counter-sorters) are often inappropriate for computer usage. Most newer research centres require data in a computer compatible format and this is increasingly true as original researchers move toward the use of computers initially and away from employment of unit record equipment in order to gain more speed, efficiency, and fuller data processing and statistical capabilities.

The following chart suggests the flow of data from input through archive status ready for distribution to users, the associated table elaborates the steps necessary to assure the usability of that data by secondary analysts. It is only after an investment of this kind, and it is a large one, that it is possible to provide the variety of services demanded by a diversity of users.

USER SERVICES

Archives are called upon to prepare duplicate data sets for users. Unlike the conventional library which loans or gives access to original copies of the information desired and leaves it to the user to prepare and take away that subset of information which he needs, the data archive produces a new copy of the data (or subset of the data) which the user may then take away to his own analytical facilities and proceed to use as he sees fit. There are also occasions when the data processing facilities of the analyst may be limited and he may ask the archive to supply analyses in addition to raw data. Thus archives must be in a position to do data processing on request as well as simply data duplication, and increasingly they are being called upon to provide training. As archives become visible centres for the conduct of quantitative social science research and due to the special skills and abilities often represented on their staffs, they are increasingly called upon to take on broader functions than originally envisaged. They are asked to provide consultation in mathematics, statistics, methodology, data analysis, and even study design. This frequently leads to the development of seminars specifically designed to identify the needs of users

and to respond to them. One response has been a growth in the scope and number of courses and training programmes offered by archives.

Data archives facilitate the current awareness by scholars of work currently underway in their disciplines by providing what amounts to a new form for the pre-publication of results. Long before any articles or books exploiting a particular data set may be published, the catalogues of various data archives reflect their existence. As scholars search archives for relevant materials, they are thereby directed to others engaged in original work who have already gathered data but have yet to publish analyses of it. The combination of resources, expertise, training and research programmes can - and often does - give an independent life to archives. Pressures are continuously generated to expand services which will recruit more users particularly where usage is a justification for funding or for other continued support. As ancillary services grow and the organization becomes more complex, it may become more and more difficult to change practices and procedures and this, in turn, may raise some difficulties in relation to other archives. This point will be considered later in some detail, but the reader should sense the naturalness of the pressures for archive development along the lines outlined above.

It must be recalled, of course, that the constituency of an archive may be far-flung, indeed. As a result, archives are often engaged in very mundane matters as well as the kind described so far. At a later point we will also return to consider the problems associated with transmitting data over long distances and working with users at a great physical remove, and the organizational consequences stemming from this condition. Yet the need for codebooks as the basis for any retrieval is undeniable and the arguments for investing the resources to make them machine readable are very persuasive. While traditional publishing practices would recommend the initial publication of multiple copies of any document - such as a codebook - and storage of this inventory for distribution on demand, this is probably an inappropriate strategy for data archives. Codebooks are often modified and updated long after they are initially created, as new information about the original study comes to light. Modification of the machine readable source is much easier than the multiple editions in a "hard copy" inventory. In addition, the space required to store a machine readable source such as a magnetic tape is usually much less than the space necessary for storing more than a very few printed copies of the codebook. Machine readable documentation, then, seems an inevitable part of data archive operations. Yet as shall be seen later, it is a costly one as well. Once the decision has been made to invest resources in the production of machine readable codebooks, however, the reliance on automated retrieval procedures increases markedly and this, in turn, begins to limit the flexibility of an archive with re-

FLOW CHART OF IDL AND RS FUNCTIONS

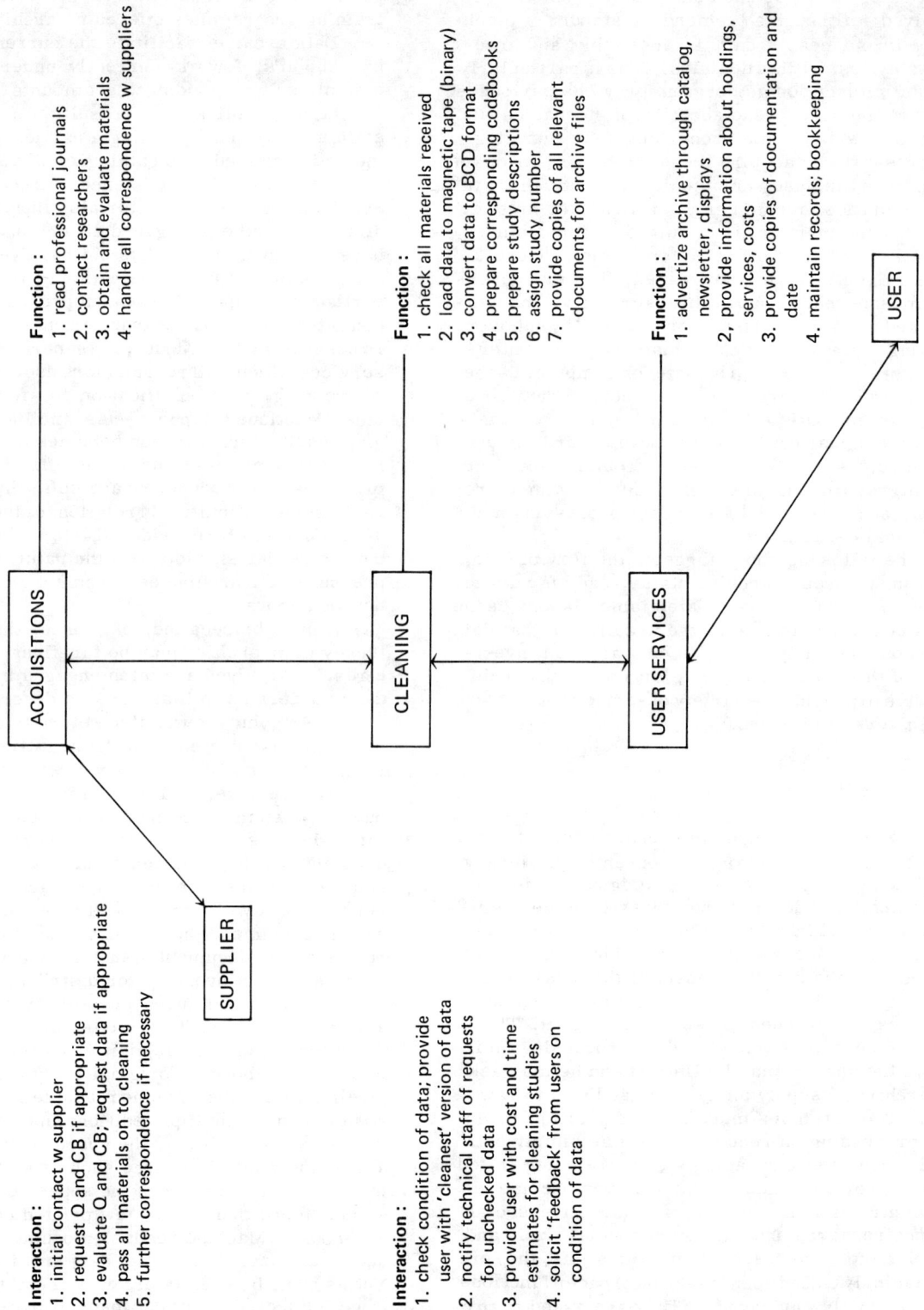

Function :
1. read professional journals
2. contact researchers
3. obtain and evaluate materials
4. handle all correspondence w suppliers

Function :
1. check all materials received
2. load data to magnetic tape (binary)
3. convert data to BCD format
4. prepare corresponding codebooks
5. prepare study descriptions
6. assign study number
7. provide copies of all relevant documents for archive files

Function :
1. advertize archive through catalog, newsletter, displays
2, provide information about holdings, services, costs
3. provide copies of documentation and date
4. maintain records; bookkeeping

```
                    ACQUISITIONS
                         |
                         |
         SUPPLIER        |
                    CLEANING
                         |
                         |
                    USER SERVICES
                         |
                       USER
```

Interaction :
1. initial contact w supplier
2. request Q and CB if appropriate
3. evaluate Q and CB; request data if appropriate
4. pass all materials on to cleaning
5. further correspondence if necessary

Interaction :
1. check condition of data; provide user with 'cleanest' version of data
2. notify technical staff of requests for unchecked data
3. provide user with cost and time estimates for cleaning studies
4. solicit 'feedback' from users on condition of data

18

OBTAINING AND PREPARING DATA FOR DIFFUSION

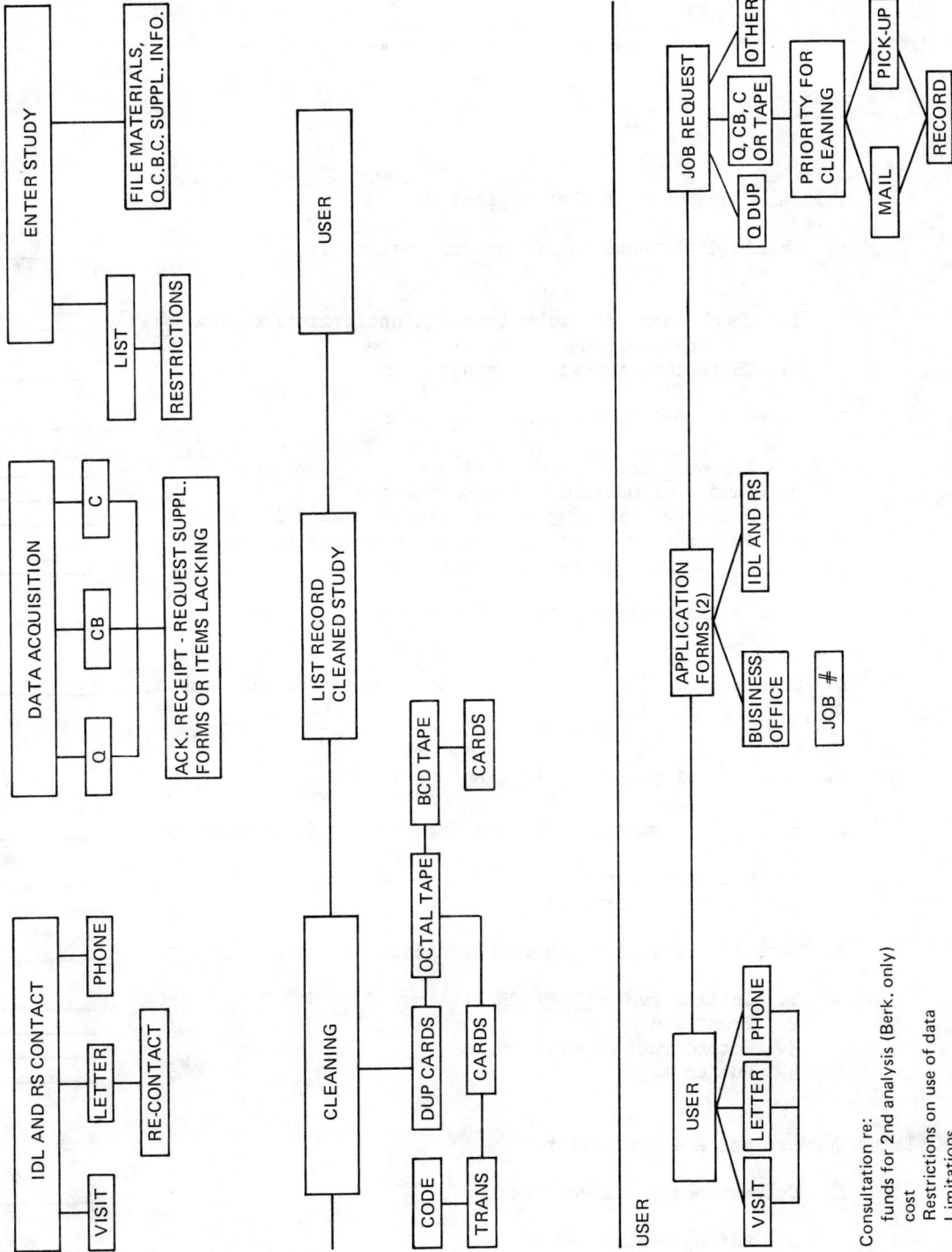

ENTER STUDY
— FILE MATERIALS, Q.C.B.C. SUPPL. INFO.
— LIST
— RESTRICTIONS

DATA ACQUISITION
— Q
— CB
— C
— ACK. RECEIPT - REQUEST SUPPL. FORMS OR ITEMS LACKING

IDL AND RS CONTACT
— VISIT
— LETTER
— PHONE
— RE-CONTACT

USER

LIST RECORD CLEANED STUDY

CLEANING
— CODE
— TRANS
— DUP CARDS
— OCTAL TAPE
— CARDS
— BCD TAPE
— CARDS

USER

JOB REQUEST
— Q DUP
— Q, CB, C OR TAPE
— OTHER
— PRIORITY FOR CLEANING
  — MAIL
  — PICK-UP
  — RECORD

APPLICATION FORMS (2)
— BUSINESS OFFICE
— IDL AND RS
— JOB #

USER
— VISIT
— LETTER
— PHONE

Consultation re:
funds for 2nd analysis (Berk. only)
cost
Restrictions on use of data
Limitations

19

I   Initial Inspection of the Original Data

    A. Obtain distributions of the original data: _____

       1. Check these distributions against criterion data
          and published materials _____
       2. Check them for wild punches _____

    B. Check the original codebook format for _____

       1. Improper use of codes: + and - _____
       2. Number of multiply-punched columns _____
       3. Number of singly-punched columns, using 13 codes _____
       4. Number of columns containing responses to two
          or more questionnaire items _____

    C. Obtain the maximum number of responses per column: _____

    D. Select Study ID   to be used for all decks: _____

II   Revision of the Original Codebook

    A. Revise the original codebook format on a Xerox copy _____

       1. Coding conversions _____
       2. Column conversions _____

    B. Have the revised codebook keypunched _____

       1. Initial run: CODEBOOK listing _____
       2. Proofread _____
       3. Second run: double-check _____
       4. Put on tape _____

III   Conversions and Corrections

    A. Convert codes and columns: _____

       1. Set-up control cards _____
       2. Test run control cards and double-check for: _____

          a. Number of columns per new deck against MPRCDE _____
            format cards
          b. Coding conversions against revised codebook _____

    c. Consistent coding of missing data   _____
    d. Consistent coding of contingency columns   _____

  3. Correct control cards and make final runs for   _____
      each old deck

B. Match-merge reformated data and put on tape: _____
   CARD-TO-TAPE, SEQUENCE CHECK

C. Obtain frequency distributions of converted data: _____

  1. Double-check revised coding format against   _____
     these spreads
  2. Correct, if necessary   _____

D. Build analysis deck: _____

  1. Check spreads of C above for wild codes and   _____
     consistency errors
  2. Set-up "T" control cards for all columns   _____
     containing these types of error
  3. Call for stylized codebook, if the revised   _____
     codebook is finished and on tape
  4. Run program set-up and build consistency errors: _____

E. Run checks for wild codes and consistency errors: _____

  1. (Optional) Obtain aggregate frequency distri-   _____
     butions of consistency errors:
  2. Set-up control cards for all columns noted in   _____
     D1 above
  3. Test run these control cards and double-check   _____
     for format errors
  4. Make final run on analysis deck   _____

F. Correct wild codes and consistency errors found: _____

  1. Correct wild codes and consistency errors in   _____
     the analysis deck by referring to the
     original interview schedules
  2. Rerun set-up (E4) on the "cleaned"   _____
     analysis deck (F1) above
  3. Make a final check for any uncorrected or   _____
     processing-generated errors and correct
     by updating, if necessary

G. Clean the reformated data of consistency errors and _____
   wild codes:

  1. Set-up control cards for program and double-check _____
     for correct matching of columns
  2. Update the reformated data with the corrected   _____
     analysis deck (F3)

III   Final Versions of the Data and Codebooks

    A.   Obtain frequency distributions of the updated data: _____

        1.   Make final check for wild codes and consistency
            errors and correct, if necessary   _____
        2.   Generate codebook distribution cards at the
            same time   _____

    B.   Merge corrected frequency distributions for the
       revised codebook on the final version: _____

        1.   Run program   _____
        2.   Have final codebook with distributions run on
            multilith paper and have the final version   _____
            printed
        3.   Put the final codebook on tape in the manner
            prescribed for other Archive codebooks   _____

---

spect to its ability to respond to shifts in the interests and demands of its users.

PROBLEMS AND LIMITATIONS IN THE DEVELOPMENT OF ARCHIVES

There are, of course, many problems and limitations to the whole archive concept but perhaps the thorniest of them all arises from the fundamental need to create adequate, detailed descriptions of the archive holdings based upon analysis of the substantive content of specific studies. Although several attempts have been made to devise an adequate cataloguing scheme, it seems clear that for surveys, at any rate, the appropriate unit to be described is the question. The problem of retrieving appropriate questions is a difficult one. Most machine-based retrieval systems have a limited set of instructions and are not as flexible as a clerk might be who can actually read through the various codebooks in search of questions or variables. Those machine-based systems actually developed have suffered from the limited supply of machine readable codebooks - or other documentation - which would provide an adequate test of their versatility. Thus many of the test runs have been carried out on a restricted set of codebooks and, usually, the very set used to design the retrieval system. Re-

trieval requests were then made by the system designers themselves and the results are not surprising.

The further difficulty with the archive enterprise is that of co-ordinating activities within each archive with those of other archives. Such matters as assuring the systematic and regular announcement of new acquisitions must be dealt with so that potential users can be connected with the appropriate data source - if it already exists - rather than each archive undertaking anew the quest for data sets already available elsewhere. Establishing the criteria and the priorities for acquisitions is even more important for every archive yet the requisite division of labour among archives has been, in the past, a matter of intense and sometimes acrimonious debate. There are relatively few examples of successful accords reached on this matter. Inter-archival agreement must be reached on technical standards as well, such as developing conventions to be utilized for signifying missing data or handling extremely large files. If extremely large files are created (such as those created by the census), the necessity arises for developing appropriate analytical programmes that deal with these special data forms and for apportioning this responsibility among the various archives dealing with such materials. As it is very easy to adopt conventions facilitating the solution to technical problems in one institution which exacerbate them in another, the need for continuous, co-ordinated collaboration is obvious.

Policies have to be developed and promulgated so that archives do not get into the position of competing with each other for scarce resources. For example, data must never be allowed to be treated as something to be bought and sold. The consequences of a failure to develop such a policy is apparent as the acquisition of new data becomes impossible. Suppliers, aware of inter-archival competition, hope that several archives will bid the price up to ever higher levels, and in this way the supplier can finance his own research. Archives themselves are under strong pressures to finance their own operations by restricting access to their data, paradoxical as this may seem, by insisting that a data set may only be loaned out, that strict accounting be kept on all copies made, and that the data set must be returned to the archive once the original purposes for which it was borrowed have been met; it is possible to obtain continuing revenue for archive operations by repeating this process over and over. Inter-archival collaboration and exchange, needless to say, is surely restricted where such policies are allowed to develop.

Another problem of inter-archival co-ordination arises from the competition among archives to obtain data sets, even if these sets are different, from the same supplier. The organizational pressures to corner acquisitions by denominating the source of supply - usually by establishing some sort of exclusive franchise arrangement - are very pronounced and some collective effort must be made to control the inter-archival competition for franchise-like arrangements. Particularly as the nature of the competition often takes a form injurious to other archives such as impugnation of their reliability or even of their motives. Even where data is obtained, the cost of adequate documentation of the data is often prohibitive, requiring extended correspondence, occasional travel, extended telephone inquiries and costly translations.

In general, the appropriation of data for re-analysis is an extraordinarily expensive proposition. It is so expensive, in fact, that if only one, or a small number of users ever makes use of an archived data set, it might actually be cheaper to have conducted the investigation anew than to acquire it for an archive. Where appropriate inter-archival co-ordination is missing, of course, the same investment in cleaning and cataloguing may be made several times over as the same data set is prepared independently by several archives. Where there are even slightly different formats for archival use (as is currently the case), each archive may invest heavily in preparing data for its own unique analytical system even when that data has been independently prepared already for the analytical system of some other archive. Perhaps the greatest problem to be overcome in the entire field of social

science data archives appears to be in the political rather than the technical realm as the problem of inter-archival co-ordination has yet to be solved.

UNANTICIPATED CONSEQUENCES OF ARCHIVE DEVELOPMENT

Many of the consequences associated with the development of data archives in the social sciences are anticipated by the archive developers. Consideration of some of these consequences, however, reveals why support for the archive movement has persisted even in the face of the difficulties outlined above. Perhaps the most important consequences have been in the area of original investigations. As a result of the possible inclusion of data in an archive, researchers are becoming more sensitive to the problems of providing adequate documentation of the data gathering and coding processes used by them in their own work. This is particularly true where funding agencies have insisted that research could be underwritten only if prior arrangements were made for the archiving of resulting data. In such instances research workers have been forced to arrange with some archives for the eventual acceptance of the data they intended to produce and the archives have insisted that thorough documentation be available at that time as well.

With the growing availability of data already in archives, researchers have had an increasing opportunity to review already the available instrument for data gathering in a much more systematic and thorough manner. They have also been able to examine the consequences of utilization of those instruments in a way that published results alone do not permit. Many feel that this has resulted in an increase in the level of sophistication exhibited in research design due to the new possibility of examining more carefully techniques which have been fruitful in the past in order to build upon them.

A further consequence has been a general improvement in the standards invoked for judging the theoretical importance of materials. As the availability of data in an archive becomes some sort of certification of the quality of that data, researchers are more and more pressed to justify the inclusion of their materials at the expense of others. This is necessitated by the scarcity of resources and the need of archives to establish acquisition priorities. Potential donors of data have responded by trying to make the theoretical relevance of their work both more explicit and of a higher order.

As collections of data have begun to emerge and to be classified along substantive lines, the existence of gaps and areas of problems for which appropriate data does not exist have become much more apparent. In many cases data archives, particularly those closely allied with research centres, have become the progenitors of interrelated programmes of research designed to fill in missing aspects of the data collection. Utilization of existing data to test theories and to suggest where more data is required has been, of course, one of the goals of archives from their very inception.

The availability of existing data has also shaped the way in which funds have been made available for new data gathering. It has become necessary to demonstrate that relevant data on the topic to be investigated is not already available as well as to assure the funding that if new source data is gathered it will be made available to other scholars - typically by placement in an appropriate archive. In many cases, pressures from archives and inter-archival organizations have been instrumental in getting major funding agencies to adopt these policies. The availability of data in archive setting has also led to the development of new techniques for constructing new variables and documenting this process automatically. Particularly as archives are prone to store only basic data and the algorithms for generating derivations rather than the numerous derivations themselves.

In general, social science research has been promoted and facilitated by diffusion of information in a rapid and economical fashion on a scale that simply was not possible prior to the advent of data archives in this area. In addition to the traditional modes of publication in a scholarly form, data and knowledge about data has become available months and even years prior to its availability via the completion of more traditional diffusion processes. In some cases data has become available for which traditional analyses were never published.

Even the structure of the social science disciplines themselves have been affected by the development of archives. Attempts to inventory and catalogue materials utilizing machine readable codebooks in order to facilitate automated retrieval of stored information have forced a close examination of both traditional categories within the disciplines and emergent ones reflecting new patterns of data usage. In the efforts to impose some order upon the great variety of materials in their collections, the archivists are leaving the influence in shaping the definition of the major categories of the social science disciplines as it is to these categories to which reference must be made. In general, then, archives can and have had an important impact on upgrading the overall quality of research in the social sciences.

FUNDING THE OPERATION OF
DATA ARCHIVES

Carrying on the archive function is an expensive endeavour and the problem of funding is a complex one. Funding for archives has come from a variety of sources. Initially, funds came from individual research projects in their efforts to gather together the relevant data for their own needs. In some cases grants were made by suppliers of the data in return for the service of archiving the materials produced by them and handling the requests for access to that data. As the demand for archive services grew, foundations (and in some cases governments) were approached to underwrite this activity. Universities have been, in most cases, an interim source of support useful until external funds could be obtained. Perhaps the most stable and viable arrangement, however, has been to derive operating funds directly from groups of users and potential users. This kind of funding has had a very strong and salutary influence tending to assure the responsiveness of archives to the needs of the user community.

Although it may be, perhaps, the most obvious source of operating funds, experience has shown that there can be some difficulties associated with charging individual users for the services rendered to them. One problem associated with this arrangement has been to arrive at a fair charge to users for the costs involved in the actual processing of the data necessary to make it useful to them (translations, documentation, cleaning, etc.). These costs can be prohibitively expensive if they must be borne by only one - or just the first user. Yet it is often difficult to predict the total amount a data set may eventually be used in order to amortize the preparation costs over all users. If some form of amortization is considered, however, the pressures are on the user to amortize his costs by resale of the data as they are upon the archives to prohibit such resale. This leads to attempts to sell data to users as if it were a scarce commodity. This policy, as mentioned before, has at least two very undesirable consequences. The first is to create pressures on the archive to control the rediffusion of data and thereby make it a scarce commodity, able to fetch a higher price, and provide more income to the archive. This operates of course in direct contravention to the whole principle of maximizing the utilization of data by as many scholars as possible, which is fundamental to the data archive rationale. The sales policy also tends to price users out of the market as the initial investment is rarely amortized over many users and pricing policies end up so that the cost is carried individually by each user. This policy also leads to a great deal of subterfuge on the part of users who, because of the very nature of material in machine readable form, are prone to create their own copies of the borrowed data. Although they may return the original data to the supplier, a black market in data obtained from archives which restrict the rediffusion of their materials is soon flourishing.

As mentioned above, the process of archiving, in general, is an expensive one and it is not only expensive to establish an archive but to maintain it as well. The final budget for 1967-1968 of the survey archive alone of the Inter-University Consortium for Political Research, for example, amounted to $425,000. That of the Roper Center for Public Opinion Research was approximately $100,000 during this time and that of the International Data Library about $75,000. These are three of the world's largest user-oriented archives, and they are efficiently run. These figures represent about the minimum costs necessary to provide the kinds of services that they provide. The initial starting cost for each of these archives was much higher, of course, reflecting travel on the part of archive directors to establish supplying contracts, obtain materials, recruit and train personnel and carry on developmental activities during periods when productivity was very low. All of these factors contribute to the extraordinary initial costs of establishing an archive.

A more detailed description of the same costs for one archive dealing with survey materials from several countries can be found in Appendix 1.

THE VARIETY OF ARCHIVE TYPES

Of course there are many different kinds of archives and not all of them require the same staffing or financing. There are special purpose archives whose contents focus on some specific regions such as Latin America or Germany or focus on some specific subject matter such as health or politics. Data may consist of roll-call votes, survey responses, census materials or biographies. An archive may contain only a single data file that is constantly being kept up to date over some period of time. The Project Talent Data Bank has a great deal of psychological, sociological and educational information on a sample of half a million American youth, for example, and this file is constantly revised and kept up to date. Data may be in punched card format or on magnetic tapes. It may even be on microfilm of a type specially coded to facilitate retrieval. It may be organized to preserve the products of host organizations and be not particularly suited to the demands of external users, or it may be set up to be specifically responsive to users' demands.

Special purpose archives are relatively common, but multipurpose archives are somewhat better known. Archives of this type focus on various combinations of areas and contents. They may deal with problems of population in developing nations, for example, or with political behaviour in industrial societies. They may combine forms of data storage; magnetic tapes and microfilm may both be employed in the same archive. And, of course, they may deal with both users and producers of data and may be concerned with the acquisition and storage of data as well as its processing and diffusion.

Some archives are particularly concerned with the servicing of a local clientele. The local clientele may actually be quite dispersed geographically as it may consist of the members of some user association, or use may be restricted simply to members of an archive's host institution. In general, local service archives are characterized by some restriction on access to their facilities and only

under exceptional circumstances can an individual or institution gain access to those facilities if not already a party to the local service clientele arrangement or at least willing to join it.

In contrast to the above are the general service archives characterized by the open access to their facilities and operating without restrictions on the class of their clientele. Both local and general service archives, however, usually do have some classes of data, access to which may, in fact, be universally restricted. It is common practice for many suppliers of data to request that the data sets contributed by them not be made available for redistribution until some specified date in the future. Knowledge of the data's existence is widely diffused but the original researcher maintains control over access to it until, for example, he has finished his own analyses. General service archives also tend to be somewhat broader in the functions they perform and often provide data gathering as well as data analyses facilities. A list of some of the better known archives is presented in Appendix 2 in which the general service, local service distinction is made. A few examples are described below, however, to clarify the discussion somewhat.

Perhaps the oldest, largest and best-known local service archive - with a clientele spread throughout the United States and Western Europe - is the Inter-University Consortium for Political Research located on the Ann Arbor campus of the University of Michigan. This archive specializes in materials useful for the study of politics and includes a variety of data such as aggregate voting statistics, records of roll-call votes, and public opinion surveys from various historical periods and from numerous locations. It is a local service archive, however, in the sense that as its name implies, it serves a consortium of universities. Facilities are not readily available to individuals not affiliated with member institutions. The Roper Public Opinion Research Center at Williams College which specializes in the collection of survey data from commercial polling and market research organizations is, by this definition, both local and general service. While individual clients may obtain the services of this archive, their costs are markedly reduced if they are connected with an institutional affiliate of the Center's International Library Association. The International Data Library and Reference Service of the University of California's Survey Research Center serves a worldwide clientele of individuals and has no membership organization. Data and analyses from the collection of survey materials from Asia, Latin America and the United States held by the Berkeley archive have been obtained by individuals from throughout the world regardless of their institutional affiliations - or lack of them. The Political Science Research Library at Yale, by contrast, while responding to external requests, is particularly designed to meet the needs of scholars at that institution. Another local service facility which has grown, however, to serve a broad clientele - is the Data Program and Library Service at the University of Wisconsin. Although specifically oriented to serving local data needs, this archive serves an international clientele in the identification and location of computer programmes particularly suited to the needs of social scientists.

Clearly, the number and diversity of archive organizations is great enough so that the problems of inter-archival co-ordination are serious indeed. The following section deals with this need and some of the difficulties that have been encountered in trying to meet it.

INTER-ARCHIVAL CO-ORDINATION

Some mechanisms are necessary to co-ordinate the process of data gathering and data exchange among archives. The diversity of organizations and variety of individual interests which must be served suggest at least seven areas which require some sort of inter-archival elaborative endeavour.

The problem of exchanging information among the various archives themselves suggests the first of these, since in order to accomplish such exchanges requires knowledge of what materials are currently available in the various archives, and where precisely they are stored; it is of little utility to have materials stored in an archive and have no one aware of their existence or to know of their existence but have no actual location.

Another factor central to facilitating the exchange of information among archives is agreement on some standards for the indexing and storing of the information contained in those archives. If each archive classifies its holdings in a unique fashion, it is difficult indeed for the user, or for other archives, to discover whether the materials held are relevant to the user's needs. Similarly, there is a need for agreement on the methods to be used for storing data so that the form in which data is stored in one archive, with only minimal alterations, will be compatible with the machinery for utilizing that data employed by other archives or users.

The importance of free flowing exchange of information among archives cannot be overemphasized. It is not only the sine granoir of the operation of a network of archives and users, it is also a prerequisite for the development of new archives. It is by means of the actual exchange of data that the standards developed and agreed upon in theory are actually implemented. New archives are under considerable pressure to adapt their policies to the existing practices of established groups so that the proliferation of archives is an integrated rather than an idiosyncratic affair.

A second area in which some co-ordination is necessary is that of contributing and publicizing the general activities of archives. It is necessary to have some central, visible source for users to gain access to the variety of existing archives. This gives the archive network much greater visibility and aids in co-ordinating their public efforts - such as the production of a comprehensive inventory of archive holdings - in a mutually beneficial manner.

And a third area is that of creating a scholarly professional association for the archivists themselves. Such associations provide a unique opportunity for professional workers in the archive community to meet together on a regular basis and permit the reaffirmation of their community of interests. They also permit them to share technical ideas, discuss policy matters, and, in general, develop a reference group. It is only by this kind of activity that the strongest pressures toward coordination and co-operation are produced and it is probably the case that the existence of such a group is an absolute prerequisite for the development and exercise of the sanctions necessary to enforce the policies agreed upon.

The initiation of new research to facilitate the actual exchange of information among archives is, clearly, a fourth area heavily dependent upon successful inter-archival co-ordination. Collaborative arrangements are required in order to explore at any length the actual basis of information exchange utilizing such devices as telecommunications experiments. Yet development of this technology appears very useful indeed in order to accomplish such tasks as permitting distant users to discover what materials are actually held by which archives. Similarly, the extensive and heterogeneous data base combined with a broad collection of users that is necessary to develop and test an adequate information retrieval system for archive use is most easily acquired through the collaborative efforts of several archives.

Archives, however, like other organizations, do not always exist in perfect harmony. The need to resolve inter-archival conflicts constitutes the fifth area of concern. Experience has shown that it is most effective when the archival community is a party to resolving conflicting claims and interests between two or more archives and it is necessary for the archival community in general to be involved in such conflict-resolving activities. Certainly establishing general policies to anticipate and avoid conflicts is a vital activity and when an inter-archival organization is operating well it functions to anticipate these conflicts more often than to resolve them.

Perhaps the most important area of anticipating these conflicts is that of establishing priorities for a division of labour in archive functioning among the general potential competitors for scarce resources such as fiscal support, personnel, regional or substantive data suppliers and users. Without such an agreement it is difficult to provide potential funding sources or supportable rationale for the development of new archives or the further development of existing ones. Co-ordination at this level, if achieved, avoids costly duplication of special purpose, local service facilities and establishes priorities for the creation of new archives.

In the effort to create a division of labour among existing archives or to consider the creation of new archives, there are at least three dimensions of specialization which have been employed. There is, obviously, a geographic basis; the contents of archives may be organized around local, regional, national, or international concerns, but always with a focus upon a specific location or set of locations. Archives may also focus upon political, sociological, psychological, economic and historical materials, thus providing the basis of what may be called a substantive division. Other archives have been organized to focus upon some problem of special interest, bringing together materials from different disciplines and different regions.

Each kind of archive may serve a different type of clientele. Users may be drawn from all parts of the world - from agencies, individuals, and international non-governmental bodies. Users may also consist exclusively of national governmental agencies or collections of agencies or they may be confined to individuals who are located in the immediate region of the archive itself.

Two major approaches have been made to solving the various problems generated by the need to co-ordinate archive activities in order to maximize their utility to such a heterogeneous body of users and to meet their often conflicting demands. The first approach has been the centralized agency where one organization co-ordinates the functions of all the others. The Council of Social Science Data Archives, for example, shortly after its founding, created several sub-committees; one dealing with the technical standards to be employed by all archives, another treating the problem of developing a centralized inventory from all archives, a third facing the problems of the division of labour among existing archives as well as priorities for the creation of new archives. The Council was concerned in general with the articulation of its two dozen member archives, and by its centralized nature, was able to carry on the problems of co-ordination and fitting together the diverse activities of its sub-committees in a reasonably efficient manner. The standards sub-committee, for example, was able to deal with the problem of how to create codebooks for survey data in a way that was compatible with the demands of the inventory committee for utilizing those codebooks for purposes of automated retrieval. A centralized form for the co-ordinating agency also permits it to have a life of its own. It is possible, as a consequence, for the agency to be somewhat less responsive to the diversity of interests of the broader clientele since agency personnel work most closely with archives and archive managers, not with the archive users themselves. In addition, the problem of any single agency is that it is very difficult to bring together on a permanent basis individuals with the depth and breadth of expertise necessary to deal with the variety of problems emergent in the archive movement. Without the promise of a continuing career involvement, a relatively dear line of advancement and rewards as well as some sense of security, it is very difficult to get experts who will deal with the problems of co-ordinating the development and functioning of archives on much more than a transitory consulting basis. Without continuity, however, the requisite direction and impetus cannot be obtained.

A second strategy to promote inter-archival co-ordination has been to adopt a more decentralized approach. In this way, different agencies become responsible for specific functions. In a later stage of the Council of Social Science Data Archives activities, for example, Berkeley became responsible for the problems of inventorying the materials contained in the member archives, Wisconsin for the problems associated with acquiring and developing appropriate computing programmes in the social sciences, and Michigan dealt with the general problems of acquiring and cleaning data. In this way the various problems were reduced to a more manageable size and it was possible to bring together a greater concentration of effort on each particular problem by professionals working in the field on a continuing basis. Unfortunately it also led, in many cases, to duplication of efforts and in some instances to some internal conflict where, for example, the interests of the host organization with the specific function and the requirements of performing this function for all archives indicated different strategies.

Thus, even with this decentralized arrangement some of the general problems persisted. Archives have a diverse motivation to collect and store data of different types and of different levels of quality. As a consequence there is generally a great deal of difficulty in arriving at some standards of storage, cleaning and documentation that are universally acceptable. It is felt, for example, that data gathered for only the most cursory descriptive uses need not be documented as carefully as those which are to be used in more extensive analytical probes. In general, archives devoted to obtaining data for highly specialized purposes are willing to invest only that minimal amount of their resources necessary to make the data useful to its own specific users. Data are not, in general, prepared for a variety of users with different interests and purposes in mind. In some cases an archive may have solved its acquisition problems by making arrangements with the producers of data and may have agreed, for example, to accept all the data produced by one or more organizations on a regular basis. This strategy can result in the collection of an immense amount of material - most of which is of very low utility. The costs of indexing, storing, cleaning, and documenting this material are prohibitive, particularly if these tasks must be carried out to a relatively high level of perfection. Thus, the volume of information may be great but its utility might be quite low and the costs of adopting archive-wide standards prohibitive.

Furthermore, depending upon how dependent a particular archive is upon the success or failure of all archives in general, archives may be more or less responsive to efforts promoting inter-archival co-ordination. This is particularly apparent where an archive attempts to gain a monopoly in some area. In such cases it may appear to be to the best interest of that archive to thwart the development of other archives which appear, in some way, to be encroaching upon its territory. Where archives are more dependent upon the success of the movement in general, however, and to the growth of secondary and comparative analysis, they tend to be extremely responsive to efforts at co-ordination.

A second type of problem which remains despite the creation of co-ordinating agencies are those due to general limitations on the availability of computing facilities to maintain and process very large data bases. Without computing machinery readily available to transform large amounts of data into machine readable form, for example, it is a very expensive project indeed to reanalyse much of the social science data that is actually collected. Many classic and important data resources are not in machine readable form at all but persist as text. For example, in many cases data have traditionally been hand-tabulated on sheets of paper. There is no inexpensive way, as yet, of transforming these great collections of heterogeneous data into a form suitable for the modern data archive. Perhaps with the further development of optical character recognition devices, this problem may be resolved, but that type of development is really quite remote. Even with its development, the costs of transformation, at this time, would appear to be almost prohibitive.

Even where the data is available in machine readable form, general purpose programmes for their analysis often are not. In many cases if programmes are available, they do not function well. This lack has sometimes led archives or archive-related organizations to make large investments in programmes and programme systems in order to facilitate the analysis of their data. Once this has been done, it often happens that the archive has a strong desire to maintain the analytical style which shaped the programme design and to store data in a form particularly compatible with this analysis programme. This then inhibits the exchange of data unless, of course, others adapt the same analytical programme system. Unfortunately, in many cases the programme system of one archive is not suitable for the resources that other archives have available locally.

Thirdly, computer resources are not yet so widely available as to justify the costs of elaborate, machine-based information retrieval activities. There are vast differences in the local costs of computing and hand labour and the tendency has been for archives to develop local retrieval systems based on the local cost structure. Thus, where there is a scarcity of computing machinery and a surplus of relatively skilled labour, the information retrieval systems developed tend to rely heavily upon the skills of sophisticated coders who introduce materials into an index system so that studies are pre-categorized and pre-classified in a variety of ways. This is an efficient approach and permits extremely rapid and low cost retrieval yet it is unpopular at institutions where the cost of skilled labour is very high and access to high-powered computing machinery is relatively easy and comparatively cheap. In this latter setting, archives have tended to develop retrieval systems which rely only on semi-skilled labour for the introduction of standardized materials into the computer and then rely upon sophisticated retrieval systems based upon elaborate and complex programmes to get the desired information out again. One difficulty with the machine-based retrieval systems is the necessity for the user himself to develop some facility with the system, whereas in the human-based systems the user need have little or no facility in this area. Archive staffing, of course, tends to reflect the needs established by the retrieval system locally adopted. Unfortunately, the two approaches described above are often incompatible with each other. As the vested interests of the archives which have pursued a particular approach become greater day by day, the possibilities of synthesis diminish and the problems of co-ordination increase.

A fourth problem remaining in the area of co-ordinated archive development has to do with the politics associated with the acquisition of new data. It has been the case in the past that the competition among archives for new materials has led some investigators to develop a false sense of the intrinsic value of their data. As a consequence these investigators have artificially inflated the value of the data, sometimes to an astronomical level as a device for financing their own research. In this same area of politics are the difficulties archives encounter by their possible contamination on the basis of the sources of their funds or the nature of their users. It is often difficult to serve both scholarly purposes and the demands of governmental agencies at the same time. This is particularly so if the governmental agencies are military or political ones. To acquire or provide data for military or political purposes restricts access of an archive to data sources for strictly scholarly research. The general problems associated with who is to be served are not easily solved even by inter-archival co-ordinating agencies.

As archives develop they inevitably specialize in their functions and the very fact of their specialization, while increasing the need for co-ordination, makes the co-ordination more difficult. Development of an area of expertise, for example, often leads to difficulty in co-ordinating efforts due to differences in terminologies, priorities, documentation and indexing systems, data processing procedures and computer programmes, depending on the needs of diverse areas of specialization. These differences inhibit the cross-flow of information. As a consequence, archives tend to recruit and to train personnel with rather narrow specialities, that is, to staff archives with substantive, area, or technical expertise which in many cases is not interchangeable. Familiarity with the materials available and data gathering activities underway in industrial nations, for example, does not necessarily keep an archive staff properly advised of the situation in less industrial or less urban societies.

Further problems in the co-ordinated development of data archives arise directly from a sense of nationalism. Officials in many countries feel that data collected in that country is a part of their national patrimony and, consequently, should not be made available to scholars anywhere outside of their country. For this reason it is not possible, in some areas, to obtain reciprocal arrangements for the exchange of data at this time. Yet for many archives data exchange is the very basis of their acquisition procedure.

There are also problems of co-ordinating archive activities associated with the costs of data diffusion. For example, if the financial structure of the archive depends upon the sale of data as a revenue-producing activity, as noted previously, there are strong pressures on the archive to do whatever it can to inhibit the unrewarded rediffusion of that data. These efforts can produce many difficulties in the attempt to co-ordinate activities among archives as those archives whose income is based upon the services they render to the community must react to the strong pressures to rediffuse data rather than to inhibit its rediffusion which is directly contradictory to the interests of archives of the first type. Where there are basic differences in the organizational structure of archives it becomes more difficult to co-ordinate their activities.

The problems of creating compatible technical standards, terminology format, cleaning procedures, etc., have been referred to before individually but it is important to recall that the adoption of standards in any one of these areas has important consequences for the other areas of archive functioning. Thus the way in which the data is stored or documented will have a strong effect upon the system utilized for information retrieval and upon the way in which the inventory of archived materials is actually maintained. As mentioned earlier, machine and programme capabilities produce vested interests which lead to difficulties when changes require abandoning systems that have been developed at great expense. If the data is cleaned, stored or documented in a form specifically suited to local machine or programming capabilities, it is indeed a prohibitively costly undertaking to transform entire collections to some new system. Very often early decisions in this area profoundly shape the direction of later development since a commitment to one or another type of data storage device or format may limit the alternative devices which can be employed at some later point in the archive's development. Good examples of this, perhaps, are

the persisting incompatibility among various magnetic tape formats such as the use of a seven or nine track format, or the commitment by an archive to unit record machinery and multiple-punch conventions as opposed to computer and magnetic tape conventions; the use of different conventions for the writing of characters on tape, or even very different physical forms for punched cards such as the Power-Samas type machinery used in many parts of the Middle East and Southwest Asia and IBM compatible equipment used in many parts of Europe and the United States of America. As each decision is made in the development and equipment of a new archive, careful consideration must be given to the ramifications of the policy adopted or the machinery acquired for the possibilities of inter-archival exchange. It is important to recall the difficulty of erecting a functioning archive de novo. Many of the equipment decisions must be made long before the machinery can be delivered and many of the programmes and procedures developed long before the actual processing of data can be begun.

These technical barriers, of course, are not the only kind which exist. The more traditional barriers of distance, bulk and weight continue to inhibit exchange of materials among archives. As mentioned, there are often incompatibilities among various computers so that it may not be possible to ship information in most compact form possible. It may be necessary, for example, to send copies of the punched cards. In many instances these are extremely bulky and subject to damage or destruction in the shipping process. The costs involved, if based on weight or volume, can be considerable.

In addition to such physical barriers there are often procedural barriers. In some cases customs is unwilling to admit magnetic tapes containing information to a country without the payment of a large duty levied on the tape itself - regardless of the contents. This raises the price of data exchange considerably. In other areas certain types of content cannot be sent. Policies about national patrimony, as mentioned before, inhibit the shipment of certain kinds of data out of countries. In other cases, the personal self-interest of the original scholar prohibits the diffusion of his data until he feels that he is completely finished with his analysis, which may take a long time indeed.

In addition to technical, political and physical barriers to inter-archival co-ordination, some important cultural barriers also remain. Besides problems such as language or differences in emphasis and style within academic disciplines, general professional style may differ so radically as to make collaboration almost impossible. In some instances, for example, the very idea of sharing data gathered by an individual scholar is simply not legitimate. Nor is the utilization of data gathered by others for secondary or comparative analysis considered to be acceptable scholarly in many places. As a consequence, there is very little support from potential donors or users for the establishment of archives and archives activities. In such circumstances a great deal of preliminary work would have to be undertaken before a local data archive could function as anything more than a "private" research facility for a very small number of users.

DATA ARCHIVE ORGANIZATIONS

At least two major organizations have been created in the effort to overcome the problems outlined above, and to promote the co-ordinated development of archival activities in general. In the United States, the Council of Social Science Data Archives was established in 1965 for several very specific purposes: to aid scholars to replicate their findings with different data; to verify, reject and accept hypotheses and theories by broadening the data base available for this scientific work; to facilitate quantitative, historical and empirical research; to improve training in the methodology of the social sciences; to develop data resources regarding social issues at international, national, state, regional and local levels; to promote experimentation with machinery to enable rapid and accurate inquiries, retrieval and exchange of machine readable social science data over great distances with minimum delay; to facilitate the acquisition of data from various sources and the development and use of various computer-based analytical capabilities; and to develop and maintain a regular inventory of the holdings of all member archives that would provide a description of the materials held by each as well as outlining the procedures necessary to obtain them. The Council also hoped to co-ordinate the development of "software" of computer programmes related to the needs of archives and their users, as well as co-ordinate the development of an information retrieval system to be used, particularly, for teaching and research purposes. In general the Council hoped to standardize the forms of data storage and documentation (such as codebooks) in order to facilitate social science research.

The CSSDA was funded initially by the National Science Foundation of the United States Government and existed for about five years before its eventual demise. It was a centralized organization located initially at Columbia University with technical offices at the University of Michigan. Both offices were later combined and moved to the University of Pittsburgh. Although the Council committees produced several technical reports on standards, a first attempt at a comprehensive inventory, conducted several technical workshops and, in general, moved toward the goals it had set for itself, it finally collapsed due to its basic inability to resolve the conflicts of interests represented by its two dozen or so member archives.

The mark of its failure was its inability to produce some kind of guidance (reflecting a consensus of the members) concerning priorities for development

in the archive area. Continued emphasis upon the development at individual archives was never replaced by a concern for the overall archive movement.

There is some possibility, and certainly it would be useful, that if the activities initially undertaken by the CSSDA were to be reorganized within an international context, some of the problems could be overcome by the separation of the funding sources for policy planning and for archive functioning. From that perspective, such an organization could supply funding agencies interested in the archive movement with guidance concerning relative priorities for activities such as telecommunications and inventory development, or provide criteria for choosing archives to be developed on an international basis; in general such a group would have a better basis for considering problems of the sort the CSSDA encountered without success.

A second major independent effort at promoting inter-archival co-ordination was inaugurated in 1966 through the establishment of the Standing Committee on Data Archives of the International Social Science Council. Membership in this committee has come from Europe, the United States, Latin America and Asia. Its purposes have been to promote the selection, rediffusion, and utilization of social science data and to help develop good relations among suppliers, archives, and users. Like the Council, the Standing Committee hopes to develop procedures to be followed by archives for data preparation, storage, processing and retrieval and to explore the rôle of archives in graduate education as well. Part of the plan has been to establish networks of archives and in particular the Standing Committee hoped to organize theoretical, methodological and technical efforts to deal with the many problems of comparative, cross-cultural and cross-national research. The Standing Committee also has expressed a wish to aid in the development of an infrastructure of research facilities for social scientists. In general, the Standing Committee has worked to improve data bases for international comparisons. Finally, like the CSSDA, the Standing Committee has worked toward the development of consensus on a standard for the description of archivable data holdings.

Several task forces have been established. One is to deal with inventories and produce a format for the description of data files. A second deals with information retrieval techniques and has been concerned particularly with problems associated with the application of textual analysis to this end in order to deal with files of variable names and to locate and examine data generating questions. They have also been concerned with developing general schemes for describing archive holdings with access systems, software, hardware, the amount of and type of use and other activities related to archive functioning. A third was to deal with ecological archives and to treat the technical and methodological problems associated with archiving and utilizing aggregate rather than individual or survey data. A fourth was to promote the sharing of information on computer programmes and software packages and the fifth was to promote the development of archives in the Third World.

Currently there is a task force on archive development in Latin America which has been moving slowly toward developing a programme of inventorying the available data in Chile, Argentina, and Venezuela and there is some possibility of collaboration with research institutions in Peru. Other activities related to this task force include a data inventory programme on social science research projects which is moving ahead in India and an interest that has been expressed in promoting archive activities in Japan. Not all the archives are in the Third World, however, and the task force has noted activity in establishing permanent files on selected data from Polish Poviats (local governmental units) and an interest in establishing an historical series of such data for the last hundred years. The Polish group is also working toward creating archives for surveys which will be organized to facilitate communication and exchange with other archives. Canada has an active archive facility in Toronto and Germany has seen the development of the Center for Social Science Information which produces a yearly inventory of research in progress as well as a clearing house for requests about research projects and personnel to provide a bridge between information needs in political activities and available social science knowledge which might be of use in meeting such needs.

The second major task force of the Standing Committee has emphasized archive management and has been carrying on surveys of regulations applying to users of archives as well as surveys of possible ways to improve the dissemination of information on archive holdings and promote the international exchange of holdings in general.

The data retrieval sub-committee of this task force has created a systematic comparison of various retrieval systems available in three European data archives and is moving toward specifying the changes of over and under retrieval (obtaining all relevant as well as much irrelevant material versus retrieving only relevant - but perhaps not all the relevant material in an archive), given a specific structure of the material to be retrieved and an appropriate structure of the inquiry pattern. In particular this group has been exploring the translation of various schemes based on taxonomic classifications of subject areas and has been trying to discover the possibility of linking selective dissemination of bibliographical information with retrieval systems for data archives purposes.

The Committee on Ecological Analysis and Aggregate Data has done some modest development in computer programmes for ecological analysis but recognized the need for further development and is planning for a follow-up of their 1966 symposium on quantitative ecological analysis in the social

sciences to be held sometime in 1972.

The Historical Data Archive Sub-Committee has explored the use of quantitative material in historical research and organized meetings of historians on problems of computer processing of historical data and has worked developing contacts between Eastern and Western European scholars as well as between Europeans and Americans.

The Sub-Committee on Program Libraries and Computers has worked on creating an inventory of computer programmes for the social sciences. This work has been carried out to a large extent by the National Program Library and Central Program Inventory Service for the Social Sciences at the University of Wisconsin. In general, this group has been trying to obtain technical descriptions of programmes and the machine configurations necessary to utilize them, and it has made suggestions for systematic compilation of users' experiences concerning how adequate a programme is for some specific data or analytical purpose.

The task force on training in secondary analysis has been dissolved since the activities it felt to be relevant are now institutionalized within various archives and research facilities.

The task force on machine readable archives of data in textual form has been working on the development of general tools for content analysis utilizing newer technical developments such as advanced optical scanning equipment.

The International Social Science Council's Standing Committee has held several conferences on archiving punched card data from sample surveys and developing co-operative arrangements among European archives and has carried on projects developing an inventory of data and of available computer programmes. In general a great deal of the resources of the Standing Committee have been devoted to information services of this type. This is best represented by its contribution to the section on Data Sources in the journal, Social Science Information, which the Council publishes. In addition to promoting contacts between researchers and promoting the flow of documents between institutions, the Standing Committee has also provided a structure for relations between national bodies and international organizations. The Council recently sponsored in Paris a workshop on computer programming and systems for the social sciences. Currently the Standing Committee is planning a workshop on programming systems and related problems, which will involve the development of social science data archives and computing facilities in Italy, and an evaluation of competing data management and data analysis programing packages.

A second workshop is planned on data preparation, touching on topics such as standards for cleaning, documentation and the problems associated with reformatting data to make it compatible with computer use. A conference on ecological analysis is also planned which will deal not only with substantive problems but technical problems, such as computing programmes suitable for eco-logical analysis.

By and large the Standing Committee has worked through task forces on specialized topics as well as being a plenary body on topics of central interest to social science data archives as an institution, and in this way they have attempted to treat the archive movement as viewed by user, supplier and funding agency.

In many ways, then, the Standing Committee has dealt with problems similar to those identified by the CSSDA. The list of its activities is long and impressive. Although the Council (CSSDA) had fiscal resources far in excess of the Standing Committee and in many areas, it was unable to produce as much as the international group; an examination of some of the reasons for those differences may be instructive. Perhaps most important is a consi-deration of the membership structure of the two groups. The Council was made up of organizations - functioning data archives - the Standing Committee is a collection of individuals - many of whom are not, in fact, directly connected with an operative archive. Thus the former group tended to reflect organizational and the latter individual interests.

The Council had money - quite a lot of it - and was able to commission expensive projects. It could, and did, bring together all its members annually and its executive committee with even greater frequency - something the Standing Committee cannot do. Meetings of the Council Executive Committee, then, often revolved about the allocation of Council resources, including the allocation of those re-sources to some member archive in order to carry out some specific technical task - such as an inven-tory. Standing Committee meetings, when they are held, tend to focus less upon the allocation of re-sources since these are small, already committed, and difficult to reallocate. Instead, energies can be devoted to developing specifications for technical work to be done by task forces - utilizing the inter-nal resources of the task force members. With the difference in the fiscal implications of these two structures it is not too surprising that the Council was only able to produce a few, relatively small concrete sub-committee products in addition to several widely attended, extremely successful national conferences. Task forces of the Standing Committee, working largely on their own, have, in contrast, produced several important products, yet no appropriate structure - such as a conference of archive managers - has ever appeared to permit discussion, improvement, and promote implemen-tation. Task force reports have tended to be simply statements by one or two interested parties who did work on their own they probably would have done anyway but with the Standing Committee's blessing.

American archives struggled among themselves both for the resources of the CSSDA and with that organization itself as a fellow competitor for basic support from the National Science Foundation.

Decisions made by this body made a real difference not only for the everyday procedures of archives but for their long-term funding as well. Yet all the member archives of the Council received support from sources independent of the NSF and the Council - often a host institution. The combination of these conditions contributed greatly to the para-lysis and eventual death of the Council. This was due primarily to the inability of Council members to agree upon a set of priorities for the develop-ment of the archive movement in general rather than to attempt continuously to utilize the Council itself as a direct or indirect instrument for enhancing specific archives.

The Standing Committee task force recom-mendations, on the other hand, have little to recommend their adoption except their reasonable-ness. The almost total lack of powers to reward or to sanction archives for their collaboration or lack of it has resulted in the production of excellent task force reports and recommendations but rela-tively little in the way of concrete products. Thus even the development of totally new archives and archive networks in Latin America and in India tend to take place with little or no assistance from the various task forces of the Standing Committee. Although most of the efforts toward the develop-ment of functioning archives in these areas has yet to bear fruit, it is possible to note how readily acknowledgement of the principles of inter-archive and international co-operation are made - and then must be subordinated to the exigences of local needs and local funding. This can be seen quite clearly in considering the efforts to promote and develop social science data archives in Latin America.

Archiving developments in this region have centred about the work of the Latin American Council for Social Sciences which was established in 1967. Of particular importance here is a con-sideration of its working group on data archives. This group has expressed an intention to develop a network of data banks throughout Latin America based wherever possible upon the further develop-ment of already existing data bases. The origins of this effort were closely linked to the formation of a Latin American Consortium of data archives. In an early meeting the working group agreed to adopt methods and technical norms which would make the developments of individual archives mutually compatible and to share information and provide complete accessibility of data. Unfortu-nately, the sub-committees created to formulate these technical norms and to establish such things as inventories, standardized interchange of data, and promote multilateral contacts, did not meet again. Meanwhile, the directorship of the council has moved from Buenos Aires to Minas Gerais, Brazil, to Bariloche, Argentina. Perhaps one desirable consequence of this latest move is that it may facilitate the integration of Latin American and North American activities somewhat as the host institution, the Fundación Bariloche, has a prior arrangement with the International Data Library at the University of California regarding the policies and technical procedures for the exchange of data and information. It is worth noting, however, that the norms regarding data documentation which apply to this particular arrangement do not coincide with those agreed upon by the Working Committee - yet practice often pre-empts policy in these matters.

An effort has been made to inventory the activities of the various Latin American social science centres with support from Unesco and the Rockefeller Foundation, although the "Directory" published by the group in 1968 reveals no data archives ready to function at an inter-institutional exchange level.

An ad hoc consortium of seven Chilean institutions was formed with holdings of both aggregate data and surveys obtained from 10 different institutions, but no programme for external exchange. In Argentina, the two organizations of major importance in the archive movement, the Instituto Torcuato di Tella and the Fundación Bariloche made efforts to co-ordinate archiving activities at a national level by naming an inter-centre data archive committee and attempting to collaborate on an inventory of archivable data. They also intended to provide a communication channel among the institutions in Argentina in order to keep the inventory of available materials up to date and to stimulate the interest of producers in sound archiving methods. Lack of funds, however, prevented the completion of this project.

A sub-committee of the Latin American Social Science Council undertook the preparation of a manual for providing documentation necessary for the appropriate storage both of aggregated data and of historical data without results. Although the survey has not yet been carried out, there was an interest expressed in determining the future priorities for the Working Committee; this was to be done by conducting a survey among Latin American researchers in sociology, economics, social history, social pysychology, cultural anthropology, demography, urban and regional planning and allied fields. In addition, the Committee hoped to co-ordinate their work with the work being done by researchers in similar fields from other geographical regions who have working interests in Latin America.

The Committee also planned to work on a set of exemplary rules to deal with the problems associated with providing differential access to archived data. This is, perhaps, a more general problem than the data archiving problem itself, but the results have not yet been promulgated. The formation of a committee of social scientists on the basis of the archive network was considered in order to establish rules for relationships with local institutions. Several countries already insist that visas be made unavailable to foreign researchers unless those researchers make arrangements to assure the co-participation of local scholars in the research process at the highest levels. As will be seen below, implementations of this policy can create pressures for archives to be established. In addition, the Working Committee of the Council hoped to deal with the problems of the division of labour among archives by attempting to arrive at inter-institutional agreements with respect to the production, archiving, and utilization of data sets.

The Latin American Council on Social Sciences and the Latin American Studies Association did reach an agreement on a minimum set of rules for non-Latin American researchers working in that region. Central to the emergence of these rules was the requirement that copies of the data produced by foreign researchers be left behind upon the departure of the foreign researchers. This could only be done in some useful fashion if archives were available to accept, store, inventory, maintain and make available the data thus left behind. As a consequence the growth of data available for archiving in Latin America and perhaps other areas of the world in which this kind of policy is adopted may be faster than would be anticipated by the level of local research alone. But the policy remains unimplemented and the pressure for archive growth unrealized.

The Latin American Social Science Council expressed a desire to extend its inventory operation to other countries and to incorporate all existing data archives into their working group as well as to work toward the establishment of new archives in the Latin American region. In particular, there was an interest in co-ordinating data gathering activities in such a way that research groups and archives interested in obtaining comparable data series might be supported more easily. It was planned to distribute print-outs and a periodical bulletin describing recent acquisitions and developments. Such a periodical would certainly aid in the desirable goal of creating consensus about and interest in archival activities and would aid in the incorporation of new institutional, national and disciplinary areas, however issues were produced. A periodical series of technical seminars was planned and the Committee moved forward to a formal agreement of collaboration with the German Institute for Latin American Research in order to establish communication that would permit ready knowledge of the research currently in progress and of the researchers currently working in Latin America. The agreement called for publication and transmittal of research results in both Germany and Latin America and would establish joint seminars as well as determining the status of visiting researchers, systematizing collaboration and establishing joint research projects. So far, however, there has been very little in the way of concrete evidence produced of the kind planned by the Latin American Committee. There are many reasons - perhaps the most important is simply a

lack of funds. But it is also worth noting that no-
where in the staffing arrangements that were
developed was there an individual with a pressing
need for the desired results. The projects never
became the "crusade" of anyone in particular.

In Brazil, for example, a data centre at the
Federal University of Minas Gerais was established
whose purpose was to provide data bases of and a
common empirical framework for social and political research projects by the faculty, trainees and
graduate students. In particular, a common focus
on municipios as the unit of analysis was maintained
and all work done by faculty and students focused
upon obtaining, evaluating, systematizing and cleaning social and political aggregate data within these
units. The effort was to gain socio-economic data
from demographic, economic and educational censuses; electoral data; and municipal, State and
national government input and output data. Although
an eventual aim was to widen the geographical basis
of the archive to include data from all Latin
America and to diversify the units of analysis to
include survey data and historical documents, this
goal has not yet been reached. Work on the Brazilian
data continues, however, as local teaching and
research activities have been set up to utilize and
augment this particular resource.

In Asia, at the moment, perhaps the most
advanced efforts toward developing social science
data archives can be seen in the work of the Indian
Council of Social Science Research (ICSSR). This
group has established as its objectives review of
the progress of social science research in India
and a willingness to provide advice to users of
social science research. It also has agreed to
sponsor social science research programmes and
projects by administering grants to institutions
and individuals for this purpose. It gives financial
support to associations, journals, and organizations
for conducting social science research; and provides,
on occasion, technical assistance for the formation
of programmes and the design of research projects.
Work is underway toward the organization and provision of training programmes in research methodology and to indicate the areas and topics in which
research should be promoted in order to further
scientific and practical knowledge. The Council is
in a position to co-ordinate many of the research
activities in the social sciences and to encourage
programmes of interdisciplinary research since it
is, in fact, the major source of funding for this
type of work in India. It has been able to take steps
toward establishing a network of centres for documentation and analytic services, and intends to
maintain the supply of social science data in India.
The first edition of an inventory of data has been
distributed and a national register of social scientists is planned. The Council has organized and
provided financial support for workshops and conferences to promote research and utilization of
research in India. It has also begun the publication
of a newsletter, and eventually will expand to

digests, periodicals and journals of social science
research in India. The Council has instituted and
now administers scholarships, fellowships and
other awards for social science research for students,
teachers, and research workers and plays a vital
rôle in advising the Indian Government on social
science research and collaboration with foreign
agencies.

The Council's first task, now completed, was
to commission a survey of social science research
in India. A working group on data archives was
also established and produced a recommendation
to develop a series of data libraries with arrangements for co-ordination and co-operation among
them.

The data inventory programme referred to
above was done by Unesco in collaboration with the
International Social Science Council and several
regional and national bodies, among which is the
ICSSR. Its first collection included a survey of
several hundreds of research projects categorized
along eight dimensions: the structure of the data,
the phase of the research, the objective and type of
study, the research methods employed, and period
during which the field work was accomplished,
the sampling and processing procedures, the
storage and accessibility of the data, and the
resulting publications. The ICSSR has also considered the possibility of a programme to transfer
to punched cards some of the vital data of India
which is currently available only on a non-machine
readable format. It has recommended that programmes be undertaken to carry out content
analyses of published and unpublished documents
and create a bibliographical research unit as well
as a unit to appraise the research design. Note-
worthy here is the ability of the ICSSR to produce
concrete results by providing the financial resources
to individuals or organizations with an intrinsic
need for the successful completion of the designated
task.

One of the most developed of the research
facilities of social sciences in India, for example,
is the Data Unit of the Center for the Study of
Developing Societies. It contains aggregate data
on socio-economic and political indicators as
well as survey data for secondary analysis of
social and political behaviour, community and
organizational data, case study materials (often
in the form of documents), and biographical data
on political and administrative elite, both historical and contemporary. The Center engages in
comparative studies across regions, examines
temporal trends, and searches for correlational
and cross-variable factors so that it might project toward the future. In particular, the focus
of this Center's work is on social change, areas
of stress in contemporary society, and problems
of the future. So far it has produced monographs
as well as the creation of the specialized data
banks.

The Data Unit of this centre provides assistance

to research staff with processed and unprocessed aggregate and survey data, collection and organization of data on education, communication, political activities, social movements, economic modernization, ecological and electoral variables, and is currently reorganizing and computing data on political variables as they are intercorrelated with social and economic indicators. It has underway a study of urbanization, migration and unrest, as well as studies of nomination selection procedures for candidates and it is engaged in aggregate analysis of responses to family planning programmes. Considering the nature and level of activity of such a centre it is not surprising that the administration of it would seek out support in order to carry out many of the ICSSR projects, as these projects serve its own immediate needs. This principle of providing support for projects directly to organizations which, themselves, require - not just desire - the results, seems to work well.

The Indian experience also shows that problems such as data access and the patrimony of the State versus the needs for professional autonomy for researchers are not unique to any one country. Creation of an archive or services of data centres may be considered in response to many kinds of problems. The type of archive to be created as a consequence may vary considerably according to local needs. In the Indian case, for example, consideration has been given to the establishment of three types of data centres, with several specimens of the first two types. The entire network would then be co-ordinated by a standing committee of the Indian Council for Social Science Research.

The first type would provide a focal point for user demands and services. Transforming data into machine-readable form, providing data processing facilities and serving as a repository of analytic expertise would be the major functions of centres of this type. They would be distributed about the country and provide regional centres for social science research activities. Their primary emphasis would be to facilitate the utilization of existing data.

The second type of centre would be somewhat more oriented to the production of social science data. They would provide the infrastructure within data producing organizations to transform data to machine-readable form and to store it. It would fall upon them to provide newsletters on data centre activities, conduct and publish inventories of quantitative social science data projects, and commission and publish working papers on quantitative data from their centres in order to permit much earlier access to those materials, than would be provided by more conventional publication procedures.

The third type of centre would have only a single cell and would be related directly to the Council itself and would serve that body in pursuing its own data needs. This would include transforming selected data into machine-readable form as well as indexing, preserving, and disseminating data for which no immediate user demand existed but which it was agreed was of great potential interest or historical value. All of these centres would facilitate the utilization of existing quantitative social science data. One of their central functions would be to provide training programmes for research scholars, as well as serve as repositories of data in order to safeguard, index and disseminate it more fully. The centres would also provide areas where the social science computing needs of the country could become highly visible and clearly articulated. In an undertaking of this size, then, organizational and functional as well as substantive and geographical types of division of labour should be contemplated in the creation of data archive networks.

Clearly there is a tremendous variety of activities currently being planned for or actually being carried out under the aegis of data archives. The preceding sections have provided an overview of these activities and the organizations carrying them out. Let us now turn to a more systematic consideration of the functions performed by data archives and the details of their operating structure.

OPERATIONAL CONSIDERATIONS OF ARCHIVES

DATA ACQUISITION FUNCTION

Data archives, like their more traditional counterparts continuing published works, perform a variety of functions. Foremost among these, of course, is that of acquisition - obtaining new materials for archive holdings from some continuing sources of supply. This activity requires the establishment of both formal and informal arrangements with institutions, departments or bureaus that produce data on a regular basis in order to obtain some or all of their production. It is often much more convenient for a potential supplier to negotiate some arrangement to supply all or all of some class of his data to an archive on a regular basis than for him to go through the difficulty, time after time, of selecting what information is to be archived and what is not. An arrangement of this kind has important consequences for the archive and these are dealt with at some length later on. In the meantime, it is enough to note that making such an arrangement quickly forces an archive to establish priorities for the investment of as scarce resources in selecting materials for cleaning or preparing for later use, or even for storing them where space itself is at a premium.

In addition, when arrangements are made to supply all or much of the output of a data generating activity to a single archive, it is usually the case that the producers of the materials require assurance that their data will not be used for purposes harmful to the client who initially sponsored the research. This is, of course, a difficult thing to foresee. Thus some mechanism has to be established to control the distribution of data and for deciding who will be given access to what data and under what circumstances. Archives generally press for more universalistic rule, for example, that a particular data may be available only upon the expressed permission of the donor, for example, thus putting the burden of approval upon the donor To avoid the complications associated with such policies, many archives will not accept data without the assurance that within some specified period of

time that data would become freely available to all who ask for it. That is, the data would move from a more restrictive to a less restrictive category on an automatic basis, usually within a standard period of time.

Even when a data set is not freely available, however, its existence within the archive, and knowledge of its existence, can serve a very important function by advising other scholars of the kind of material that does already exist on a topic and by opening up to them the identification of and possibility of negotiation with the original donors. Such negotiation can often provide some insights into the problem, even if direct access to the data itself is still prohibited.

It should go without saying that archives must be scrupulous in their respect for the wishes of the data donors if only to continue receiving data. One policy that has worked well for this purpose has been where data requiring permission for its use or distribution is simply never made accessible to anyone - close friend, staff member, important colleague or prestigious person - without a formal letter in the archive files signed by the donor himself and stating explicitly that the specific user in question, person or institution, may have the data for the purposes specified. This practice puts pressure upon the donor, especially where a data set is in great demand, to change the status of the materials, to make them freely available so that he will not be bothered by the need for constant review of the status of the materials. Usually donors are informed on a regular basis of the requests for and utilization of data supplied by them, and this is often enough control so that they are willing to remove barriers to the free accession of their data.

It is important that the archive sensitize regular suppliers to the growing need of a great variety of users for raw data. Efforts along these lines have resulted, in many cases, in the suppliers' standardizing the format of their own works so that cleaning and indexing operations are greatly facilitated. As a result, suppliers are also provided with the previously unexploited possibility of exploring topics over time with data initially collected only for a single purpose at a single moment. Thus the archive in the attempt to satisfy its own, internal needs, can and often does have an impact upon the data suppliers. The most important of these effects is an increase in the degree of standardized preparation of data and its preparation in a more regular and reliable fashion. The resulting consequences for cleaning and indexing are profound.

Of course, not all suppliers produce a regular and continuing stream of materials. Many times new materials must be obtained from suppliers who may produce only one or a small number of studies on a very irregular basis. In order to keep in touch with sources of this type it is necessary for an archive's staff to be engaged in a constant review of the literature in a variety of disciplines examining for news of field work recently completed, undertaken or even in the planning stage in order to identify potential sources of data. When a potential supplier has been identified, correspondence must be initiated. This often leads to a situation where, after preliminary negotiations, it is necessary for the archive staff to keep track of and to keep in touch with the potential supplier over a period of months or years, in various locations, as he goes through the continuing stages of data collection, preparation, and analysis and publication. The burden of this pursuit has led, in at least one instance, to the development of an automated correspondence review system where for each instance of correspondence with a potential supplier (or even a potential user) that is still outstanding, i.e., to which some response might be anticipated although the response might be months or years away, an entry is made on a magnetic tape and this tape is reviewed monthly. In the review process the archive staff is notified of all past correspondence which should be reviewed during the current month, and the status of the correspondence file is then automatically changed to show that a new letter was sent out during this month. Using such a system it is possible to review, regularly, all of the outstanding correspondence, still unanswered, from the previous month or months, or even a year or more, and to delve once again into the problems of revivifying the correspondence with the suppliers. An elaborate system like this is necessary where there is a great deal of correspondence and many suppliers who, after being contacted in the early stages of their search, ask that they be contacted again at some future date when they are ready to think about giving their data to an archive. It is unrealistic to place the burden of contact on the potential supplier and expect him to contact the archive when he is ready.

While the central thrust of the initial correspondence is the necessity of explaining the concept of archives to a potential supplier and convincing him of the desirability and advantages of donating his data to an archive, the skills required for such activity are not inconsiderable and the amount of work involved may be enormous. It is often the case that correspondence alone is insufficient integrity to inform the potential supplier adequately or to convince him of the archive. In such cases some sort of face to face interpersonal contact is absolutely essential in order to obtain the data itself. A great deal of energy must be devoted to providing assurances that the supplier can maintain some control over access to his data. Although total control can be exercised by him for some fixed time period, he must be convinced that eventually, usually within a period of from 2 to 5 years, his data will revert to the public domain. Because of the timing involved and the matters of mutual trust and confidence, much of the acquisition from individual suppliers must actually be done via personal contacts; correspondence alone is not enough. Since many of the data sets have an ephemeral quality to them, it is necessary for the archive personnel to be well integrated into the world of research so that they can learn about and begin acquisition of potentially useful data sets before the data itself is actually lost or destroyed.

Of course obtaining new materials from a variety of suppliers, each of whom is producing only a small number of very different kinds of studies, means that the form in which data arrives at the archive itself varies tremendously from supplier to supplier and from study to study. Obviously, this complicates the cleaning and indexing processes considerably. At the same time, as archives become more common and scholars are more prone to utilize them prior to their entrance into the field for data gathering, it is becoming more common for them to make some effort to adapt their own format to that used by some of the major archives. This movement to adopt archive conventions for personal endeavors reaches its ultimate when funding sources require that arrangements for archiving be made prior to the actual release of funds for the research itself. Without such pressures, unfortunately, the diversity of personal styles in documentation of machine readable social science data tends to increase as more research is done by more people on an occasional or one-time basis.

An essential consideration in the area of data acquisition for archives is the necessity to establish priorities for the kind of data and the nature of the data to be acquired. Every archive must have some policy for selecting materials to be added to its collection. Whether or not the policy is actually expressed in a written statement, it is reflected in the decisions made on a day-to-day basis by the management. The implications of the acquisition policy are far reaching indeed and should be carefully considered and constantly reviewed. Since the cost of processing and maintaining a data set for the archive's collection usually is far greater than the cost of acquisition of the material, selections must be made with great care. Unlike pamphlet material or reprints which are easy to preserve, ephemeral or frequently replicated data sets which are widely available elsewhere should only be acquired when there is a concrete need for them as they are likely never to be needed. There is a very high probability of being able to obtain popular data sets elsewhere if a local need for them actually develops; the costs of acquiring, cleaning, indexing and maintaining a data set should be considered in relation to the likelihood of there being multiple users for it; the possibility of acquiring it at some later date if the need should arise then; its availability at a reasonable cost and with little delay from some other source; the amount of overlap with the existing collection and the intrinsic significance of the data. There is often considerable pressure upon the archive to acquire data in order to complete some set, fill some gap or develop some potential for a special kind of analysis (comparative or time series, for example), simply because these are "reasonable" materials to have and should be of interest to professionals in various disciplines even though no specific interest has actually been expressed. The argument is made - quite correctly - that few scholars are as aware of the kinds of data available as the archivist is and if only the materials were available they would be used. This is a compelling argument and must be balanced by the cost of maintaining materials which are not, in fact, used. The most effective means of resolving the dilemmas of assigning priorities for the acquisition of data sets, then, is the establishment of an archive user's advisory committee. In this way the archivist's up-to-date knowledge of the availability of materials can be tempered by the researcher's knowledge of likely data requirements within their fields of expertise.

A criterion not to be overlooked in establishing acquisition priorities is that of methodological adequacy. Considering the costs involved in acquisition, storage, maintenance, indexing and cataloguing of the materials, archivists have often decided to pass up studies of great substantive interest which appear to have been done in such a poor manner, utilizing such sloppy and shoddy techniques of data gathering or documentation that despite the interest of the subject matter, the data set is not worth acquiring. The tension between the need for methodological adequacy and substantive interest is one that reoccurs constantly in the battle for establishing priorities for acquisition.

Operating policy should include a list of criteria which studies should meet if the data set is to be considered acceptable. At a very minimum the following documentation should be available for each study:
(a) Complete and accurate codebook or description of the data structure;
(b) Description of the data format;
(c) Illustrations of structure and format;
(d) Total size of data set;

(e) Complete and accurate description of the organization of the files for the medium in which the data are stored;
(f) Precise definition for each data element;
(g) Complete explanation for all codes used;
(h) Sample of documents used in data gathering;
(i) Descriptions of sampling procedures employed, with intended and resultant sample size;
(j) Summary of training provided field workers and coders;
(k) Description of data collection procedures;
(l) Name and current address of study director.
The ephemerality of the original source was mentioned earlier as one of the criteria to be considered in acquiring data. It is sometimes necessary to acquire a data set which may or may not actually be kept simply because the data set is about to disappear, and unless acquired by an archive there will be no possibility of assessing its actual level of methodological sophistication or the degree of substantive interest which may be expressed in it. If the data set is not acquired at that moment it will never be possible to acquire it. Naturally it is more important to acquire complete data sets than sets where important sectors or segments of the data are missing. Hence completeness is also a criterion for acquisition.

Finally, it is necessary to give some thought to the accessibility of data once it has been prepared. While a case might be made for acquiring and preparing materials which will not be available for general access in the foreseeable future, it would seem that the amount of data to be acquired that would be available for use and is of recognized importance is so great that the acquisition of materials which could still not be readily accessible to scholars should have a low priority indeed.

THE DATA CLEANING FUNCTION

Once data has been acquired, the archive usually must then perform a second major function, that of cleaning the data, that is, placing data into a format that is easily handled by computers, and identifying and correcting possible discrepancies between the actual format of the data and the descriptions of that format. This is necessary because, in many instances, data is acquired on punched cards where the format was designed to facilitate analysis on unit record machines. It is a rare computing installation indeed that is prepared to handle material prepared in this way. Typically, this data is often multiply-punched, that is, more than one punch has been placed in a single column of a single card and unusual combinations of punches have been employed or blanks have been used, for example, to stand for some kinds of information as well as the zero to stand for other kinds of information. At many computing installations it is often difficult to read multiply-punched data or make a distinction between zeros and blanks. Even where the data set is already in a form suitable for processing by one type of computer, it may pose difficulties for another. The 1960 one-in-one-thousand sample of the United States Census, for example, was available on magnetic tape in either of two forms - neither of which was readily compatible with the types of computing equipment most generally available to scholars and analysts. As computing machinery evolves, furthermore, steps must be taken to guarantee the continuing compatibility of archive holdings with available machinery. The rate of development has been so rapid that, in some instances, two transformations have been necessary to keep already cleaned data in a usable form. If modifications are not made to accommodate the format demanded by each major computing development, adequate transformation at a later date may become very difficult.

Thus some effort must be devoted to the problems of making data legible as it is received by reformatting and by maintaining this legibility by further reformatting when necessary. Once this is done, it is also necessary to make sure that the codebooks, that is, the description of the format of the information, duly corresponds with the data itself. If, for example, the codebook says that in the ninth column of the second card of the data for a given individual, the sex of the respondent is signified by a one-punch for a male and a two-punch for female, this must be the information that is punched in that column of that card or represented in the appropriate manner on the magnetic tape. This process often requires some rather sophisticated sleuthing on the part of very competent social scientists who are also sophisticated in the area of data processing. They must examine the distribution of the punches for each column to see if in the example given above all of the cases have either a one or a two-punch and that a large portion of the cases do not have, say, 3's, 4's, or 5's. In this latter instance, some suspicion might be aroused that one was looking at something other than the sex of the respondents since for that particular case only three legitimate punches are possible: male, female and undetermined or don't know. Once this step has been completed, it is necessary to examine the data in order to locate and correct contingency errors such as responses to questions that were not applicable to the particular respondents or returns for an election that was not held in a given year. Data must then be stored in a format that permits easy storage, easy retrieval that is accurate and economical in a form which is, in turn, usable at other computing installations.

Although, in general, archives try to reduce errors in the data which can be attributed to coding and keypunching to less than about one per cent, it is not entirely clear what the standards for the minimum degree of cleanliness are. A legitimate debate among archivists has evolved about this very point. On the one hand are those who see the user

community as being represented by those with relatively limited facilities in the area of computing (and sometimes in the area of expertise as well) requiring as a consequence that the archive do as much as possible to facilitate their own work. On the other hand, it is pointed out that the users of archive materials are very sophisticated indeed and have access to the most advanced kinds of equipment available. As a consequence, the archive should do no cleaning at all but allow each user to do that which he feels is minimally necessary for his own work, and of course the user is the best judge of what that minimum is. Eventually, if the results of the cleaning operations of various users are fed back to the archive, the data will actually be cleaned by those with the greatest interest in its being cleaned - the users themselves. The archive's ability to synthesize and document the cleaning activities of several different users requires, however, some extremely sophisticated procedures and equipment.

THE CONVENTIONS AND STANDARD FUNCTION

In order to facilitate the process of utilizing data initially prepared by others, it is necessary to establish conventions for coding and standards for describing the data sets themselves. This third function of archives is necessary in order to permit combining information from different collections in some reasonable way; to combine samples from different studies in order to increase the number of cases; or to make comparisons among data sets. Thus many archives have moved toward a common, standardized way of handling the same type of information, particularly missing data or non-responses and this facilitates later analysis considerably. These standards as currently used by many archives are attached in Appendix 3. All archives face the problem of obtaining descriptions of the study design, the sampling procedure, the field work methods and other information that is not contained in the data itself, and of course it is crucial that this information also be included somewhere in the data description. Researchers about to enter the field have been aided considerably by prior examination of the documentation and coding practices adopted by archives. The solutions to common dilemmas have made their work easier.

DATA PROCESSING AND ANALYSIS FUNCTION

A fourth function of data archives involves the actual manipulation of data for the user's purposes. This most often revolves about the problems of reformatting, i.e. providing materials to the user in a format compatible with his local facilities as contrasted to a format which the archive adopts as an aid to its own convenience for storage purposes. Archives must be able to provide users with punched cards in 80-column (or other) format, in rectangular, round or other type of punching configurations, on 7 or 9 track magnetic tape, at different densities, and at different parities, all as a function of the capabilities of the computing installation to which the user has access. It is sometimes necessary to provide users with specially prepared data sets rather than simple copies. Typically in such a data set only a fraction of the information is provided - such selected cases or selected variables - whatever is needed by the user, or prohibited to him by the donor must be taken into account.

Occasionally it is necessary for archives to provide some sort of hard copy, that is, printout or partially processed machine readable output of data, aggregated, for example, from individual to organizational or from small political to large geographical area. This may be because of user needs or because of supplier restrictions. Very often it is necessary to aggregate data in order to protect and assure the confidentiality of the original respondents. In this situation archives may retain data on individuals but only distribute information on groups of individuals.

Archives are often requested to provide actual data processing and statistical analysis service for users who do not have access to appropriate facilities of their own or where the user has no reason to obtain the entire data sets when a single analysis will suffice for his needs. Many researchers who work with a national census can serve as examples. It is unreasonable to expect such a user to acquire an entire collection of census materials in order to carry out a small number of analyses. It is also necessary, on occasion, to perform sophisticated analyses for a user simply because his own facilities are not adequate for carrying out the kinds of analyses desired.

THE DISSEMINATION OF DOCUMENTATION FUNCTION

A fifth function of archives is to develop and disseminate codebooks and other material describing available data. As mentioned before, a codebook relates the data content to the data format. Often the original researcher's own documents may require a fair amount of translation as localisms and special usages may not be intelligible outside of the context in which the research was initially carried out. The availability of this kind of material provides a great pool of examples for other studies and it is possible in the development of new research instruments to examine the kinds of measures that have been used previously and to ascertain their utility for describing some groups or making some distinctions within others. Codebooks also provide the basis for indexing the contents of archives. Many studies, particularly surveys, are so heterogeneous in their content that any attempt to use the entire study as an indexing unit are almost hopeless.

Rather, it is necessary to examine and catalogue individual variables within studies. It is also necessary for archives to maintain, if possible, related materials, especially those derived from the original study in order to provide examples of how the data has been analysed already and clarify ambiguities in the interpretation of it. It is common policy for an archive to request a copy of every publication resulting from the utilization of data obtained from that archive to augment their collection of any publication of the original supplier of the data.

THE STORAGE AND MAINTENANCE FUNCTION

Perhaps the most obvious function of an archive, the sixth here, is that which all archives perform, and that is the storage and maintenance of the data itself. Materials can deteriorate slowly, such as questionnaires or printed matter, analyses, data descriptions, and even punched cards, or they may deteriorate more rapidly as in the case of magnetic tapes. Consequently, it is necessary to establish appropriate facilities for dealing with materials of each of these two types. Heat, humidity, rodents or other parasites may well attack materials of the former type, but magnetic materials must be insulated from magnetic flux and physical shock as well. Even with these precautions it is necessary to recopy magnetic tapes on a periodic basis in order to assure their continued utility and, where usage is very heavy, to protect against deterioration due to machine-induced wear. Internal procedures must be established in an archive to identify the current storage location of all materials. In most cases there is nothing in the material itself that identifies it. Unless a special labeling convention has been adopted, it is usually not possible to pick up a deck of cards, leaf through them and ascertain from the patterns of punches what in fact those punches refer to or to discern the contents of a reel of tape. It is necessary to have cards securely boxed, and labeled in a way that will insure unambiguous identification of the contents. Similarly with magnetic tapes. In this latter case, it is possible and, in fact, desirable to label not only the tape reel but to have as a precaution a machine-readable label as the first part of every file. If this is done, however, it will usually be necessary to remove this label from any copies of the material being sent elsewhere unless special arrangements have been made in advance to handle the label. Most computer programmes presume that they will be encountering only data and not descriptions of data and will not function properly if the label is not taken into account.

THE INVENTORY FUNCTION

All of this suggests the seventh function of an archive, that of maintaining a rather elaborate inventory of the studies contained within it. The inventory of studies should be indexed not only by general topic, but also by specific questions. This facilitates the reassembling of data sets to user specifications by assuring the inclusion of all required items without the necessity of duplicating unessential information. It is also necessary to maintain an inventory of studies and questions available through other archives so that users need not be routed on large and sometimes fruitless searches leading from institution to institution in a quest for appropriate materials. It should be possible for a user upon his approach to any archive to be informed of what is available in every archive. In most cases inventories have been based on codebook contents, and the stage was passed long ago where the number of studies and the number of questions permitted manual indexing. These numbers are so great that only automated devices are capable of appropriately keeping track of and indexing the extraordinary variety of materials already in existence.

Two devices have been used so far in developing codebook-based inventories. The first depends upon the tagging of every question with some label or labels in order to classify it appropriately in terms of the substantive variables with which it might be associated. This requires an elaborate and extensive categorizing scheme that is, at the same time, inclusive of the interests that the great variety of users may and actually do express as well as exhaustive in the categories' coverage. In addition, use of such a system requires a staff of clerks with a sufficient command of the various disciplines involved to make an accurate assessment of how the specific question should be appropriately tagged.

A second approach to the problem of indexing has relied upon the actual words appearing in the questions themselves. Automated procedures are then employed to produce concordant indexes of these words. Thus every question from every study in an archive containing the word "vote" or "voting", for example, would be listed along with the proper identification of its source. This indexing procedure is so voluminous in its output, however, that it soon becomes necessary for users to develop a capacity for interacting with the data base in such a way that they can specify strings of concatenations of words which, when they appear within a question, cause that question to be selected as a possible source. Combinations of these two approaches, that is, human-based question tagging and automated indexing, are desirable and, in fact, have been used with success.

A third approach to inventorying, which also depends upon some degree of intervention by skilled assistants at the time of creating the codebooks, involves writing of summaries which can then be searched - either automatically or by the individual user. These usually consist of a summary description of the major purposes of the study and a listing of the crucial variables employed but do not contain any reference to specific questions. Clearly an important problem in creating an index of archive holdings is to arrive at an appropriate division of labour. The question is, should the archive on cataloguing place great emphasis on detailed cataloguing or is the burden more appropriately placed on the user to develop more sophisticated searching strategies. This is not a question that has yet been resolved to a degree satisfactory both to archives and to users.

It should be noted that it is not sufficient to stop with the identification of only those materials that are readily available to users when creating archive inventories and indices. It is also necessary to include references to data which is not yet available either because it has not been acquired, has been acquired but not yet cleaned, or even though acquired and cleaned, distribution of it is restricted in some way. An inventory can serve as a useful device for users even where they may not actually obtain the data itself by alerting scholars to others in the field with similar interests as well as permitting the articulation of new data gathering offerings with already existing ones.

THE RETRIEVAL FUNCTION

Retrieval is the eighth function of archives. Archives are required to retrieve various types of information. Archives may retrieve a total data description such as the codebook and summary for a study. It may retrieve partial or total data sets and, in some cases, may be asked to retrieve parts of several data sets in order to create integrated, multi-file data sets. For such a request, the archive must bring together data from a variety of sources (typically in a variety of formats) focusing upon a given theme, problem, event, or location. This often requires the archive to search not only its own holdings but those of other archives as well and, where necessary, obtain from other archives those materials required to solve the needs of the user. In this way the collections of archives gradually come to be more overlapping and integrated. It is not reasonable in every case to expect a user to assemble his own data file from bits and pieces of data available in many forms in a variety of archives. It is more feasible and practical for the archives to do that for him and have, as a result, materials that could be used by many investigators.

THE DIFFUSION FUNCTION

Perhaps the function of data archives which differs most fundamentally from that of their more traditional counterparts is the diffusion of data to users. In the conventional archive the user is often required to come to the archive in order to examine the rare materials stored there and then, perhaps, to copy those he needs but only using specified non-harmful means, the data archive specializes in copying its own collection and making it available to the user at his convenience, in the form most suitable to his purposes. The preparation of materials to user specification, then, can require quite a bit of sophistication on the part of the archive staff and does require access to, if not direct possession of, a variety of sophisticated machinery. It must be possible for an archive to prepare data according to almost any format that the user might desire. Although international competition in the computing area may change matters, current possibilities of reducing materials to only on standard data format are not very likely.

Once materials have been prepared there still remains the problem of shipping it out to a distant user. This can be difficult in areas where the postal service is not particularly oriented in this direction. A carton of data cards weighing sometimes more than 20 kilograms would be difficult to ship through the mails of many countries and other shipping devices are both expensive and, on occasion unreliable. The problems of sending magnetic materials by courier are now complicated by airport search procedures where passengers are passed through a magnetic field. If prior arrangements are not made, this procedure would serve to obliterate the information carried on a magnetic tape. Although soluble, practical problems of this type must be considered in the development of archives and steps taken to overcome them.

In the process of making data available, archives must still maintain control over access to their materials in accordance with any wishes of the original donor. Very often this leads to problems of controlling illegitimate rediffusion. This happens, for example, when one user acquires material for a specific purpose and then makes this material available for another purpose to a second user to whom the material may not have been available in the first place. It is for this reason that it is probably the best policy to make each user contact the original supplier directly for any special permission and thus place himself openly on record about the purposes for which he intends to use the data and his willingness to abide by any restrictions against rediffusion. The only sanction available to archives for dealing with those who ignore such procedures is to limit access of that user to other archive materials in the future. Often that is not much of a sanction at all. The problem of illegitimate rediffusion can be heightened even further where, as in the case of some archives, the sale of data is the source of revenue for the archive. By the illegitimate sale or redistribution of data by users the revenue-producing potential of that material is totally destroyed for the original archive. This sensitive area must be thought through carefully by archivists and only with the help of a well-organized archive and archive-user organization can practical policies be worked out.

The diffusion activities of archives place actual and potential users in contact with suppliers and with each other. Thus it is possible to promote the research enterprise by the maintenance of files of inquiries so that people with common interests can be told of their common interests and contacts between them facilitated, particularly when they are working with a common data set. This activity is also facilitated by the creation and utilization of an archive newsletter, for example, in order to advertise the contents and services of the archive as well as inform potential users of the kinds of uses being made of data held by it.

THE TRAINING FUNCTION

Archives must also train users, suppliers and other archivists. They must train users in the exploitation of this new type of social science information resource; teach them how to make a query, where to make a query so that the appropriate data can be obtained, and once the data is obtained, how to utilize it; teach them the devices available for processing, the strategies to be employed for analysis, and the kinds of interpretations that can be made from such analyses.

Suppliers must be educated in the preparation of their data for other users. They must be impressed with the need to document their work and need to be shown the methods for doing so. They must be instructed in the methods available for storing data and the necessity for giving consideration to the storing problem when establishing the format in which they will gather and process their own data originally.

It is also necessary for archives to provide training to archivists themselves. They must be trained in the procedures for establishing and maintaining an archive. There is a need to discuss not only the techniques involved in daily operation of social science data archives, but also the general policy questions which are generated by an activity of this sort.

THE PROGRAMME DEVELOPMENT FUNCTION

The eleventh and final function of archives is to engage in the development of new programmes, particularly in the collection and creation of specialized data sets on a substantive and temporal basis. Often it is only archive personnel who can have the overall perspective and resources necessary to generate collections of this kind. Even though individual users may not have a need for the material at the moment, collections of users and potential users may be mobilized by archive staffs in order to pursue this kind of information. A further area in programme development is for the archives to encourage - and sometimes engage in - the creation of new computing power. This can be done by underwriting the programming for analysis and information retrieval themselves, of course, but also by clarifying to potential programmers and even to manufacturers of information processing machinery the currently unmet needs of social science data analysts. That is, archives can provide a device for concentrating the interests, requests and needs of a variety of users into a single spokesman capable of articulating them and making strong representations to the computing industry about the creation of appropriate machinery, and strong representations to programmers regarding the potential for development of new analytic aids.

STAFFING FOR ACQUISITIONS

Perhaps the most difficult task in the establishment of a social science data archive is that of staffing the organization. For each of the 11 functions cited above, it is necessary to obtain highly qualified personnel - yet relatively few opportunities exist for individuals to be trained or to gain experience in these activities. Consider first the problems associated with obtaining staff members capable of carrying out the acquisition function of an archive. Individuals involved in this activity must have sufficient competence in the substantive areas of the archives specialization and be able to judge the relevance and assess the possible utility of a variety of data sets encountered in many different settings. Continuous awareness of new and developing data sources is a further requisite for this job and requires constant scanning of an extensive literature as well as continuous correspondence and personal interchange with research workers in one or more substantive areas. In addition, the acquisition function must be performed by individuals sufficiently sophisticated methodologically to permit their assessment of the adequacy of any potential acquisition in terms of the procedures utilized to gather it and the kind of essential supporting information and documentation available for it or the likelihood of obtaining such information from the suppliers in order to make the acquired data of any utility.

To perform these activities well, it is necessary that the individuals responsible for acquisition have sufficient status within the organization of the archive to permit easy and flexible contact with suppliers as the situation may demand. This is often necessary in order to enable him to convince the potential supplier of the reasonableness and desirability of donating data to the archive. This often calls for a fair amount of professional status on the part of the archivist himself for his argument to have any legitimacy. The acquisition function must be performed by individuals having sufficient status within the archive to guarantee its responsibility with regard to the use and rediffusion of donated data. Frequently it is possible to obtain data only if initial arrangements can be accomplished in person

and takes on many of the qualities of a personal exchange. As a consequence, the acquisition function must often be performed by an individual free to travel to the supplier and he must be able to carry out the mechanics of obtaining copies of data and documentation as well as help determine the politics of obtaining access to them. In order to do this, of course, the archive staff member engaged in acquisition must be reasonably conversant with the cultures in which he will be working in order to deal with the mundane problems of data duplication and transfer as these are, in many cases, problems that the supplier himself has been unable to solve. It is also necessary for him to be capable of translating supporting materials to assess their adequacy or, when it is necessary to have them translated, to be capable of judging the quality of the translation. Data without documentation is of little utility and documentation adequate for the original scholar is rarely sufficient for the secondary analyst. Consequently, considerable effort must be expended in obtaining - often by interviewing the investigator and his assistants in the field - adequate documentation for the data being acquired.

STAFFING FOR DATA CLEANING

Once the material has been obtained and delivered to the archive itself, responsibility usually shifts to specialists concerned with the problems of cleaning data sufficiently so that it can be used by other scholars with a minimum of confusion and delay. This function must be performed under the supervision of an individual who knows enough about the substance of the materials being cleaned to identify logical inconsistencies in the data. It is through this process that the relationship of the documentation to the data itself is clarified and it is during this process that correspondence or even further direct, personal contact must often be initiated with the supplier. The cleaning process must be done by someone capable of deciphering ambiguities and illegibilities in the documentation - sometimes by comparison with the original data gathering documents themselves, if they are available. In addition, the substantive competence of the personnel responsible for data cleaning operations must be sufficiently great to permit the integration of complicated data structures into more usable forms. Thus it may be necessary to create an integrated collection of studies dealing with the same topics at different times or bring together into a single data file a focus on the same problems using different analytical units. It is clearly necessary that the person responsible for data cleaning operations have some technical competence in the area of data processing in addition to the substantive skills described above. The cleaning process requires recoding and reformatting of data, (i.e., the removal of multiple-punched, and, in many cases, special symbols such as the plus, minus or even the blank) depending upon local conventions, and the reconstruction of documentation sufficiently detailed to permit easy utilization of the data by secondary analysis. This task may be complicated by such common occurrences as unidentified redundant cards in the data set as a result of attempts by the original investigator to weigh this or the absence of some subset of the population due to an oversight in the duplication process. The individual in charge of data cleaning must have the technical competence to identify and resolve such problems as separating original cards from duplicates. The cleaning process usually requires close examination of frequency distribution for every field or every variable identified in the codebook to check for wild punches or to identify possible systematic discrepancies between data and documentation. In many instances it is necessary to match the respondents in different waves of panel studies or match respondents in subareas with the characteristics of larger areas. All of the tasks require a constant shuffling back and forth between codebooks, data, original protocols, and computer printouts, and frequently results in the need to communicate with the original researcher once again. All of this may illustrate how important it is for the cleaning function to be conducted by individuals combining both substantive and technical expertise, who are articulate, and capable of facile communication with a broad range of scholars and researchers, suppliers and users of data.

THE CODING AND DATA PROCESSING STAFF

Frequently materials are received by an archive in a form that is not immediately suitable for machine manipulation. Some coding and preparation is then required. To the extent that the materials received are in non-machine readable form, some individuals on the staff must be capable of creating a coding scheme that represents the data in coded format with a minimum loss of information. Provision must also be made for the original materials to be coded into that scheme and then transformed to machine readable form. These skills are not at all identical and it is often the case that a staff member capable of conceptualizing a particular set of codes is unwilling or unable to do the tedious coding job itself. The task of code creation requires a sufficient substantive knowledge to generate an appropriate set of coding categories that summarize the information and are particularly suitable for analysis. The coding task itself requires no substantive skills at all, simply careful attention to details and meticulous workmanship. The actual transformation to machine readable form via keypunching, microfilming, or other procedures such as optical scanning requires the services (often available on outside contract) of specialists in order to be economically feasible. However, even if the data has been acquired in a machine readable form, it is still necessary for a staff member to create a duplicate

copy for backup purposes and to carry out any transformation in data format required by local hardware or machine considerations. Again, this can be done by technicians who have no substantive sophistication but who are familiar with the operations of the local computing installation.

It is important that someone on the staff, usually someone directly associated with the coding and machine preparation activities, is capable of identifying the needs for data processing equipment and procedures currently unmet at the archive installation. It is in this way that the archive data processing operations can have an impact on the rational development of computer programmes and policies to aid in archive functions. Thus the data processing specialist should be able to articulate as well as identify unmet needs in this area, give guidance to programming specialists who carry out the actual developmental work, and represent archive interests in computer centre policy planning situations.

STAFFING FOR DATA ANALYSIS

Data archives are often called upon to carry out some aspects of the data analysis for users who may not have the facilities or the competence to do so themselves. This requires the presence on the archive staff of, or ready access by staff members to, a consultant with a fair degree of statistical competence; someone who is capable, when required, of suggesting appropriate analytical procedures as well as the capacity, when required, to perform or supervise the production of specified data processing tasks and statistical analyses for users. This is a delicate area and the archive staff must be sensitive to the problems of the user. Whenever feasible the staff should make the effort to train users to perform such functions themselves.

THE DOCUMENTATION STAFF

None of the analytical functions can be performed, however, without the availability of adequate documentation describing the data in its archived format. This requires the presence of staff members capable of writing and editing codebooks. In addition this staff must oversee the production of the codebooks themselves in machine readable form, usually by keypunching. Machine readable codebooks are increasingly an absolute necessity as archives become more complex and varied in their contents, as they provide the most feasible approach to indexing the archives content via the automated machine-based analysis of the codebooks themselves. Even prior to this step, however, it is often necessary for the original documents to be translated into the archive's official language and some capacity - usually external to the archive must be developed for this task.

A further technical consideration for the every-day operation of an archive involves transportation of bulky data to and from some remote storage location, in order to provide at least one copy of the data as a backup in the event of some local disaster. A courier engaged in this activity may also be employed to transport work to and from the location of the computer, if that is necessary. All that is required of personnel at this level is responsibility and hard work. The employee should be capable of keeping careful track of the location of specific items in storage and it should be possible to rely upon him to be faithful to the performance of his duties.

THE INVENTORY STAFF

Once the archive is in existence, the necessity to keep a continuous record of its contents in a form oriented toward the demands of users is fundamental. The preparation and maintenance of such an inventory requires the attention of someone with sufficient substantive knowledge to be able to catalogue items in an appropriate fashion and to keep that catalogue up to date. It is better if this is done in a form that articulates easily with the inventories and catalogues of other archives. In this way, users, when addressing the problem of locating data, can turn to the inventory specialist at the most convenient archive and discover not only what is available of use to him at that installation but what exists in other archives as well.

Archive inventories, increasingly, are based upon an index of variables or even the questions included in the archived studies. These are also summarized in some fashion and constitute the basis of the study descriptions. The archive must have someone on its staff responsible for this work on a continuing basis. In practice, archives managers discover only too often that the knowledge of the archive's contents resides uniquely in the mind of that individual who has painstakingly examined each study - and each variable within each study - with the care and attention necessary for the cleaning process described above. There is a great temptation to allow this person to perform all of the indexing functions as well. This is only desirable if the index entry is made absolutely explicit at the moment the study is finally accepted into the archive in its cleaned form. This procedure does mean that studies not yet incorporated into the archive are not indexed in any way, and it should be noted that this category may, in fact, include the bulk of the materials in the archive's possession. By relying solely on the efforts of the data cleaner to produce its index an archive is placed in an extremely vulnerable position should something happen to the individual who carries on these two activities. It is a wise policy decision to create organizational procedures that assure a widespread knowledge - even at the informal level - of what is actually

contained in the archive. In practice, a great deal of reliance is placed on this informal knowledge to supplement that available, formally, through the inventory or index to variables.

STAFFING FOR RETRIEVAL

The mere existence of an index and an inventory is not enough, however, to place the desired data in the user's hands. There must be some provision for an interface between the user and the archive staff to facilitate this. An individual performing this function must possess sufficient substantive knowledge to translate user requests which - typically cast in abstract theoretical concepts - into the specific terms required by the local retrieval system. Fulfilling this rôle also calls for sufficient technical knowledge to use any automated retrieval systems in operation at the archive. The basis for most functioning retrieval attempts is the variable rather than the study, for example, and the best retrieval systems are those which permit the identification of the variables of interest in all the studies where they occur. A simple reliance on the recall of an individual expert is usually insufficient when working with anything but the simplest collection of materials. The ability to extract a formulation of needs from the user which can be translated into the terms of the local system requires tact as well as skill and considerable substantive expertise.

STAFFING FOR DIFFUSION

Once the appropriate materials have been properly identified, located, and retrieved, the mundane but essential tasks of producing a copy of the data for the user, packaging, shipping, and accounting for these activities still remains to be done. This may require dealing with international shippers as well as local postal services. It will require the creation of - often substantial - packages of punched cards or printout. The physical tasks involved in packing (occasionally crating) and preparing materials for shipment as well as the materials to do so must be readily available. The accounting, of course, must be done scrupulously. Some structure must exist within the archive to facilitate billing users when applicable, in order to recover the costs incurred on his behalf. It is better if the accounts are machined in an itemized fashion so that archive managers as well as users, will be sensitized to the relative contribution to the final cost in each step in retrieval and diffusion. Perhaps, the most important aspect of the diffusion function, however, is maintaining user awareness of the constantly changing contents of the archive and, in particular, promoting interaction with the archive by new and old users alike. This requires a staff member capable of describing the newest developments in archive services as well as the newest archive holdings. In some cases performance of this function requires staff members to utilize automated systems for the selective dissemination of information so that potential users who have already expressed a continuing interest in specific kinds of data will be assured of notification immediately upon the archive's acquisition of materials related to their interests. Staff personnel must also take explicit responsibility for introducing potential users to the procedures for obtaining materials from the archive and, in general, encourage their exploitation of this resource.

Finally, to have staff capable of handling all aspects of data diffusion adequately, it is necessary that someone take the responsibility for controlling access to the materials in the archive. In all instances, this means maintaining control over physical access to all archive materials. Given the extraordinary ease with which extremely costly materials can be inadvertently destroyed, the need for physical security simply cannot be overstressed. Day to day operations require a tactful but very firm staff member capable of exerting enough authority to exclude unauthorized personnel - even those of high status - from the areas in which unique copies of materials are stored or being worked on. An obvious corollary here is the desirability of maintaining copies of materials in disparate locations to lower the risks of a total loss due to the inadvertent destruction of all given data sets or part of one. In addition to the physical access problem there is still that of maintaining other kinds of security as well. Donors often place materials in an archive with the understanding that these materials will be diffused only when explicit permission has been given for diffusion and permission must be sought for each request. In some cases donors request that materials will not be diffused under any circumstances prior to some specific data. Clearly, it is essential for the integrity of the archive that requests of this kind are respected; someone must take explicit responsibility for the actual act of distributing data and be able to assure donors that their wishes will be respected. Although this would appear to be a trivial task, the individual charged with it is often placed under rather extreme pressure by colleagues, friends, status superiors and potential employers to make special exceptions - usually very reasonable ones - for them. Ability to withstand such pressure is not universal and staffing of this function must be done with care.

STAFFING FOR THE TRAINING FUNCTION

Social science data archives are a new phenomenon and, as a consequence, there are few people sophisticated in their development, management or utilization. Unlike more established enterprises, it is necessary for archives to engage in a variety of training activities in addition to those required in order to deal with an established user community. It is necessary to introduce potential users to the procedural elements of archive usage, for example, teach them how materials may be obtained from archives and impress upon them the kinds of restrictions that must be honoured in so doing. Potential users must be introduced to the vocabulary as well as the technology of archives. They must even be introduced to the many ways in which archive materials may be of substantive interest to them. There are many scholars and other potential users of social science data (perhaps the majority) to whom it is not at all obvious how archive materials can be turned to their purposes and there are few, if any, existing programmes outside the archives themselves designed to introduce potential users to this material. Archives must maintain some staff, then, capable of organizing appropriate instructional programmes, recruiting the necessary faculty if the archive itself is unable to provide it, securing materials, recruiting students and bring these elements together to maintain some continuing visible activity.

An independent, but equally vital sphere of training is that related directly to the problems of development. Since social science data archives have such a relatively short history and since there are so few archives in actual operation, there are very few people indeed who have had some opportunity to work in and to learn about archives of this kind. The need to replace archive personnel who, for one reason or another, must depart, and the need for supplying trained personnel for new archives are continuing ones. It seems that only the archives themselves are currently in a position to fill the demand for training personnel to fill these demands. Some provision should be made within the structure of every archive for training potential archive technicians and managers as well as users in the proper operation and utilization of these resources. The staff members charged with these responsibilities must have some ability as teachers in addition to command of operating procedures that experience alone can give combined with an awareness of the subject matter that only a scholarly or research involvement can provide. Since many of the trainees in an archive will be individuals of considerable status in their own professional spheres, it is important that any formal teaching be done by someone whose status is at least the equivalent of his pupils. Needless to say, individuals fulfilling all these requirements are in very short supply.

PROGRAMME DEVELOPMENT STAFFING

Finally archives must engage in the development of new research programmes in substantive or area specialization as well as those related to the computing needs of the social sciences. It is always necessary for archives to carry on with the integration of data sets, the creation of integrated documentation systems and comprehensive indices. The changing needs of users require flexibility in these activities and provide a continuing demand for the attention and development of appropriate programmes. Responsibility for identifying the need for synthesis of data sets or the inauguration of a focused programme of acquisitions must be given to individuals with some command of the substance and sensitivity to the emerging needs of users. This activity often requires the identification of gaps in the existing collection as well as the ability to identify new areas in which data should be gathered.

The development of new computing programmes, of course, is also a continuous process that derives, in part, from the emergence of new analytical models as well as the need for new procedures to handle ever larger and more complex data sets. Someone within the archive must be specifically responsible for maintaining an up-to-the-minute awareness of the variety of data processing and analytic packages available not only in order to produce archive data in a form suitable for analysis by any of these packages, when requested by a user, but also in order to exert an influence upon the designers of future packages to assure that they deal appropriately with the kinds of problems emergent from the archive situation as opposed to those faced only by the isolated user. Archives, after all, must often deal with incoming material in a variety of formats and typically, produce data for rediffusion in a highly standardized format. The nature of that format is shaped, in large measure, by the archive's knowledge of and commitment to one or more of these packages. Clearly, it is vital that someone in the archive take the pains to have some influence in shaping the development of new computing programmes which may become widely adopted, so that archive operations (e. g., retrieval) can articulate as closely as possible with user needs.

THE ACQUISITION PROCEDURE

Let us now consider in greater detail the procedures necessary for performing each of the 11 functions for which a staffing need has been identified, turning first to that of acquisitons. In order to determine the major sources likely to supply data sets to archives, it is necessary to identify and examine all of the institutions regularly engaged in the production of the type of data to be archived. Since new institutions do not appear too rapidly, it is probably not necessary to continue this review once it has been completed, but simply note the emergence of potential new data sources as they emerge. It is necessary, however, to review the literature on a continuous basis. The literature, in this case, includes lists of contracts and grants given and received as a means of identifying individuals engaged in the production and analysis of data relevant to the archive. The literature also includes,

of course, more conventional scholarly outlets scanned for a similar purpose. Surveys are also conducted of archive users as a means to identify and contact potential suppliers. In addition, however, it is usually necessary for someone from the archive to travel frequently to areas where research is being done and data is actually being gathered as this is the only reliable device to learn of unpublicized data-gathering activities. It is frequently the case that a fair amount of information is being obtained for special purposes, governmental or commercial, for example, knowledge of which may not become wide-spread through conventional channels for a considerable time, if ever. Thus, continuing on-the-spot review is really a necessity. Sometimes this function can be carried out by local correspondence, of course, but in order to do this it is necessary that the individual on the scene is particularly sensitive to the development of new data sources.

Once potential sources of supply have been identified, a problem still remains in establishing contact with the suppliers themselves. This can be done by correspondence but personal contact has proven to be a far superior method. Careful negotiation is necessary at this point to assure a clear and unambiguous understanding on the part of donor and archive regarding the terms of both acquisition and diffusion of the data.

The final step in the acquisition process then, after all arrangements have been made with the supplier, is to provide for the duplication, shipping and receipt of the data itself as well as their passage through customs where necessary and payment of any costs involved. Production of a duplicate data set is sometimes possible by the supplier himself. Where this is not possible, however, the person performing the acquisition for the archive must know enough about the availability of local data-processing installations, either commercial, governmental or academic, to which access might be obtained for duplication purposes. Often the local supplier is unaware of these resources. This means the archivist himself must do his own research on these matters. Similarly, there may be very little local experience with the long-distance shipment of data. The archivists must make any arrangements necessary to circumvent erasure of tapes by airline security measures, damage to card by storage of materials to be shipped in an exposed place, and similar disasters. In a similar manner some arrangement has to be made for the receipt of data in magnetic tape format, for example, where (as is currently true in some situations) duty must be paid upon the magnetic tape itself. This duty may be considerable, regardless of the fact that a tape is simply the medium on which information is carried and not a commodity itself. And, of course, there are often problems in reimbursing suppliers for their costs due to such things as currency restrictions requiring careful prior arrangements.

DATA CLEANING PROCEDURES

Upon arrival of a shipment of data to an archive, a careful review must be made to assure that all parts of the shipment actually have arrived prior to beginning the data cleaning process. This review includes making a complete inventory of the study itself, including not only the data but the documentation that is supposed to accompany the data as well, and extending to the location of any publications which may have resulted from the original study. Copies of relevant publications should be obtained if possible. A comparison of the codebook with the original data gathering instrument is always necessary to insure that the sequence and the wording of this document are, in fact, appropriately represented within the codebook. This must be followed by a review of sampling procedure itself, if one was employed. Weighting procedures utilized must be made explicit to enable identification of any duplicate cards that might be present. These steps are usually carried out prior to the move to load the data onto magnetic tape. This is done not only to make storage easier but to facilitate the remainder of the cleaning process. In the effort to load the data to tape, unless special provisions have been made with the local computing facility, the archivist will often encounter the special difficulties associated with trying to read multiple-punch cards with the usual computing hardware and discover that the task cannot be accomplished without a special "binary read" capacity and associated computer programmes. If previous arrangements for the specialized programmes and hardware to allow reading of cards in a column binary fashion were not made, the loading process must be exported to an appropriately equipped facility, if one is readily available. If proper arrangements have been made, cards can be loaded to tape and a frequency distribution for each column or each variable of each card image (or in the case of data arriving initially on tape, for each record) is obtained. If acquisitions are made from diverse sources around the world, provision has to be made for the transformation of the original data into a locally acceptable format. That is, if data arrive in a form suitable for the use of Power-Samas machinery or Remington Rand machinery and the archive has available to it only IBM or IBM-compatible machinery, some intermediate effort must be made to translate the data into the IBM-compatible format. Similarly, provisions must be made for handling different track magnetic tapes, written at different densities and using different character conventions.

Once the frequency distributions have been obtained, the next step in the cleaning process is to correct or annotate discrepancies between this distribution and the study codebook. An examination of the punches outside the legitimate range can indicate the accuracy level of keypunching and, in some cases, draw attention to mislabeled variables. When, for example, a solid proportion of cases have illegitimate or undefined values for some variable, it is often desirable, although seldom possible, to refer back to the initial documents in order to resolve any discrepancies discovered at this stage, but it is more common that they must be resolved by correspondence with the original supplier. The next step is called contingency cleaning, where someone checks carefully for logical consistencies in the responses. Where such inconsistencies can be identified and resolved by recoding, annotations to this effect are made in the codebook. These serve to warn potential users of possible dangers in this area.

The data is then sorted on the identification field and card or record member to check for any missing, as well as any duplicate records. As a part of this process, a complete listing of all the records is produced and this is saved as one part of the permanent file of documentation for that study. A frequency listing is performed by variable from tape and a check is made of all fields unspecified in the codebook in the search for unlisted indices or variables that might have been created in the donors analytical efforts but which remain undocumented. The distributions for each variable are compared with the codebook once again to make sure that they now fall within the valid range specified for each variable and that no wild punches remain. A significant number of out-of-range punches suggest that the punches outside the legitimate range are not there due to keypunching error but are the result, instead, of some unspecified new category and a further annotation is made of this fact in the codebook.

Multiple punches must be recoded or spread into a single-punch column format. This can be done by using a binary tape that has been sorted and checked to assure merged card images; that is to say, when there are multiple records for each respondent, all the records for that case appear together and in serial order. Frequency distributions are obtained for each of punched category and multiple punches are then redistributed to new columns. That is, the original variable is turned into a series or a list of new variables with one for each value of the initial variable. The respondent is then indicated as having had or not had each of the specific values of the original variable, column by column. This, of course, requires as many columns in the new format as there were alternative punches in the original. A revised version of the codebook must be prepared to reflect this new arrangement.

The data cleaning procedure continues by recoding only listed variables where "plus", "minus" and "blank" codes have been employed as legitimate punch categories. This is done because many computing installations either cannot accept some of these punches or will not distinguish between blanks and the "zero" codes. In the process of recoding variables to make them more acceptable to a greater variety of computing installations, some archives always recode responses into a consistent direction, so that category values (1, 2, 3...) always go from weak to strong, low to high, etc.

The basic reason for following the steps outlined above is to create a cleaned and well documented data set but in so doing an entirely new codebook must also be written and edited. This final codebook includes more than simply the wording of the original questions and the description of variables and their location on cards or tape. It should also include a general description of the study and the procedures used for gathering the data. A set of codebook conventions has been adopted by many archives to make sure that such information is included and the results may be seen in the sample codebook presented in Appendix 4. The conventions are described more fully in a following section devoted to codebook writing. Specific variables may be identified according to their conceptual categories when producing the final codebook in order to facilitate the retrieval process later on. The new codebook is then written on magnetic tape or punched on cards and loaded to tape and a sample copy of the codebook is printed out from the computer. It is important to note here that when data from several studies has been combined to produce a merged data set, this requires a special type of codebook wherein a single question, which may have been asked in many different response waves appears only once in order to eliminate the redundancy that would result from a more conventional format. The final frequency distributions are now run and a check is made against the preliminary version of the codebook. When every discrepancy has been resolved, the marginal figures themselves are merged into the new machine readable codebook by punching and sorting or using a special purpose programme and multiple copies are produced for distribution.

In general, archive policy has been to encourage the distribution of codebooks even where data are not available for further analysis. In such cases the codebook can still serve a useful function for potential research workers, and every effort should be made to produce these codebooks in the greatest possible detail and give them as wide a circulation as possible.

CODING PROCEDURES

In those instances where a decision has been made to acquire data that is not already in machine readable form, it is necessary to go through some prior steps in order to produce the end result of a machine readable, fully documented data set. Where raw data is to be made into machine readable data, it is necessary to derive an appropriate set of categories for each response and to assign fields for the storage of that information on tape or in card image format. Once this has been done the actual coding process must be carried out; the field and the category for every value of every variable for every

case is determined and noted. As in the case where data arrives in machine readable form, it is desirable to avoid multiple punches as well as "plus", "minus" and "blank" punches, and code responses in a consistent direction if possible. Where necessary, a consistent identification for missing data should also be employed.

In order to identify the variables in the study each question or each variable may be assigned to some position within some classification scheme if a retrieval system based on such tagging is to be employed. Classification schemes of this type often consist of several dimensions with several possible values on each dimension and the resulting multidigit tag is then made a permanent part of the question. Some alternative retrieval schemes based on analysis of the text of the variable descriptions or wording of the questions themselves do not require such tagging but are in no way hindered by its presence.

In addition to coding variables it is also necessary to produce some description of the study as a whole to facilitate retrieval operations. This is usually done simply by preparing a list of the variables in the study and writing a summary of the study occasionally using only a restricted, standardized vocabulary of key words. Retrieval systems based upon the analysis of study summaries depend heavily on the skill of the summary writer for the adequacy of their retrieval.

ANALYTIC PROCEDURES

The fourth procedural area is that of analysis. Sometimes a user may request the analysis of the data directly rather than access to the data itself. Although an appropriate analytical model is usually supplied by him, this is not always the case. When the user does not specify the model, specialists on the archive staff should be able to make this determination. In practice it is sometimes necessary to suggest to the user, who does have something in mind, alternative models that may suit his purposes more fully. Once the analytic model has been determined, it is necessary to locate an appropriate computing programme, if one exists. If it does not, one must be written. Most frequently the user is able to identify the model he wishes and to utilize and suggest the computing programmes to be employed. In such a case it is simply necessary for an archive staff technician to carry out the requested operations. However, it often happens that the model suggested by the user is inappropriate for the data at hand and other alternatives must be made known to him. Care must be exercised to avoid distorting the proposed analysis to fit the available computing power rather than developing the computational resources necessary to accomplish the tasks dictated by the user's theoretical structure.

WRITING CODEBOOKS

No analysis is possible, of course, without the existence of adequate documentation. The most important documentation is the codebook which relates the location of information on magnetic tapes or punch cards to the substance of the study. Often the original documents are in languages that may not be commonly spoken or understood by the archive's users. In such cases it is necessary to translate the existing information into some more common language. As mentioned before it is necessary to include more than simply the tape storage location of every variable in creating a codebook. It is also necessary to include descriptions of the study itself - information not contained within the study. Naturally a title must be included, and should be chosen with care. Titles are often the basis of a variety of first-level retrieval efforts. Literary allusions are of little utility in this procedure. It is also common practice to include somewhere in the codebook the name of the project director and his organizational affiliation at the time the study was done as well as his current affiliation if at all possible. The need for this is vital when later users have reason to contact the original data gatherer. Because of scholarly mobility, regular updating of this aspect of the codebook may be required. Users should be able to determine the original sponsor of the data from the codebook if only to obtain permission from the sponsor for access to the data. It is always proper to keep the sponsor advised of the uses that have been made of the data. In addition to the sponsor, codebooks should include the name of the organization which actually collected and processed the data. Ambiguities discovered in the analysis but missed in the cleaning process can be then resolved by returning to the original agency doing the field work for clarification. The dates that the data collection was actually effected must be included for each wave of data. Both the dates of start of work and termination are necessary so that historical events which might alter the interpretation of the data in some way can be taken into account by the analyst.

Information about the location of the sample, of course, is fundamental. Not only the country but the region or state, the city, even the actual sections within cities, must all be specified if possible. The most difficult task often is that of specification of the sampling criteria and the method of sampling employed by the original researcher. Usually for social science research the universe has been defined in terms of criteria such as the following: sex, religion, nationality, position within the family structure, income, occupation, and the social status of the respondent (with some elaboration of how that is determined). The region and number of sampling points, and, where particular organizations or institutions were used in defining the sample, this must be specified as well as any other special criteria employed.

The actual method of sampling employed must be specified in detail in order to distinguish between full probability samples with random selection of respondents and more common techniques such as quota or even samples where the most available respondents in some area is selected by the interviewer at his own convenience. Information about the sample should include such things as the probability of selection of sampling points, and quotas used to control selection of the respondents. When some other form of systematic sampling has been employed it is obviously necessary to specify the system employed. All procedures must be specified in great detail. The definition of the universe and the specification of the elements in that universe must be made as explicit as possible. The original sampling frame should be described and the selection and replacement procedures employed must also be clarified in order that the secondary user may have some sense of the utility of the data for his own purposes. Where possible, the intended sample size and the number of actual respondents attained should be included, as well as some description of the method of data collection. Using this information, potential users can decide if the data from a self-administered questionnaire or mailed questionnaire, telephone interviews or personal interviews, observations or diaries, census or other records, or from some other form of data gathering is what he needs for his own kind of work. Where a field staff was employed to gather the data, it is necessary to include a description in the codebook of how many assistants worked on the job as interviewers, noting how many of them were continuing staff or professional interviewers and how many were new staff. If new staff were brought on, how much training did they receive, how many days of training, what kind of training and what use was made of field work supervisers. In the field work itself, how many mailings were made and how many call-backs for interviews. What was the language of the initial questionnaire and interview and, if translations were made, from what language to what language, and who did the translating.

Where weighting procedures were employed to account for stratification in the initial sampling, these procedures must be delineated in the codebook. The potential user must be able to obtain at a glance a list of principal variables employed in the study and determine the kind of personal data obtained in those instances where individuals were the unit of study. Derived data, where it exists, must be clearly specified and the methods by which scales and indices were obtained must be set forth in detail. It is of importance to users to know what type of questions were used in gaining the information - were they pre-coded, were some answer lists provided or do the data represent these codings of open-ended questions. In the latter case, the coding procedures must also be included in the codebook. Of course any publications and reports that have issued from the work should be referenced in the codebook by the author, title, data and place of publication, so that the potential user has an opportunity to see the kinds of use that have been made of these materials and in some cases, a list of other users of the data. Finally, an abstract or summary statement should be written which clearly expresses the contents of the material and the intent for which the data were initially obtained.

DATA STORAGE PROCEDURES

Careful provision must be made for the storage of materials obtained by the data archive. It is poor practice indeed to rely upon a single, original copy of the data. The first step after acquisition, and then again after cleaning, should be the production of a backup copy. It is important that at least one copy of the data exist on punched cards rather than in any magnetic form. The backup copy and the original should be stored separately and preferably at some distance from one another so that should a disaster occur in one location, the materials would not be completely destroyed. The costs of duplication are so slight and in general the costs of storage are so small that no compromise should be made on this point.

The ideal storage space for data archive materials is cool and dry, fireproof, dustfree and free from the incursions of rodents and protected from access by unauthorized personnel. When storing a magnetic tape, the area must also be free from any large magnetic flux, either steady or intermittent, which might affect the information on the tape. Some sort of physical security is also necessary for at least one set of the data to prevent unauthorized and inadvertent use which might destroy the materials, and of course, it is necessary to have a physical control over those materials whose circulation is to be restricted in some way.

Where storage space is at a premium a common practice is to have a backup copy of the data stored in a high density, multifile tape format. This type of material should be copied over periodically (every 18 months or two years) to assure that it is not deteriorating. Other mass storage devices may also be employed depending upon local computer facilities. Finally, an additional version of the data should be printed out, bound and stored with the technical staff where they may obtain it easily for ready reference during the cleaning process or to be used in resolving any difficulties that arise during the analysis by a user.

Original documentation should of course be stored separately and should also be in a secure, dry, fireproof, rodent proof environment and should be available to users only under supervision to prevent inadvertent loss. Copying facilities should be readily available, however, for user needs. It is important to have working papers readily available to the staff in order to keep track of each correction. These papers chronicle all the steps included

in transforming the original data to its final version in the archive. A sample of a portion of such a working paper is included in Appendix 5. An inventory of the codebooks in their final format, stored ready for distribution should always be at the disposition of the user-service personnel.

INVENTORY PROCEDURES

The acquisition of each new study by an archive should always be cause for its inclusion in the archive's inventory. This inventory, of course, must include the working title of the study, and the name of the investigator. References should be made to the location in which the study was done and to the format in which the data is currently stored. The status of the cleaning procedure should also be recorded and kept up to date. This inventory should also state specifically any restrictions on access to the data, again to be revised as needed. The inventory should note the number of cases in the study as well as the number of card images it contains so that users can determine if a data set is complete, as well as to estimate costs of reproducing data set they desire. For similar reasons the length of the codebook should also be specified and a listing of the principal variables should be included. If the study description from the codebook is also included, then the inventory becomes the fundamental document in the diffusion process. It is the primary resource for a potential user and permits identification of materials available to him at a specific archive.

Naturally, when possible, it is desirable to expand an inventory to include materials not contained in the local archive, but available elsewhere on an international scale. For this purpose, it is only necessary to add to the above information the name of the archive in which the data is stored. In an ideal arrangement all of this material could be continuously submitted to a central clearing house where periodic revisions and updates would be made available to the user community. Ordinarily, an inventory is organized simply by country or region of the study; the major variables employed in the study; and the author's name. Preliminary searches are rather gross and indeed tend to obtain much more information than would actually be necessary. All of the above functions can be facilitated by using a format for the data inventory which is itself machine readable, so that the updating process can be assisted by the employment of a computer.

RETRIEVING DATA

When a request for information is made to an archive, a retrieval process should be placed in motion, which begins by determining the user's needs with as much clarity and detail as possible. This may require activities which rely on the skills of individuals. The archive must have the ability to communicate with users by correspondence, telephone or direct conversation in order to identify his needs and relate them to the capacities of the archive. Perhaps the most common outcome of this procedure is to refer the potential user to some other, more appropriate, collection of data. Where it seems likely that the archive does contain some potential materials, consultation with the archive librarian can determine which studies are in fact likely to be of use. It is at this point that a user may be supplied with descriptive lists of concept names employed within the library and the vocabulary of research terms commonly recognized by the staff. Bibliographies may also be supplied about assorted variables and collections already identified within the archive and used previously and thus already available in a convenient form.

Sometimes retrieving data requires procedures which rely upon machinery rather than personnel to facilitate rapid screening and sorting of information. In instances of this kind, the user may be referred to a listing of classifications within the inventory and then shown, for example, a keyword listing of study titles. This is certainly a useful device where considerable care has been exercised in giving the studies meaningful titles. However, a title alone is rarely sufficient to reveal the diversity of contents which the study might contain. An example of such a keyword listing used as an index is included in Appendix 6. Another device called item-tagging, has also been used with some success. Specific questions and studies are identified by conceptual tags placed upon them in the coding process. Where the conceptual scheme has been carefully developed to reflect the needs of the users, this is without question the most efficient way of obtaining an insight to the contents of a large and complex archive. User constituencies change, of course, and so do the needs of the users. The consequence of such changes for retrieval schemes which rely on the tagging of variables is their inevitable obsolescence although some become obsolete more slowly than others. A much more costly device for handling the retrieval problem has centred about the development of retrieval systems dealing with the manifest content of the variable itself, that is, the actual wording of questions or the names of variables such as race or income. Where collections are small, it is possible to produce printed indices of variables in a concordance. Every variable or every question containing a specific word or string of words is listed under that word or word combination. It does not take long, however, for an archive to reach such proportions that a concordant index of its contents is so gigantic that it inhibits rather than encourages the retrieval of information. At this point specialized question or variable bibliographies may be produced by the archive staff based upon their experience with user needs. Many users may then utilize these restricted lists of variables when they have been carefully constructed and the need for specialized (and costly) "custom" retrieval is reduced to a minimum. Selective retrievals using combinations of keywords connected by Boolean operaters may also be used with this type of system and the bulky output can be reduced by citing only those variables or studies which contain the specific string of keywords requested by the user.

When potentially interesting studies have been identified, the user should be supplied with appropriate study description plus the wording for key questions, if that is readily available. Additional information must be supplied regarding the accessibility of the data, and procedures for obtaining data on which there are any restrictions. Users must also know how clean the data is and in what form it is currently stored. The user is then in a position to make a rational decision about whether to acquire the data or to proceed with his search. If there is some possibility of actually acquiring the data the user then examines the codebooks for the study itself. If the library has the facilities the job is done there - otherwise the codebooks may be borrowed or analysed for more convenient examination. Also at this point the user should be supplied with names of others who have also expressed interest in or used the particular data set. In this way scholars with a common interest can be put in touch with one another.

On the basis of the information outlined above, the user specifies the data set or subset that he desires and the format in which he wishes it produced. It is also possible, of course, that he may simply ask for specific analyses rather than actual data. A typical request might be for all materials from a specific study or perhaps only selected variables or cases or even all the materials from several studies. An analysis of the percentage of voters casting ballots for a specific party over a ten-year period might be requested, for example, instead of the analyst obtaining the data for that ten-year period. The archive staff must produce the requested materials in the form requested and with the documentation appropriate to the new format. The advantage of maintaining the codebook in machine readable form should be obvious here as an important device for easing the task of producing appropriate documentation after partial or reformatted data sets have been requested. The final product may include a tape or decks of analysis cards containing selected sets of variables in a form rearranged to suit the special requirements of the user. Special analysis decks may also be assembled from larger matched and merged data files and entirely new measures that have been generated from sets of variables as requested. For example, complex scales or indices may be produced for analysis by the user or variables may be transformed from one type of distribution to another. Where new variables are generated at the user's request, the codebook describing the new data format should be produced in a form that permits the user, if he desires, to make multiple copies of it. This new codebook can go to the user as printed computer output or as a multilith, ditto or photo offset master, or even a deck of punched cards or magnetic tape.

Regardless of the archive's ability to satisfy the user's current demands some record should be made of his interest to permit later contact in case appropriate materials are actually acquired or should there be an independent expression of interest in similar kinds of materials by another potential user. The archive can then respond as before by placing the potential community of users in touch with one another. Maintaining a sensitive system for carrying on this type of selective dissemination is not cheap, however, and specific provisions must be made to underwrite such an activity.

DIFFUSION PROCEDURES

After all specifications for data have been made, it may be determined that the data as requested is currently inaccessible to the user. He should be informed of the procedure for gaining access - usually by securing permission from the donor - and the archive must then await general reclassification of the data or specific permission granted to the user. Careful records of the authorizing correspondence must be placed on file in order to document any later disputes that may arise and they are likely to arise. If data is directly accessible, the data set should be prepared according to specifications provided by the user. It may be necessary at this point for the archive to borrow special machinery or subcontract the work to be done. User specifications for data must be clear and unambiguous. It is good practice to provide order forms in advance to reduce potential misunderstandings. Such a form requires the user to specify if he wants his data on cards, and if so, in IBM, Remington Rand, ICT, or some other format. He must state, if he wishes the data on tapes, how many tracks, what density, what parity, and character conventions, what blocking factor should be used. If the request is for paper tapes, again the necessary information must be provided. Where the request is for analysis rather than data, it is equally important to reduce ambiguity in requests. A sample of such forms is included in the collection of prototype materials appearing in Appendix 7. Any work deck must be described by special codebooks and users must agree - preferably in writing - to archive policy regarding his rediffusion of the data he is obtaining. He should assent to a policy of giving credit for the source when this is required by the archive. It is common practice to request users to supply copies of any publications resulting from the use of materials provided by the archive. When materials are packaged for shipping, special care must be taken not to exceed size and weight limitations of the local postal service - if that is the means to be used - and materials must be wrapped in such a way that they

are physically secure. Normal handling procedures are often enough to guarantee change to cards, for example, when they are crushed or folded. If the materials are to go by some means such as air transport where special measures may affect them, special provisions have to be made in this case as well. Magnetic tapes must be protected, for example, against passage through the magnetic fields of metal detectors used in some airport situations. It is a good practice to insure all materials being shipped for the costs involved in duplicating them and to retain on file the control card setups used to produce the data. A return postcard should be included in all shipments to acknowledge safe arrival of all parts of the shipment in an undamaged form. Safe arrival provides the signal to bill the user for the costs incurred.

TRAINING PROCEDURES

Due to the difficulty of finding personnel capable of carrying out many tasks of an archive, potential archive personnel - and users - must often be trained by the archive itself. Archive personnel can also be trained for employment by other archives. A good training programme involved placing all trainees in every operational phase of the archive, including all stages of activity from packaging materials for shipment to participation in the determination of emergent policy. At each stage of apprenticeship, that is in each operational phase, the trainee should write a manual of organization and procedures. In this way a high degree of familiarity is gained with local procedures and constant consideration is given to alternative ways of solving routine problems. Trainee work on updating the archive inventory is, perhaps, the best way for them to gain familiarity with the contents of the archive. In this process he will develop a feeling for the cleaning and diffusion status of individual studies; the variety of materials contained in the archive and the form and location in which specific studies are stored. Even where personnel are to be employed at the archive in question, it is not a bad practice for them to try writing a procedures manual to clarify their understanding of the job. It is important that all levels of a data archive organization have a good picture of how the entire operation functions in order to articulate individual activities with organizational goals.

Training of archive personnel, however, is not enough to promote archival success. It is also necessary to train potential users. This is done by providing an introduction to social science information retrieval procedure and the general use of data archives. This would include an introduction to the terminology of archive usage, a survey of the available computing programmes and an overview of other archives and their resources. Users should be introduced to the technology of data processing through a survey of terminology, the availability of existing analytic programmes, and a brief introduction to the problems involved in creating new programmes where those available are insufficient. Most important, however, is the introduction of potential users to the whole idea of secondary and comparative analysis. Thus some instruction must also be provided on the general theory of scale and index construction and on the utilization of cross-tabular and multivariate statistical analytic techniques for the interpretation of social science data. The Impress primer prepared by the Impress Project of Dartmouth College (Hannover, New Hampshire, U.S.A.) is a good example of a syllabus of exercises using archive materials to examine.

PROCEDURES FOR DEVELOPING NEW PROGRAMMES

Archives are constantly engaged in the development of new programmes in various substantive areas. Development of this kind is best facilitated through continuing survey of user needs and interests as well as by surveys of available information sources. In order to assure the sensitivity of the archive to the needs of the user community and to combat the tendency of all organizations to become preoccupied with their own internal procedural concerns, the survey of user needs can be aided by the existence of an active advisory group of users. This group should have considerable power to shape the priorities and activities of the archive. It should be the responsibility of this advisory group to aid in obtaining funds for the acquisition and processing of new data, and in this way, it will influence strongly the kind of data actually acquired and the form into which it is processed by the archive. The emergence of new programmes have ramifications for staffing, of course, and the advisory committee can play an important rôle here, as well.

In addition to the continuous development of substantive programmes there is a never ending pressure for the development of computing programmes. When the needs of users - or archives themselves - require the development of special equipment or special programmes, archives can, as a focus of expert opinion, take a leading rôle in specifying the performance criteria of facilities to be developed and entertain bids for construction of the appropriate machinery of writing of programmes. Archive staff should be consulted in contracting for the writing of general purpose programmes as individual users often do not share the broad perspective generated by constant interaction with many different users.

EQUIPPING FOR ACQUISITIONS

A third archival consideration regarding the functioning of archives revolves about the actual equipment necessary to permit specific operations. For acquisitions this tends to be confined to conventional office equipment, such as typewriters, paper, desks, pencils, file systems, telephone and, in brief,

everything necessary to permit correspondence with users. Additional equipment is also required, however, in the form of scholarly journals to be scanned for potential information sources, scanning report forms so that scanners can get summaries of their suggestions to those who decide on acquisitions with ease, and, in some cases microfiche or microfilmed readers.

EQUIPMENT FOR CLEANING

Basic office supplies are also necessary in order to engage in the cleaning process. In addition some system is required for binding computer printout produced in this activity. The bound printout must also be stored in some orderly fashion. Because of the large size of most printout, ordinary file systems are not capable of handling this kind of material, specialized files are usually necessary even if they consist simply of shelving built to the appropriate dimension. Due to a constant necessity for changing the content and the form of documentary materials, a great deal of copying must be done which requires ready access to some economical photo or xerographic copying machine. A keypunch, counter sorter, reproducer and interpreter constitute the minimum unit record installation necessary for the cleaning operation. Without them it is impossible to examine the arriving data for its completeness, check for multiple punches, and search for duplicates and repair damaged cards. Access to a computer to be used in data cleaning goes without saying. The computer should have the capacity to read multiply-punched cards, however, and a binary read capacity of this type is a specialized piece of hardware not generally available at most computing installations. Special arrangements must be made in advance therefore to assure this capability. Because of the variety of data sources and data users, it is also advisable that the computing service selected or developed for archive use have the facility to read and write both seven and nine track tapes and be able to handle the general set of ASCII character conventions. It is also necessary for card conversion equipment to be accessible if there is a likelihood of new materials arriving in a variety of card formats.

Access to a computer although vital, is not of much utility if appropriate computer programmes are not available as well. At the cleaning stage it is necessary to have programmes that permit complete flexibility in the manipulation and recoding of card images on magnetic tapes. Programming as well as equipment should allow for operation on a binary tape to permit its reformatting into more conventional format in character by character fashion. Programmes of this type are better if they do not place too heavy a burden on the cleaning staff but are simple to use as well as powerful and flexible.

EQUIPMENT FOR CODING AND ANALYSIS

For coding, office supplies alone are sufficient, but for associated analyses it is also necessary to have access to a computer and to appropriate software. Once again this is a crucial point as many large and powerful computing installations do not have the kinds of programmes particularly suited to social science data analysis. They may specialize instead in computing or accounting as opposed to data processing and statistical analysis. Special provisions should be made to assure the availability of the necessary programmes.

CODEBOOK EQUIPMENT

For the production of codebooks, convenient access to text copying and keypunching machinery is fundamental. It is also important to have convenient access to a computer used for checking marginal distributions and for examining discrepancies between documentations and data. Some sort of question tagging scheme is necessary if the retrieval system employed can utilize it. Only two such schemes are currently in existence and although both of them have proven useful to the agencies where they are employed, they also have some drawbacks. Before committing an archive to a retrieval system of this kind, great care should be exercised to assure by actual test, its utility for the clientele whom the archive serves.

STORAGE EQUIPMENT

The storage function can be fulfilled by access to a fireproof and rodent-proof warehouse capable of storing cards neatly and safely in racks with a high degree of assurance that they will be kept dry. Tapes must be maintained in fireproof, dustproof, dry, cool, rodent-proof, cabinets shielded from magnetic flux. Working material, however, must be stored with the archive staff. This includes files, tape racks, microfilm storage, as well as storage for printout format. It is also advisable to have the capacity to lock up all materials or prevent unauthorized access in some appropriate manner.

EQUIPMENT FOR INVENTORY, DIFFUSION AND TRAINING

The inventory requires access to a keypunch and a computer in addition to standard office equipment, as do most retrieval systems. Facilities to duplicate both data and documentation is necessary for diffusion. This implies reproducing equipment must be available either via a computer or card reproducer. Even where documentation is produced as computer printout, copying devices are often employed to provide users with up-to-date copies of auxiliary materials. Wrapping, boxing, crating, and shipping facilities must also be available to permit proper diffusion of materials.

Training requires manuals as mentioned before

as well as sufficient office space for the students. Programme development requires no special equipment but is facilitated by access to a time-sharing computer system.

OTHER TECHNICAL CONSIDERATIONS IN THE ESTABLISHMENT OF AN ARCHIVE

The actual location of an archive is of primary importance for its utility and its success. There are several points which must be taken into consideration in determining what an optimum location might be. Perhaps the most important of all, is the resource environment in which the archive is to be placed. Few archives are capable of being totally self-reliant. As a consequence, it is necessary to give serious thought to both technical and intellectual capacities readily available in the immediate surroundings. Computer-related considerations come to mind immediately and, as mentioned before, special care must be taken to assure adequacy in the types of computing machinery and unit-record equipment available for archive use - both on a regular basis and in extraordinary circumstances. An appropriate environment is one that includes the greatest possible variety of different kinds of machinery. In this way, when special needs arise, the archive staff can take advantage of equipment at surrounding installations and use any special machinery necessary on an as needed basis. One installation may have the capacity for translating from seven to nine-track tapes and the converse, for example. Another may have the ability to deal with Remington Rand format, or Powers-Samas format and convert these to IBM format. Whatever the availability of alternative systems, however, it is absolutely essential that there be readily available an installation so similar in its capacities to handle routine archive activities that they may be continued in the case of mechanical failure at the archive's regular installation. Care should be taken to assure that this backup installation has the capacity to run the programmes that are actually used regularly by the archive as slight differences in machinery or in local operating systems are often enough to cause inconvenient and costly delays during the period required to make the programmes operational in the new environment.

The problem of computer programmes is a serious one in general and because so much of the work of archives is innovative and developmental, it is important for the organization to be located in an environment rich in computer use, as well as in computing machinery. The variety of users and the range of demands they place upon an archive is such that a variety of programmes are necessary. Many of them may be local, some of them may be proprietary, and the general problems of discovering what programmes are available to answer user needs is made more difficult if the archive is forced to rely only upon formal sources of information regarding programmes. Most documented programme development is not of the kind useful to the archivist, as there tends to be more emphasis upon problems of analysis and computation and less upon the problems of data manipulation. As a consequence, archive-related kinds of programmes are not always in general circulation.

Even where programmes exist, however, there always is and always will be a continuing need for programmers themselves. They are necessary to adapt existing programmes to the local situation as it evolves; to create special programmes as the needs arise and to modify programmes developed for the archive as changes take place in the computing environment in which the archive operates.

For there to be such programmers, there must be other programmers as well. Good programmers require the stimulation and interaction of other programmers, and it is much better to create a situation where it is possible to have several programmers working together on a part-time basis to fulfill archive needs than to rely on a single, totally dedicated programmer who is forced to work in relative isolation from his fellows. This consideration is important if for no other reason than because it is relatively difficult to retain programmers to work in professional isolation.

The importance of immersing the archive in an environment rich in technical resources, where many different computer-related activities are taking place, is of fundamental importance in making sure that the archive and its staff are aware of and able to utilize new developments in the field. Many times these developments may take place and become widespread knowledge in a local situation months and even years before recognition of their availability is possible through formal communication channels. Occasional new developments themselves have already been superseded by others of a superior nature. At the very moment knowledge of them is being diffused through conventional channels. Without contact with the computing culture, it is difficult for an archive manager to know about such developments except through formal channels.

Machinery of course is not everything, and the global interests of archivists are such that they are often called upon to communicate with and to utilize information from a variety of cultures. Consequently a linguistic capability must exist within the archive itself or in the surrounding environment. Rapid, accurate translations of semi-technical and technical material relative to the archive enterprise must be readily available and inexpensive. Although any given language may be used infrequently, or perhaps only once, the variety of languages with which a comprehensive archive has to work may be very great indeed, as original research and associated documents are often carried on in local dialects. It is difficult to have a staff capable of meeting all the linguistic demands placed upon an archive and it is therefore necessary that the archive turn to the surrounding environment for certain kinds of help. Since the required translations

are often rather technical, yet still in the social science sphere, it is of great importance that archive personnel be capable of dealing directly with the translator in order to assure the reasonableness as well as the comprehensibility of the translations. Independent translations by individuals unfamiliar with social science concerns are usually unsatisfactory and some type of archive-translator interaction is essential. These considerations suggest archives should be immersed in a metropolitan or sophisticated academic environment in order to have the requisite linguistic capability readily at hand.

It is necessary for archives of all sizes to engage in publication of codebooks, newsletters, catalogues, inventories, and a variety of regular and fugitive materials. As a consequence, some provision must be made for large-scale, low-cost reproduction and printing and binding.

It is difficult, often impossible, to deal with international shipment of materials and international correspondence from a remote location. Archive staff should therefore have ready access to a port of entry customs offices to facilitate the shipping and receiving of information from any part of the world. Also, some thought must be given to the general problems of shipping and receiving, where packing and crating facilities might be required as well as short-term storage for bulky materials.

Finally, the technical problems of billing, collection and accounting must be handled with promptness and accuracy. Again, it is sometimes necessary for an archive to depend upon the resources of a host institution rather than to maintain this specialized function for itself as the need for bringing together the component charges for services rendered may rely heavily on the larger accounting scheme anyway. Careful accounting for costs is also a central tool for rational management of the archive and should reflect the functions performed, considerations of staff time, and equipment charges.

LOCATION IN AN ENVIRONMENT OF SUBSTANTIVE RESOURCES

Technical considerations aside, there are several substantive reasons why great care must be taken in locating the archive in an environment suitably rich in resources. Most important, perhaps, is the way in which archive location affects the ability to locate potential staff members capable of carrying through the cleaning operations and the preparation of codebooks. As noted earlier, they must have some skills in the social sciences and yet they must work at what is essentially a clerical task. For there to be a steady supply of people with this level of training, it is often necessary to locate the archive in a university environment so that students willing to do this kind of work on a part-time and transitory basis can be employed. Similar staff requirements for tagging items according to a conceptual framework for indexing purposes and for retrieving information from the archive also argue for a university location as, again, this work requires a level of knowledge of the social sciences that is beyond that of the average clerk, yet the work itself is essentially clerical. Similarly, individuals who write study descriptions for the codebooks must have a knowledge of the discipline, must be familiar with the needs of users and must be willing to work on a relatively small flow of new studies on an inter-mittent and part-time basis as a backlog and need develop. Student labour is an obvious choice.

The most important substantive considerations in determining the location of an archive is the num-ber and variety of its users. The location should encourage their constant pressure. It is only in response to user demands that there can be a steady, continuous and rational development of an archive. Archives must respond to user demands for new data, thus creating programmes for completing collections where there are gaps and for extending collections into new areas. A new and more appropri-ate technology can best be developed for data pro-cessing and analysis in response to user demands and not in isolation.

USER ACCESS

Thus the second major aspect for determining the appropriate location for a new archive is consider-ation for user access. Users must have good external access with telephone and mail - easy, reliable and cheap. It must be a relatively simple matter for users to secure continuing attention to his needs as well as a prompt and reliable response to his requests. The turn around time, that is, the time between submission of some sort of request and response to that request in the form of data, analyses or simply the statement that the data does not exist, should be as short as possible. When dealing with a collection that is in good condition, no more than a week should elapse between receipt of a user request and dispatch of the data asked for.

In addition to data access, however, there should be good physical access for users. The library must be easy to get to. There should be good air, rail, bus, or road connexions to it. There must be some facili-ties - either in the archive itself or in its immediate environment - to accommodate visitors, both long and short term. There should be space for visitors to work with the archive materials, to pour over and examine them, to make decisions about the kinds of information that they need to obtain the data, to do the processing, and in fact to do all of the many kinds of work related to utilizing archived materials.

SPACE CONSIDERATIONS

Each of the above considerations has some ramifi-cations for the physical arrangements of the archive. Archive activities can actually be divided into two space utilizing modes - active and passive. Active space is use-related space. This involved such things as desk space for users referred to in the preceding paragraph as well as wall or floor space for documentation files used only under the super-vision of an archive employee; or material which is available only for duplication for example. Some provision must also be made for the storage of data being actively used. To the extent that this utilizes local computing facilities, a fair amount of space may be required for cards, tapes, and filing of printout - all used as intermediate products in analysis. Even if this kind of service is not provided there must be some spot for the storage of data in the process of being prepared for users prior to dispatch.

More important, perhaps, is the consideration of the space needed for archive-related activities. This encompasses work space necessary for edit-ing and writing of codebooks as well as desk space for the specialist in dealing with user matters. There must be a provision, perhaps wall space, for storage of all the documentation utilized in the cleaning process and this may be a large amount indeed. Despite its bulk, however, it should be possibly available when needed by staff members. Desk space for other archive functions and files for correspondence can be considered in terms of ordinary office requirements.

In addition to the needs of the archive for space in an active sense with convenient access and frequent change in the users or usage of the space, there are also needs for passive space - both for original and back-up or duplicate copies of the data. In both instances attention must be paid to appro-priate storage of materials; a cool, dry, fireproof and rodent-proof, and - for tapes - flux-free environ-ment. Depending upon local conditions, there must be additional consideration given to dust and to theft prevention or unauthorized access for any purpose. Original data is usually stored separate from the archive and from the back-up collection because it is usually on punched cards - a low density form of information storage - it is often quite bulky. This suggests a need for sufficient storage space to per-mit access to each stored data set without moving any others, which means secure racks and shelves, or cabinets. Piles of card boxes heaped in a corner will not do the job. Back-up data and documenta-tion which should also be stored separate from the archive and from the original data, may be in a high density, small volume format such as magnetic tape or microfilm requiring little space and free-dom from dust and from high magnetic flux. As this data is only to be used in time of disaster, more consideration may be given to its physical security and less to its accessibility.

ARCHIVE SECURITY

Careful attention must be paid to the problem of secu-rity for both the active and the passive collections.

In the former instance some form of document circulation control is necessary in order to prevent unauthorized loss in the latter, to prevent inadvertent destruction, theft or sabotage. Whatever security procedures are employed, however, should not unduly inhibit usage by interested parties. The dilemma of encouraging usage while maintaining the assurance that no materials are being misused, lost or stolen is a difficult one indeed. One effective way of confronting this dilemma is to make the archive facilities as much "self-service" as possible for all unrestricted information. This should be done with full knowledge that some data tapes will be damaged, some documents lost and most movable objects not properly replaced. Duplicates must exist, therefore, of everything made available in this way and some resources budgeted for keeping stock and maintaining some order. A sharp division must be made between information freely available to all - and all the rest. No intermediate category should exist. Information - whether printout, cards, tapes, microfilm or any other format - restricted in any way, should only be available through a designated archive employee to be personally checked out, used under supervision, and with a back-up copy in a safe place.

It is somewhat simpler to consider the problems of controlling the circulation of data while simultaneously encouraging its use. The first consideration here is simply preventing inadvertent damage to or destruction of the data set. This can usually be accomplished by decisions that the archive staff do only handling of the activities necessary to produce a copy of the data for the user and insistence that the worker using local data processing facilities and local data has the technical competence to do so without causing any unintended damage to other archive materials stored at that centre. The problem of preventing unauthorized use is more difficult. This requires, in the first place, physical control over the data by the archive staff. They, in turn, must rely upon a "status of studies" list, at least two copies of which should be maintained on a regular basis, kept constantly up to date. This list should indicate the actual physical location of all copies of the data, including file number and tape reel number if stored on magnetic tape, as well as the format in which the data is stored. It should indicate at what stage the study is in the cleaning process and, finally, its accessibility to users. As an adjunct to the status of studies list, there should be a continuous programme to upgrade all studies by bringing them to the status of cleaned studies, freely rediffusable, with all necessary documentation available for the user's needs. Although it is necessary to inhibit user access to restricted materials, continuous effort should be made to abolish any restrictions on the use of archived data by insisting upon written permission from the original data source authorizing the availability. To add specific user data for a specified purpose, some pressure is placed upon the original

supplier to reclassify the data and make it more generally available.

Unlike a conventional library which brings together unique copies of material to facilitate their use, it is necessary for the data archive to maintain physically separate locations for the original data collection, for active data, and for an emergency or back-up copy. It is always necessary to have at least one duplicate copy of the documentation stored separately from that which is accessible to the users. If all these collections are stored in the same location, a natural disaster such as earthquake or fire can destroy the entire collection. If they are kept at some place removed from one another, then the probability that all three collections will be simultaneously destroyed is reduced markedly.

In every instance it is necessary to maintain some control over access to the data, although, with the data set for user utilization, this control should be minimal, assuring only that whatever accounting is necessary is taken care of adequately. The data archive must never fall into the kind of situation characteristic of some traditional archives where a unique collection is carefully guarded to prevent its destruction and the process of guarding itself inhibits almost all usage of the collection. Since the fundamental characteristic of a data archive is the ease with which entire data sets can be duplicated, it is pernicious to develop excessive zeal to control access to data by users - as long as that zeal exists in control over access to the back-up copies.

Control, of course, can be exercised in several ways. Perhaps the most fundamental device is to retain control over knowledge of the location of data back-up copies by placing them in something less than public areas. Some archives have rented locked bank vaults which, while expensive, is not prohibitive considering the relatively small bulk of data stored on magnetic tapes. Bank vaults are not an adequate solution, of course, for more bulky forms of data storage and documentation. Other archives have rented warehouses in areas removed from their daily operations. Although this may complicate the problem of deposit and withdrawal, it is a relatively cheap solution to the control problem. Some care should be taken, however, to assure that at least one of the collections is stored in a fireproof setting, since even in the short history of archive operations, at least one archive has been burned to the ground with the consequent loss of its collection.

In addition to the possible loss of the archive collection itself, there is a high risk of losing the correspondence records upon which future archive development depends. As a consequence, some archives keep a microfilm or magnetic tape copy of the correspondence or of a summary of it. At least one relies upon the source of the correspondence to maintain a copy of the original and maintains only a magnetic tape summary statement of letters sent and received on specific dates indexed by topic. In the case of loss they will rely upon suppliers to help them reconstruct crucial correspondence.

ACCOUNTING

It is not possible to over-emphasize the importance of the accounting operations to the success of a data archive to assure some sort of fiscal responsibility. Yet there is an even more pressing need to devise an accurate cost-accounting system to permit a rational budget and development planning. Without data on costs for the functions performed by an archive, budgeting and planning simply cannot be carried out with any degree of efficiency. In order to have a cost accounting programme, and in order for it to operate, there must be willing co-operation on the part of all personnel within the archive. Such co-operation does not come about by simple mandate; it requires a fair amount of training for all the personnel. Instruction regrading the general basis for the accounting system is fundamental so that all can understand the importance of their co-operation. Reassurance must be given that honesty and integrity in reporting information for the cost-accounting system is not likely to threaten their security although functions may, and probably will, keep changing.

Even the most willing personnel, however, are not capable of accurately reporting the time and materials expended on different functions without a regular format to facilitate recording this information and considerable imagination must be devoted to the development of an appropriate device. Needless to say, this entire concept implies that the division of labour on functional grounds be clearly made and that personnel engaged in the performance of several different functions be scrupulous in the recording of their contribution to a project on a functional basis.

The various accounts must be gathered together in order to bill services to the user. This requires some bookkeeper or accountant within the organization as well as some mechanism for billing and collection. These needs give further weight to considerations for locating an archive within some functioning, larger institution. In that way the accounting function can be handled externally if necessary. Yet the development of an archive as a service function for some larger institution has its drawback as well, particularly if no provision is made for discretionary funds at the archive administrative level. Such funds are absolutely essential for dealing rapidly and efficiently with emergent problems. It is usually the case that if no provision has been made for flexibility of this sort, the archive finds itself unable to respond to sudden developments when necessary and does not perform its functions well.

ADMINISTRATION

We have been talking about the technical considerations of archive operation, including the location of

the archive and the need for accounting procedures. Clearly there is also a need for an administrative structure to co-ordinate archive functions and to recruit new personnel, as well as give direction to the development of new programmes. The administration should oversee the budget and use it as a device for developing and formalizing priorities. The administration in general is responsible for securing the funds to carry out the archive operations.

To accomplish these administrative functions requires careful staffing. The responsible administrator must have knowledge and some skill in the technology of information storage and retrieval. He must have expertise in the substantive and geographic areas of his archive's specialization as well. These qualities are requisite not only to insure a reasonable development of the external relations of an archive but to insure its proper internal functioning as well. Without sufficient technical expertise to converse directly with the programming staff, for example, it is difficult to assure that the direction of new developments in this area will be as useful as they might be elegant. Similarly, very careful expert judgement must be exercised in the establishment of acquisition and data cleaning priorities. Often the variety of specialized demands is too great for any one individual; thus it is important, when staffing top management positions, to secure individuals who are not only capable of working well with subordinates on the technical level but with professional colleagues willing to serve the archive in an advisory capacity.

DEVELOPMENT TIMING

In order to place an archive in operation careful attention must be paid to the timing of its development. Planning must make allowances for the amount of time necessary to get the different aspects of the archive established. The problems of scheduling various operations to the time involved in conducting the operations themselves must be carefully considered. The central problems in establishing an archive are locating, recruiting and training appropriate personnel. Unfortunately, it is very difficult to find people with a background in data archive operations. Other types of experience may not be suitable to this new kind of enterprise. As suggested earlier people who have substantive as well as technical skills at a relatively high level, who are willing to work in an activity which, as yet, has few professional rewards, are in short supply. As a consequence, it is not surprising that most successful archives are established with the expectation that there will be a steady and continuing turnover of key personnel as skilled younger people leave routine jobs to pursue more promising traditional careers when the opportunities arise. Accepting this posture implies that considerable care must be taken to establish a pro-gramme within archives for training new personnel on a regular basis, as well as a start-up operation. The time it takes to recruit a full staff may be very short for clerical personnel but may require an academic year or more for administrative and technical personnel involved in positions from which they cannot leave immediately.

Even when the personnel have been recruited and trained, however, a considerable lag is still to be anticipated before regular operations can be undertaken. This lag can be attributed to three sources. The first is simply the problem of acquiring basic materials. To the extent that the archive acquires materials from other archives, the time for this activity may be very short. If the acquisition of totally new material is undertaken, however, it may be a matter of months or years before any substantial collection has been developed. These materials, of course, may still be in a very crude form. The second component of the lag de-rives from the need to clean the data to achieve at least those minimal standards of documentation and format agreed upon by all archives as being neces-sary for use by the typical scholar or researcher. Examination of the figures given in Appendix 8 will provide an idea of the time involved for carrying out cleaning operations in an established archive with professionally trained and equipped staff en-gaged in data cleaning as an ongoing activity. The third component of the lag to be expected when establishing a new archive comes from the need to develop and debug an appropriate set of programmes for carrying out the routine operations of the ar-chive on the local computing machinery. Even where the bulk of these programmes can be obtained in an already developed form, a considerable amount of time must often be spent in adapting them to local conditions. An additional period is necessary of course for the archive staff to develop some facility in casing them. More often than not, programmes in use at other archive installations are not so rea-dily transferable. In such cases it is necessary for the archive staff to develop sufficient expertise in their own field to be able to communicate their peculiar needs to a local programming staff having no background in carrying out operations of this type. Thus sufficient lead time must be allowed for each activity to assure that it will be in operation when needed.

The problems associated with scheduling the development of the different aspects of archives functioning are reviewed below.

The developer of a potential archive should begin with a survey of the computing power available to him and in the process he should take pains to develop a feeling for the constraints that local faci-lities place upon his planned operations. Questions of costs, capacities, and access must be raised. Is all machinery available at any time or only some of it and then on a carefully scheduled basis? Can the available machinery handle input materials of

various forms likely to be encountered, including magnetic tapes written according to different con-ventions, cards that are multiply-punched using all standard conventions as well as ordinary punch-ing according to different "standard" conventions? If some of these conditions cannot be met, what steps are necessary for developing appropriate resources? Often the task of doing an adequate survey of the computing environment requires prior recruitment of personnel with the technical skill to carry out this survey. As is evident, problems of personnel recruitment and development of the technical infrastructure are closely intertwined.

After the personnel and computing problems have been solved, the problem of physical location is usually largely determined. It is then possible to begin the acquisition process.

In many cases, obtaining data promises of its availability may be made months or even years in the future. While such materials may technically be considered to have been acquired by the archive, they are not yet physically possessed by the archive. Because of this, further delays can be anticipated in the actual development of a collection available to the archive staff for processing.

Delays due to the cleaning process have been alluded to previously, but these should also be augmented by the time it takes to index and catalogue materials that have been obtained. Only when all of these operations are reasonably underway and a fair prediction can be made regarding the availa-bility of the material should advertising of archive services be undertaken.

Once in operation, attention must be paid to the time involved in servicing user responses. In particular, every effort should be made to reduce the time required to supply basic information to users by correspondence or by telephone, to an absolute minimum. A further problem in opera-tional timing is that deriving from the resources required for search and retrieval procedures. How long would it really take to make a specialized search or a specialized acquisition and preparation, and how long would it actually take to provide the information on the availability of the data to the user? By how much is this period extended by the delays involved in duplication and shipping mate-rials? In many cases, if - from the user's per-spective - the total time involved is much greater than ten days or two weeks, the utility of the data to him diminishes rapidly. Although it may be possible to serve the user's needs eventually, his own time constraints may prevent him from making use of an archive as it stands, if it appears too sluggish in its response to inquiries.

THE PROBLEM OF ARCHIVE SPECIALIZATION

In the creation of a new archive, careful considera-tion has to be given to where that archive fits into the matrix of already existing archives. An early consideration, then, must deal with how the proposed archive differs in its specialty from the others, if at all. One basis for possible specialization is that of geographical focus. Clearly a focus upon the local region has many advantages. In particular, easy access to suppliers and the ability to keep data sets up to date with ease are important. Local specialization also permits an independent check on the reliability of work done by data suppliers, which is certainly not possible when an archive specializes in materials from more remote regions. There are also disadvantages to local specialization. Depending solely on local sources, it may provide data of very little intrinsic interest and there may be very little research done on any one topic. This kind of specialization produces an archive which must deal with a variety of substantive areas, weakening thereby the strength in substantive specialization of archive personnel. Often an archive specializing in acquisition of data only from the local area must deal with data in a variety of formats and this may also complicate internal procedures considerably.

A second basis for specialization is to expand the local focus to a somewhat broader scope - that of regional specialization. This certainly facilitates independent comparative analysis and provides a broader basis for conclusions of analysis done with the archive material, yet it suffers from the same disadvantages produced by local specialization and increases the difficulty of keeping up to date on the sources of supply as well. A common solution to this problem is to make arrangements with the local data producers to acquire all of their output on a regular basis. While appealing at first glance, this solution can severely tax the resources of the archive for cleaning and cataloguing. This is particularly true if arrangements are made with suppliers that produce studies with great frequency and only a small fraction of the data are ever used again. This problem is most likely to arise when arrangements are made with a market research firm to supply all of its output to an archive.

Specialization of an archive in the collection of data at the national level of course has the great advantage of providing data of intrinsic interest, yet this strategy suffers from the disadvantages outlined above and the problem of excessive data as well. The magnitude of information may be so immense for some types of data, such as the Census, that the storage - not to mention the analytic facilities of the archive - can be exceeded. In order to deal with census materials from large nations, for example, it is necessary to develop computer programmes for manipulating data on tape in highly specialized formats where a single data file may extend beyond the limits of a single reel of tape.

The specialization of archives in the collection of data at the international level is certainly desirable as a device to permit the comparative analysis of materials; such archives suffer from the problems of dealing with materials in several languages and in a variety of technical formats. The technical procedures involved in different countries often are not compatible with archive procedures, and special pains must be taken to produce materials in a form easily used by others, and documented to facilitate their rapid location and retrieval.

The disciplinary or problem focus provides a second major dimension for characterizing the specialization of archives. By collecting all of the machine readable data on a specific problem or in a specific discipline, the possibility of making comparisons from different types of data is enhanced. Collections of this kind also facilitate the analysis of events within larger contexts and provide opportunities for independent validation of conclusions drawn from one data set by analysis of another. The methodology of utilizing data with different analytic units such as individuals and areas is not well developed, however, and a great deal of theoretical work remains to be done in this area.

Perhaps the greatest advantage of archive-specialization in a discipline or upon some specific problem is that of creating high visibility for the archive within the discipline. This visibility, in turn, encourages both donors and users of data and reduces the problems associated with establishing acquisition criteria considerably. As a consequence of such specialization, indexing is also simplified and, due to its visibility, the archive usually becomes more responsive to user needs. The problems about which archives can and have been created, however, may be of transitory interest. This type of specialization may provide very little residue for other users. Therefore in the establishment of a problem-oriented archive, considerable care should be exercised in order to avoid this difficulty.

The final dimension for characterizing archive specialization is that of the unit of analysis. Archives exist, for example, which specialize in data on countries, on individuals, on municipalities, and on political events. This kind of specialization simplifies data management considerably and clarifies the priority problem in deciding where to turn for new data, but it does raise other problems, particularly those associated with analytic units of analysis such as municipalities whose very definitions may change. This type of problem creates a need for special computing programmes to permit aggregation of data according to many different criteria so that a "new" municipality can be compared with its former self on the basis of a different aggregation of component sub-units.

INTER-ARCHIVE ARTICULATION

Archives exist in an environment of other archives as well as an environment of users and care must be taken from the start to assure good articulation of the new archive with those already in existence. Articulation takes place at many levels ranging from the problems of assuring compatible hardware to those of assuring compatible policy. At the hardware level, for example, it is absolutely essential that compatibility exist with unit record equipment at the very minimum. The standard for the world, it seems, more amd more, is that of the 80 column card with rectangular punches used by IBM and many other corporations. Remington Rand, Power-Samas, ICT and small card variants should be viewed with care. If local considerations suggest the use of machinery of "non-standard" types, some provision must be made to permit easy and economical transformation of these materials into the more standard format.

In addition to unit record compatibility, however, and perhaps more difficult because of the number of parameters to be made compatible, is that of assuring magnetic tape compatibility. In general, no standards or even common practice exists as yet about the number of tracks, the density of the parity to be used in writing such tapes for social science use. These parameters vary considerably from institution to institution. Thus the ability to handle both seven and nine-track tapes of densities ranging from 250 to 1600 bits per inch, even or odd parity, is of some importance in facilitating inter-archival exchange. There is some agreement about the representation of characters on tape, however, and the ASCII conventions are widely used. Local archives, however, usually have their own blocking and labeling procedures. Such procedures should be developed in a way that makes it possible to reblock tapes to user specifications easily, remove labels where necessary and add labels in magnetic format to the beginning of the tape if desired. All of the above remarks, of course, refer to tapes used in large computers. As yet there has been no development of mini computers for data archive work or the use of casettes for handling of large scale social science data bases. Such a development seems likely in the near future, however, and special attention should be paid to the manner in which such developments would affect the ability of archives to articulate their activities with other archives.

A third problem in promoting inter-archival collaboration at the hardware level is the need for some sort of data documentation format compatibility to facilitate information retrieval and data processing. With compatibility in this area, for example, it is possible for an archive to acquire codebooks in machine readable form from another archive and use its own information retrieval programmes to scan the contents of that documentation in response to the needs of local users.

Inter-archive articulation must also be promoted at the information exchange level. It is important that the format as well as the contents of data inventories is in some standard arrangement that will enable archive staff members and users to work with materials coming from any archive. In the same way, the information retrieval process is facilitated immensely if the format for codebooks and the contents of the codebooks is standardized as well. For examples, the International Data Library and Reference Service (IDLRS) Information Retrieval Project Codebook and the Council for Social Science Data Archives Inventory Format (this latter one is shown in Appendix No. 9) provide some of the standards that are currently widely adopted.

The actual exchange of data is another vital point requiring the articulation of an individual archive with the archive community at large. There are four components to this problem. The first and perhaps the most important is the problem of costs and cost sharing, and may be even income sharing. Where an archive has invested a fair amount of its resources in the cleaning and preparation of a unique data set, there tend to be strong pressures generated for recuperating that investment. Unless an agreement exists among a variety of archives, to mutually underwrite the development costs or to share any revenue produced in the distribution of data sets, a problem revolving about the desire to restrict the exchange of data sets is likely to emerge. The most notable manifestation of this problem is in the area of controlling rediffusion of data obtained by one archive from another. This is often a problem due to the desire of the original archive to assure compliance with special wishes of the donor regarding the use of his data. It is also a problem, however, when the originating archive has structured its operations in order to recover its investment in data preparation by controlling the rediffusion of those materials. To the extent that clear and unambiguous understandings have not been agreed upon prior to the exchange process, it is entirely possible that archives will become embroiled in rather bitter controversies over the rediffusion problem. The pressures to serve the user and provide him with data exacerbate the problem when user service is the criterion for support to an archive that holds a data set from another archive structured to gain its support from the "sale" of unique data sets.

Not all the investment of an archive in a data set is made in the cleaning of that data. Increasingly, additional amounts are invested in placing the data into a specialized format that will facilitate use of one or another computing programme. Thus materials prepared for the Berkeley Transposed File Statistical System (PICKLE) or for the OSIRIS system, the Statistical Package in the Social Sciences system or some other systems, involves an investment on the part of an archive. This leads, in turn, to the archive adopting a stance that will encourage the adoption of the analytical programme package compatible with the archive's data storage format. The relative incompatibility of these systems along with the slight differences in their ability to perform one or another kind of analysis provides an incentive for archives to develop analytical and data

63

processing packages specifically suited to the needs of their specialized users and to encourage the adoption of these systems and associated data storage format by other archives.

The third component of information exchange is that of providing leads to other archives for the possible acquisition of new data and referral of potential users to other archives more suited to their needs. There must be a constant awareness on the part of archive personnel of the activities and interests as well as the contents of other archives so that other archives can be considered, in many ways, as an extension of local facilities when referring users or making contacts for potential acquisitions.

The need to train personnel for archive operations is a continuing one. It is almost essential for personnel staffing an archive to be trained in some other archive. Articulation of archive policy and procedures is promoted by this activity as each archive provides opportunities for staff training and specialization, not only for its own personnel but for personnel from other institutions as well. At the moment the problem of underwriting this function still remains and it is not clear whether the costs are borne by the archive that will eventually employ the trained personnel, by the training archive, or by external agencies concerned with the promotion of the archive movement. There are instances of all three arrangements having taken place.

Perhaps no topic has generated more debate among archivists than establishing the basis for a reasonable division of labour and functional specialization among archives. This is a topic that is continually under discussion and for which numerous solutions have been proposed. Little has emerged from the debate, however, and it is unlikely that anything will emerge until methods are devised to encourage specialization as well as inhibit deviation from policies already agreed upon. Each archive, so far, has pursued the interests of the user community it serves, whether that serves the interests of the archive and total user community or not.

These difficulties lead, then, to a consideration of the final problem, that of developing policy for inter-archival collaboration and articulation. The problem of archive movement policy has two aspects. One revolves about the need to establish priorities and eliminate inter-archival competition to secure funds from external supporting agencies. The second has to do with getting research supporting agencies to include as a requirement for funding that provision be made for archiving data to be produced from the study prior to the initiation of field work.

THE COSTS OF DATA ARCHIVES

There are two aspects to estimating the cost of a social science data archive. The first has to do

with the establishment or set-up phase of the archive during which time extraordinary costs are incurred. The second has to do with the operational phase after all activities have become routinized. The costs involved in setting up an archive can be divided into three areas. The first has to do with the general problem of securing appropriate physical facilities. This includes the initial purchase of office equipment and supplies and the acquisition of the spaces to be used for archive operations and data storage. The third expense derives from the problems of acquiring the initial data base and preparing it for use by scholars. As mentioned before, initial data acquisition may require much more than simple correspondence with potential suppliers. It may involve a great deal of travel on the part of an archive representative to convince potential suppliers that to donate their data to the archive is a reasonable thing to do and to establish inter-personal contacts essential for assuring a continuing flow of data to the archive. There may be extraordinary costs incurred at this point in purchasing data as well. It is sometimes necessary to underwrite part of the costs of the producer in order to gain access to his data or, more commonly, to purchase data already prepared for archive use from some other archive. Exchange of data or services at a later stage can reduce these expenses considerably. The initial investment for data acquisition may be considerable. Whether data is obtained from other archives or obtained in a rough form from original suppliers also has important consequences for the initial budget for cleaning and inventorying materials. And finally, there is the extraordinary cost associated with the initial hiring and training of personnel to staff the archive and its operation.

In the operational phase the relative expenditures for each of the categories outlined above will change considerably. A sample budget is given in Appendix 10. In creating the budget, salaries and wages required for senior technical personnel as well as for clerical personnel must be closely related to the functions that will be performed by each. As the emphasis of the archive changes and as the nature of the collection develops, the expenditures will change accordingly.

Acquisition of permanent equipment diminishes with the years as most of it is obtained during the initial set-up phase. Expendable supplies and equipment, however, increase as a budget item with the growth in operations. Travel continues from set-up through the operational period, although, perhaps on a somewhat lesser level in the latter phase. A new area of expenditure develops with age - that of publications. Publications are clearly necessary to give visibility to the archive and its collection. It is often necessary for the archive itself to engage in the publication of a series of analyses based on the the use of its own materials in order to provide models of how archives can be used. Data cleaning operations are mostly a function of the nature of the archive's data sources. The budget for such activities should also include the costs of any translations necessary as well as the costs involved in the acquisition of raw data. The costs of developing computing programmes to deal with the archive's materials and the costs associated with data processing, such as the keypunching required for the production of machine readable codebooks must also be added into the total budget figure. Similarly, a budget item must be created for the costs of computing itself. Finally, there is the question of overhead. This must be included in the calculation of the costs of archive operations to whatever extent certain kinds of services, such as accounting, mailing, housing, secretarial work, postage, telephones, or any ancilliary functions, are underwritten or supported by the archive itself.

FUNDING ARCHIVE OPERATIONS

Whatever the costs may be, every archive is faced with the problem of securing funds for its operation. This activity breaks down into three major considerations - that of the magnitude of the funding, the sources of the funding and the bases of the funding - plus a fourth consideration - the need for a cost accounting scheme in order to justify the funding and continue its flow.

The magnitude of funding required by any archive is a function of the size and complexity of the archive and the kinds of services it performs, but it is relatively independent of the size of the archive's collection of data. Thus, some of the largest archives currently in operation when size is reckoned in terms of the number of studies or the number of card images for studies contained in their collections operate on a more limited budget than some of the smaller archives do because of the restricted range of services they perform for their users. A good example of an extreme case of this is the project Talent Data Bank which has, in fact, only single data file but is rather costly to operate because of the great amount of energy put into maintaining the data file and providing potential users a great variety of services.

There appear to be only two kinds of funding sources for archive operations: institutional sources or individual sources. In the former, the archive's host institution - a university or a bureau for example - underwrites the costs of archive activities for services rendered not only internally but to external users as well. Thus a Census Bureau may support an archive which actually serves a community outside the bureau itself. A variant on this is where some external institution - a foundation perhaps - underwrites the activities of an archive located in a host institution to provide services to be rendered to a more general clientele. And finally, there is the most successful form of funding wherein a consortium of institutions is created and this consortium then underwrites the activities of an archive that serves all the institutions that are members of the consortium.

While institutional funding is to be desired because of the magnitude of the funds involved and the stability of the sources, it is not, in fact, the only way in which archive activity can be supported. It is also possible for individuals to underwrite archive operations, by purchasing a membership in an archive association and thereby approximating on a small scale the kind of structure made possible at the institutional level by the consortium arrangements. Individuals may also support archive operations by paying a fee for the use they make of the archive's resources.

This brings us then to the third major consideration - that is, what is the basis of funding? The most obvious one is perhaps one of usage whereby a charge is made for each use of the archive, whatever that use may be. Thus a charge for response to a question about the contents of the archive or for the actual retrieval of information about the contents may be made. This taxes the first step that any user or potential user must go through simply to discover if there is any material of potential use to him contained within the archive. A second level for charging fees is associated with the production for a user of a specialized data set - that is, making a copy of the tape or cards and the documentation necessary to make use of that material. A third basis is to charge the user when he requests an actual analysis of the data to be performed for him. The costs rise sharply in this case as a function of the uniqueness of the request being made. Perhaps the ultimate source for user support of archive operations can be found in the growing requirement by successful archives that donors of data be required to underwrite the costs of making their donation a permanent part of the archive. This last procedure has become more and more feasible as many funding agencies recognize the wisdom of such a policy and ask that grantees make provisions for this expense in the construction of their original request for funds. When involved in this process, the supplier becomes much more sensitive to the problems of careful documentation of his work and to the standards of workmanship represented in the production of this data so that he can reduce the costs associated with depositing the data set in an archive.

A second basis for charging the user for his usage of archive services is to focus upon the unit of information required to satisfy a particular request. Thus one may charge for the number of questions retrieved, the total number of questions searched, or the number of card images over which a search has to be made. A charge may be based on the number of studies to be examined for a retrieval and, in some cases, the cost may be divided up on the basis of the number of actual or potential users of the material in question. Another basis for producing revenue is to charge users for the number of uses they make of any materials retrieved from the archive. This will be reflected in an archive charge based on the number of rediffusions of the initial data set made by other sources. By sharing revenue produced in this manner it is possible for archives to engage in the speculative development of new data sets and to encourage the rediffusion of this new material without the fear that the economic base of their operations will be eroded by free or relatively inexpensive recopying of materials initially developed by them at great expense.

An alternative way of developing a base for charging users does not focus upon the marginal costs of usage at all, but emphasizes services rendered instead. Such an archive is funded on a sustaining basis for unlimited usage by any number of researchers in the same way that more conventional libraries are organized. Thus access is permitted to all members of the institution or collection of institutions having reason to use the archive facility, i. e. there is simply open access. The need for a precise and useful cost accounting system is clear in this case and is equally important in the other cases as well. Such a system is absolutely essential in order to justify the costs charged to users and requests for continuing institutional funding made by the archive. The cost accounting system must be relatively easy to implement and must break down to small functional elements. In this way the proper assignment of marginal costs can be made as different individuals engage in the rendition of services to users. The resulting cost figures are essential for estimating the costs of developing new data sources.

Chapter 3

PROBLEMS REMAINING IN THE CREATION OF DATA LIBRARY INFRA-STRUCTURE

Problems can be identified in three major areas and these problems must be overcome before it will be possible to create an infra-structure for the development and use of social science data archives. There are problems of administration, technical problems associated with data management, and political problems related to the general use of existing data for secondary analysis.

ADMINISTRATIVE PROBLEMS: CREATING NEW ARCHIVES

Perhaps the most obvious administration problem has to do with the creation of new archives. Who is to provide the impetus for the creation of a new institution? Even where a well developed substantive need already exists, for example, there are still problems in establishing new archives in a way that will complete geographical coverage when combined with other existing archives. Of course, where a substantive need is not yet recognized the problem of gaining legitimacy for a new archive is even more severe. It is certainly easier to talk about completeness of geographical coverage than to talk about completeness of substantive coverage. If no thought is given to substantive problems in an attempt to assume geographical completeness, scarce resources will be wasted on the development of new archives whose contents will be of little or no utility at all, gathered in a fruitless attempt to obtain "everything" from a given area. Although the idea of complete and thorough coverage of all "relevant" data from a specific area or region is appealing in its simplicity, it is, in most cases, a chimera. The problem of "relevance" intrudes constantly as materials are available from so many sources and on so many topics - from bank transactions, communication flow and corporate statistics to classroom test results, municipal expenditures and individual test score results. The criteria for including materials in an archive, clearly, must extend far beyond simple geographic boundaries. A crucial step in the creation of a viable archive is the successful specification of the criteria for acquisition of data.

ADMINISTRATIVE PROBLEMS: RECRUITING PERSONNEL

Every new archive is confronted with the serious problem of staff recruitment. Where do staff members come from? The technical staff must have some substantive competence and include people capable of dealing with administrators and researchers as well as the technical aspects of computation and computing machinery. If staff members are to be recruited from other activities, the most obvious would be to recruit them from already functioning archives. To do so, however, creates problems for later inter-archive co-operation unless archives supplying personnel are explicitly engaged in training and production of archive professionals and expect them to move on. However, few, if any, archives are engaged in such training activities at this moment.

ADMINISTRATIVE PROBLEMS: ALLOCATING PRIORITIES

Recruitment of an appropriate staff is not the only element in the equation for successful operation, however. It is absolutely vital that there be an active and extensive community of users. One of the first tasks for the administrator of a new archive is to create this community. He must develop an awareness of the archive among potential users and devote energy to introducing them to the contents of archives in general as well as to their usage, and the ways in which the archives may be exploited by them. This need to develop a user community has been partially met by user training programmes. Institutions which are members of the Consortium, for example, can send potential users for training during the summer. Other institutions have sent potential users to Berkeley in order to develop their ability for dealing with archive materials, and Unesco has conducted a series of seminars in various locations designed to aid the development of a community of users.

A final concern under the general heading of administrative problems is the need to develop mechanisms for the allocation of priorities in the archive development process itself. What, in fact, is to be the archive's claim to legitimacy in the area of its data collections? Certainly one consideration is that new archives should be developed and existing archives perfected in a manner that is clearly responsive to well-developed user needs. If an articulate user community does not exist, it is difficult indeed to decide upon an appropriate set of priorities for establishing and developing new archives. It is only by continuous feedback from the users that a reasonable assessment can be made of the general direction for archive development. Too many archives have floundered by ignoring this consideration. Such feedback is not possible, of course, without contact with the user community. In addition, in allocating priorities for development, there must be some consideration given to future needs. It takes time for the development of any new programme even within an established archive. In order to take this developmental time into account, therefore, the archive administration must be aware not only of current user needs but must be able to anticipate the needs of future users as well. To do so requires a high level of substantive sophistication combined with close contact with the user community. And finally, the administration must be in a position to anticipate the needs of the archive itself as an organization in its own right in order to deal with problems arising from strictly organizational needs in collaboration with other members of the archive community. Since the organizational necessities of individual archives frequently conflict with the interests of the archive community, some device is necessary to permit a productive resolution of such conflicts. One factor for consideration when allocating resources and giving priorities to specific archive programmes must be its effect upon the general community of archives. The resolution of conflicts among individual archives and between archives and the archive community must be implemented by some organization of archives. This organization must also play a central rôle in providing guidance to archives in the establishment of technical standards and procedures. At the moment there is no such organization and, clearly there is a vital need for its creation. Only by means of an organization with membership open to all archives and potential archives can the archive community gain a clear understanding of the overall direction of its development.

TECHNICAL PROBLEMS:
DATA MANAGEMENT

The second major problem area to be overcome in creating the infra-structure necessary to promote the use of data archives by social sciences revolves about the technical aspects of managing large data files. At the moment there appear to be five obstacles of this sort dealing in turn with problems of organizing and storing large bases, retrieving information within them, analysing data once it has been retrieved, and problems associated with maintaining inventories and indexes of special collections held within data archives. In order to deal with the large volume of materials typically contained in an archive, some sort of high density format must be employed for storage. This may mean blocked binary tape format written at very high densities or other kinds of representation such as data cells or simply punched cards. Whatever technique is adopted by any one archive, however, often precludes interchangeability of stored data with other archives due to technical incompatibilities. Since local conditions dictate the most appropriate storage technique for an institution, there is a clear and pressing need for some sort of inter-format translation capability. It is not easy, in fact it is not currently possible, for individuals in the United States to process data stored on Power-Samas cards, for example, or with certain kinds of data storage formats since there is no readily available capability for translating these to a locally acceptable format.

The second problem in managing large data collections, simply stated, is the absence of a capacity to manipulate data in its stored format with facility. This capacity often requires machinery capable of reading standard input materials in non-standard ways. Because of the long history of social science research utilizing punched cards prior to the development of high speed computing machinery, a common practice has developed as a device to facilitate data analysis using unit record machinery (or to conserve expensive card materials), whereby information about two or more variables is punched into a single column of a card. When this has been done, considerable difficulty may be encountered in attempts to process such cards by most computing installations unless a special piece of hardware (a binary card reader) has been included in the machinery.

Even where it is possible to read data and get it into a form readily manipulatable by computer, normal archive functioning - data cleaning in particular - requires some generalized programmes for manipulating tapes and characters on tape. Two examples of general programmes of this type are the Berkeley Transposed File Statistical System (PICKLE) designed by Merrill Shanks and Harvey Weinstein of the Survey Research Center, University of California (Berkeley) and the CRAB computer programme prepared by the Survey Research Center for the University of Hawaii, for recoding and reformatting of data.

TECHNICAL PROBLEMS:
DATA RETRIEVAL

Once the problems of storing and manipulating data have been overcome, the data archive user is still faced with locating and retrieving the materials he needs from a store of information, often so great as to be overwhelming. In many cases he must seek mechanical aid. A major task for archives is to help users identify their needs. This may be done either by a system based upon technical-mechanical capabilities, where the user has the responsibility for learning how to utilize the system, or by a system based on the knowledge of the archive held by some particular expert able to guide the user to the materials he needs.

Among the machine-based systems for identifying user needs, perhaps the most common example is the "selective dissemination of information" idea. Such systems rely upon the ability of the user to develop a profile of his needs and on the archive to develop a constantly updated index of its contents as well as a mechanism for matching the index with the user profile. It is essential that users have an opportunity to communicate to the archive his assessment of the relevance and the pertinence of materials retrieved. This feedback permits a continuous modification of initial profiles. Users construct initial profiles on the basis of key words or concepts used by the archive in its indexing scheme. This profile is modified by the user as his interests shift or as he becomes more aware of the adequacies or inadequacies of the profile and retrieval system available to him. Of course it is possible to have interest profiles for groups as well as for individuals, and in some cases these profiles are automatically updated and modified as a function of user response to the utility of the materials being retrieved. These comments are used to reshape the specific profile more closely to expressed needs.

Clearly a great deal depends upon the indexing and selection strategies used by archives in creating retrieval systems. These systems often depend upon the creation of a thesaurus which permits the translation of a variety of words into a few key concepts. Reference to any one of these words or strings of words in the index - or codebook - is then equivalent to use of a computer to examine and create an index according to the thesaurus concept or using some specific set of rules that permit the assignment of specific words and specific phrases to specific concepts. "The General Inquirer" is an example of a programme of this sort. Another way to create indices is to insist that all materials placed into the computer in textual form must use only a restricted vocabulary of key words for which standard meanings have been agreed upon. There are advantages and disadvantages to each of these systems. In general, the more restrictive the indexing, the more rapid and the more economical is the retrieval resulting from it. At the same time, a restricted set of concepts will become less reflective of the needs and concerns of the user clientele over time. Difficulties of expanding and modifying a classifying system once it has been established are considerable, however, and serious thought should be given to this particular disadvantage

when invoking an index system of this kind.

Searching of material is a third aspect of selective dissemination of information. The search process is clearly determined by the depth of the indexing carried on in the initial review of materials. It is not clear that it is better to invest large resources in indexing materials to great depth, assuring thereby that everything conceivably of interest to the user is retrieved as this also raises the probability that many of the citations will be of no interest whatsoever. The optimal level of indexing can only be determined through active feedback from users.

In text searching procedures in contrast to using indices for retrievals, it is possible to specify terms that must be present, absent, or present in certain combinations within the text itself. Each of these terms may have different degrees of importance in making retrievals. But, as always, with each step in relying upon machinery for processing, the costs must be considered. The more text to be searched the longer it takes to search, of course, and costs go up accordingly. Yet the search time is relatively unaffected by the complexity of the search system. Some technical help is always required for preparing actual search requests and for their computer implementation. A good deal has been written on various technical searching strategies which will not be gone into here, but the important point here is to decide upon a retrieval system that optimizes relevancy, pertinency and cost. Very often users are caught between the problems of maximizing relevancy at the cost of pertinency or the other way around. In both cases, however, the user also will try to minimize his costs and an appropriate retrieval system will permit this.

Clearly all of the preceding remarks require constant feedback from users. There are certain minimum requirements from every user. He must learn to utilize the indexing and retrieval scheme, participate in it and give back information necessary for improving the scheme. He must, in many cases, be able to make his initial request for materials in machine readable form. Successful machine-based retrieval systems must be able to respond to users with peripheral interests yet cope with increasing user interest in general and a rising number of requests. Throughout is the problem of evaluating the adequacy of the service. Continuous feedback from user by means of comments upon the quality of the materials received and the quality of the indexing is fundamental but should be supplemented by a series of more abstract and carefully designed tests.

Costs must be carefully weighed against relative benefits. It is still the case, in many instances, that it is far more efficient for an assistant to search materials - or for an analyst to search the materials himself - than to invest in the development of a retrieval system which relies heavily upon a mechanical infra-structure.

Machine-based retrieval systems require the development of a set of computer programmes for their operation. At present there are several retrieval techniques and a variety of classification systems. There is no industry-wide standard language or procedure for information retrieval. Although compatibility among the various kinds of retrieval processes and the various kinds of data stored in social science archives would be desirable, such compatibility is not widespread at the moment and there is no organization working toward this goal. As each archive develops its own system, its vested interest in promulgating that system grows. A good example of the politics of programming can be seen by examining the indexing programmes from institutions with sharing computer systems using remote input and output devices. Indexing programmes utilizing this capacity are based upon an entirely different philosophy than is advocated at institutions not having a similar mechanical capacity.

If and when more computer-based information retrieval systems are developed for data archives, it will be possible to examine user requests as a form of data itself. If preliminary arrangements are made so that user requests are gathered in some sort of compatible form, it will be possible to search for materials at a variety of institutions. Gradually there should emerge a clearer picture of the community of scholars who deal with and are interested in specific kinds of analytical problems. Selective dissemination of information systems are operating successfully covering a variety of fields. There is no reason, in theory, why such a system cannot be extended to deal with machine readable social science data. The problem that must be faced again and again, however, is the extent of the systems coverage. A comprehensive, global, machine-based social science information retrieval system would appear at this time to be impractical.

The second major strategy for retrieving information relies heavily upon responsible experts instead of a machine. There is no question about the speed and efficiency of such systems. They are often faster and better than machines. However, there are limitations upon the capacity of even the most capable individual. In particular, the content of archives grows more quickly than can be assimilated by any individual. While an individual may be extremely competent, the range of his competence may be narrower than the range of inclusiveness of the archive materials. Entrusting all of this information to a single individual is also a great risk for the library administration since accidents can and do happen to individuals. With the loss of an individual can go the loss of access to the materials in the archive. The great advantages of using individuals, however, often outweigh these limitations. The ability of a sophisticated archive expert to reformulate user requests in a way that will exploit an archive more fully is particularly important. In addition, browsing and scanning materials while looking for other kinds of information often provides unlooked for and unexpected materials of great utility to the user. Machine-based systems do not provide this capacity.

Once positive identification has been made of materials for a user there remains the general problem of actually retrieving precisely what is needed. This may involve the selection of specific cases and/or specific variables according to some reasonably complex set of criteria. As this is done, the difficulties with providing adequate documentation become more apparent due to the absence of adequate automatic documentation devices.

TECHNICAL PROBLEMS: ANALYSIS

Even where the appropriate materials can be obtained and where they are adequately documented, there are serious limitations to most of the analytical systems currently available, that is to say, with most of the systems used to provide specific summaries or analyses of the output obtained from the data archives. They tend to be costly or limited in their analytic ability. To the extent that these particular limitations have been overcome, such analytic systems are often unavailable or dependent upon specific machinery that is not widespread so that they are actually of little utility. Another great difficulty with many existing analysis systems is a requirement for some special data format that must be employed, that the dependent variable be the first field of analysis, for example, or that variables may occupy only a single column of a card. The programmes are difficult to modify. Many of the existing systems which are in fact widely employed are not particularly user oriented. They require the user to employ a complex syntax and to employ awkward and non-standard keywords in his research, inhibiting thereby the utilization of these resources. An additional problem of many analysis systems is the inability to link different files so that materials from different studies, for example, can be brought together during the analysis. Finally, almost all existing systems have difficulties dealing with problems of textual materials, such as descriptions of biographies. Thus a great deal of programme development work is necessary before data already available in archives can be utilized. Only a collective effort can accomplish this and, once again, the absence of a central co-ordinating agency to facilitate such an effort is sorely noted.

TECHNICAL PROBLEMS: INVENTORIES

The fundamental tool for the utilization of archives consists of an inventory or inventories. This permits the user to locate the materials and facilities that he needs. There is currently a need for several kinds of inventories. The most fundamental is an inventory of archives or institutions holding collections of available data. Clearly these inventories must contain the location of the archive as well as a general description of the collection or data contained therein. In addition, there must be a complete description of the methods for user access to the collection: an outline of the procedures that the user must follow, a description of the restrictions which may be placed upon dat contained within the archive, and either the pricing for specific data sets, which is sometimes possible, or more common a formula for calculating the costs of any specific type of data set that the user might wish to obtain. The format in which materials are available must be described in this type of inventory, as it is possible that only certain output formats can be constructed. At any specific archive, the user must know in advance what options he has available to him for the form in which he obtains materials for his own use.

A second type of inventory that must be produced, again focusing upon organizations, is that which lists the producers of data. This would characterize their specialties and competencies and identify the location of the organization, as well as the methods of access to it. Once again, it is necessary to include any restrictions that might exist about ways of getting access to these organizations, some consideration of how costs can be calculated in advance, and a statement including the variety of output formats that are available from each of the different data producing organizations.

A third type of required inventory would list the user community and identify the special interests of users and potential users; connect the data sets that people have used with the user in order to facilitate communication among scholars interested in the same kinds of materials, and identify unfulfilled data needs.

The last and perhaps most common kind of inventory required is that of studies themselves - something akin to a library's union catalog. These inventories must contain the content of the studies as well as the identification of where they are stored and, like other inventories, must specify the way in which access can be gained to the contents of some specific study. That is, what are the accession methods, what restrictions are placed upon the accession to the data or use of the data, and what are the costs and available output format?

Two other types of inventories are also worthy of consideration, and in both cases there are currently archives or organizations working in this area. One is an inventory of analytic and data processing programmes. The National Program Library Service of the University of Wisconsin performs this function and has been able to accumulate a large number of programmes suitable for social science research. They have documented these programmes and tried to develop ways in which they could be used on machines other than those initially considered in their design, and have been able to function as an archive of programmes rather than data. They do not publish for external consumption an inventory of their own holdings. There are, however, older groups, not so specialized in the social sciences which do publish such inventories. The most well known of these is the Society to Help Avoid Repeated Effort, or the "SHARE" association of the IBM Corporation and its users, which publishes a listing of available programmes.

A second of these computer-related inventories is that dealing with the location and availability of specialized hardware - such things as optical character recognition so that it is possible for the users to locate and gain access to specialized hardware for one time or occasional use if he finds that necessary. This kind of listing is available on a small scale from several places, including the Organization for Economic Cooperation and Development, Directorate for Scientific Affairs in Paris, which conducts a survey on computer utilization in member countries and, as a result of this has published a listing of the location and availability of machinery and related activities.

There are, however, several obstacles to the creation of any one inventory among the many that need to be created. Perhaps most fundamental is the lack of descriptions and summaries for the various studies which are incorporated into existing archives. If we consider, for the moment, only inventories of studies, the obstacles to the creation of such an inventory can be seen to be substantial although not insurmountable. In order to permit constant updating and revision of the inventories, and of course that is the nature of inventories, it seems essential that the inventory itself be created in a form suitable for manipulation and revision, utilizing automated computing machinery. This is particularly true as the magnitude of the inventory increases and need grows for help in the searching process. This makes the need for automatic machinery for searching even stronger. At the moment, however, there are very few descriptions of studies and summaries of studies that exist in a machine readable form. These inventories usually contain only the most elemental kinds of descriptions about the nature of the studies available even in archives, and after a preliminary search of study listings it is usually necessary for the user to obtain more elaborate documentation.

At the moment, at least two archives have experimented with the development of codebooks for the studies which are themselves in a machine readable form. In this way it is possible to use a computer to actually search through the questions or question wordings in order to identify the specific studies that may be of interest.

This does not solve all of the problems, by any means. There is still no generally acceptable system for categorizing the questions or the variables that may occur within a variety of studies. This is particularly problematic where there are large data bases dealing with very broad substantive interest. In more specialized collections the problem is not so acute. Two schemes used with some success are the one developed at the Roper Center for Public Opinion Research and the one created by the Zentralarchiv at the Institute for Empirical Social Research in Cologne. Both rely heavily upon the availability of rather sophisticated workers who are able to categorize the variables within studies according to the scheme as presented. In many places such classifiers are in short supply.

Even where the classifiers exist in abundance and it is possible to utilize the question-tagging or variable-tagging system of this sort, all inventory systems face the problems of updating and the possible obsolescence of their categorizing scheme. The need for constant change, that is to say, the constant acquisition by archives of new studies, the constant production of materials by suppliers, the constant shift in the user base, and the constant development of new and unmet needs, certainly suggests that an orthodox printed format for the inventory is not the most desirable format due to its inflexibility. Yet, the actual rate of change may be much slower than the theoretical maximum and it may well be the case that it is more reasonable to print a hard copy core to the inventory with regular update or modifications being circulated as needed. The relative advantages of these two systems are still being debated, but it would seem that during the earlier stages, as the rate of increasing knowledge is very rapid, and the need for a rapid diffusion of the information into the field is most intense, that at this time a machine-readable inventory is to be desired. At later times a more permanent version may serve the purpose better.

A further consideration, assuming the existence of a machine readable inventory base, is the possibility for people to gain access to the central inventory service from remote positions, treating it as if it were in fact a local service. There is much comment about this feature, except that the cost may be prohibitively high. Again the interposition of human beings in the system may reduce costs considerably so that the central inventory may maintain its own files in machine readable form but respond by mail to the requests of a great variety of users as interpreted by local inventory or the central inventory staff.

Finally, a major problem in getting an inventory into operational form has to do with the nature of the category headings themselves that are contained within the inventory.

This brings us to the problem of the inventory index. At the moment, there appear to be three major types of strategies for creating an index to an inventory's holdings. The first relies heavily upon the presence within the study titles of key words which reveal the nature of the study's contents. If, for example, the titles are especially written by trained abstractors using a restricted vocabulary, it is possible to sort the titles in such a way that they are arranged alphabetically by every key word appearing in every title. This system has been used with some success by some archives, but there are problems in that titles assigned to many studies do not in fact reveal much of their content.

A second major strategy has been that of attaching to each study a series of concepts which are central to a specific discipline or set of disciplines. Although this technique has been used with some success, the contents appropriate to some disciplines are not appropriate to others, and where the user base is sufficiently heterogeneous, the number of concepts can become enormous. The conceptual scheme itself, of course, has to be assigned with the possibilities of revision and modification which is very often a difficult thing to do.

Indices can be created automatically by creating a concordant indexing of words appearing in various questions, thus requiring only minimal decisions as to the nature of trivial words to be excluded from consideration. With this system, every question or every description of a variable appearing within a codebook is listed under each of the non-trivial words appearing within that variable description or question-wording. This technique also has its limitations, not the least of which is the cost of such a system, but it is often the case that many questions in surveys, for example, can be used as measures of some specific variable, without the theoretical term, such as mobility, ever appearing explicitly within the question-wording. Rarely, if ever, is there a question asking about the social mobility of a respondent in those terms, yet there may be many questions dealing with social mobility, although asking about occupation and similar things. There may be a need for some combination of question-wording and concept-tagging and perhaps even key word summarization besides, in order to have an adequate index. All this is possible on the basis of existing programmes that rely upon machine readable codebooks or inventories for classification purposes, yet there are very few machine readable descriptions of studies currently available. Even with the number that is available, there is not the large base of users from which to develop a great deal of expertise in the use of indices. Clearly, without a central organization to promote comparable development, progress in this area will be severely hampered.

The lack of users is, in fact, one of the best indicators of the kinds of political problems which are associated with the establishment and maintenance of data archives in the social sciences. As matters now stand, it would appear that the cost of maintaining the social science data archive system in the United States may actually exceed the costs of doing new research on the topics of interest. In other words, the potential of the archive movement is simply not being fulfilled. This is due, in part, to a lack of awareness; many scholars do not know about archived materials. This problem could be resolved if there were better inventories available, and wider diffusion of data repositories. Under-utilization is also due in part to the ignorance of many social scientists regarding the techniques of secondary analysis. They are not aware of, or familiar with, ways in which existing data can be reanalysed for their own purposes. Whether it is a cause or consequence is not clear, but in many places the absence of research utilizing data collected for other purposes is also associated with a great deal of hostility toward secondary analysis on the part of traditional academics. In those institutions most preoccupied with the traditional forms, (frequently institutions of lesser quality) secondary analysis is not considered to be "good research". Students are not encouraged to develop skills in this area or to learn about ways they might utilize existing data for their own purposes. There are the further problems arising from a lack of faculty informed in the techniques of secondary analysis and a great lack of teaching materials, particularly examples of how secondary analysis might be utilized. The user shortage is exaggerated, and exacerbated in many instances by an academic hostility and secondary analysis has not become as popular as had once been hoped.

An additional problem area derives from the political barriers to inter-archival exchange of materials. In many cases, the format of storing data - the way in which documentation is arranged - varies from archive to archive depending upon the unique interests and capabilities of the local staff, equipment and user base. The lack of standardization makes exchange difficult indeed. For example, if materials at one place are maintained in multi-punched cards and another archive has no facilities for dealing with multi-punched cards, it is difficult, if not impossible, for them to exchange data.

A second major problem has to do with the desire of some archives to maintain control over the use of materials deposited within it. Where material is initially obtained with the understanding that there will be some restriction on the rediffusion or utilization of these materials, archives must exercise control religiously. In order to maintain their credibility with potential donors when materials are given to another archive, control over rediffusion is considerably weakened, and many managers of many archives feel threatened, quite rightly, by the possibility of unauthorized rediffusion of data. As a consequence, they are reluctant to provide data to other archives and in any situations where their control over its use will be weakened in any way.

An additional barrier to inter-archival exchange of materials arises from the simple economics of trying to recover a costly investment or to use the sale of data to obtain operating funds. For many archives, the sale of data constitutes a major source of income for developmental purposes or regular operations. To the extent that once the material has been sold it can be easily copied, (and of course that is the very nature of machine readable data - it

is very easily copied) it can be distributed by others at a lesser cost or in a manner more convenient to the local user. The archive that initially obtained the materials or that invested efforts in their preparation, cannot recover its investment if it cannot control rediffusion. Consequently, archive managers become very concerned about, and hostile to, the idea of making data available to other archives.

Such conventional concerns as threats to their uniqueness perceived by archive managers when other archives operate within their areas of specialization should not be overlooked - these threats may be geographical, institutional, substantive, or having to do with individual suppliers - anything that an archive has come to feel as being its right and proper domain. As a consequence, archivists are often reticent about supplying crucial information to other archives. While such information might encourage the development of science, it might also weaken the bargaining position of the archive. This happens where all participants are men of good will and there is widespread concern for the sharing and promotion of materials.

Sometimes opposition to the release of data may be due to national policies in this regard. Some government officials feel that to make certain kinds of data about the country available to others is not wise, and consequently, data may not be released. But without reciprocal arrangements for the exchange of data, it is difficult to obtain data from external sources. This problem is similar in many ways to that facing commercial firms who do not wish their data made available to competing commercial interests and thus are very reticent to make data available to archives unless given absolute assurances about control over its diffusion and use. This has the consequence, of course, that archives become very strict about their willingness to let any of that data get out. As these are among the problems remaining in the creation of an infrastructure for the use of the Social Science Data Center, serious consideration must be given to the political as well as to the technical barriers to be overcome before such a task can be accomplished.

Even where the problems of inter-archival exchange have been overcome, political problems associated with obtaining data by donations still remain. Who should bear the cost of data acquisition, for example, the donor, the user, or the archive? Who carries the archive developmental costs: who should underwrite the process of cleaning, of creating an inventory, or maintaining an index? And of course, who should have control over access for the materials contained within the archives?

The access problem has been resolved in several ways. One is by permitting the control over access to remain with the data donor for an indeterminate period of time, and the donor must be available to make a determination about each proposed use of the data. This system has worked reasonably well where the donor is an agency or an organization of some kind. It is more desirable, however, to insist that the donor's control lapses after some fixed period, whether it be one year, or five years or twenty-five years. After that time, data deposited in the archive is, by agreement, available for general use. The third possibility here is for the archive alone to maintain control over access to the data. There are several concerns associated with this policy. What are the bases for permitting access to be and how are they derived? If data access rules are created, how is this done so that suppliers accede to them?

In the general area of data donations, steps have to be taken to prevent the development of inter-archival competition for specific data sets - such competition creates a false sense of the commercial worth of the data. There have been incidents of this in the past, and as a consequence the cost of acquiring data has been driven up considerably. As a result, the selling of data was seen as a way of financing further research. It would seem that this must be considered to be inappropriate practice as it artificially inflates the cost of secondary analysis and makes it economically unfeasible.

One development in this area that seemed to hold a great deal of promise was the attempt by the Council of Social Science Data Archives to get agencies, whether governmental or private foundations, supporting original research, to adopt a policy requiring that provisions be made for the archiving of all data generated using their funds. This should be one of the conditions for all funding, and it is not without its consequences. One consequence would be to require the investigator to get a commitment from an archive to accept his data. This permits the archive to exercise some control over standards of documentation that must be met before the data can be deposited. Secondly, where archive policies have limited the amount of time during which exclusive control of data utilization is maintained by the donor, there is a tendency to put pressures upon the donor (original researcher) to publish materials as rapidly as possible, with a consequent acceleration of the flow of scientific information.

In summary then, several difficulties must be kept in mind when considering the development of a Social Science Data Storage and Retrieval Facility, whether in a developing nation, for specialized users, or to serve the world community of social scientists. These include the shortage of available administrative personnel; the needs for developing appropriate technical systems for the management and retrieval of data, a similar need for data analysis, the need to devise techniques for maintaining inventories and indices of data to inform potential users about the availability of data. In addition, problems must be overcome in the political area, such as prompting donations by users, facilitating exchange of information among archives, and, most important, increasing demand and usage by making secondary

analysis more acceptable within both academic and policy settings. With these problems in mind, let us turn now to a consideration of some possible solutions of them.

SUGGESTIONS FOR OVERCOMING THE PROBLEMS FACING THE SOCIAL SCIENCE ARCHIVE COMMUNITY

Perhaps the single most important factor to be considered in the solution of all the problems outlined is the location of stabilized, long-term, large scale funding. This would permit the recruitment of skilled personnel; training of personnel in specialized procedures; development of an appropriate technical infra-structure; and acquisition of materials and equipment necessary to carry out the work of a data archive. As matters now stand, most large archives are confronted with the funding problem either continuously or every few years. They find it difficult to make long-term plans, or they are forced into the undesirable practice of funding their activities on the basis of the sale of data. As we noted before, this practice has negative consequences in general and is not a viable solution to the funding problem.

There are two possible sources of stable funding. The first, of course, involves users or potential users in the formation of a consortium. In this way, large scale long-term funding can be arranged if a user community in fact exists. Such consortia are based on common substantive interests, thus they may focus on social problems or the study of politics or the needs of census users, as long as all members recognize the need for support of the archive in order that they might be able to use its services. A consortium, however, requires an organizational framework in order to persist. The first problem is that of establishing archival priorities. Thus some sort of organizational device, such as a special sub-committee of users, must be devised so that data acquisition priorities as well as technical developmental priorities can be established, and whereby conflicts between priorities of organizational development and substantive richness can be resolved.

A second function of such committees is to assure the responsiveness of the archive organization to the needs of its users. Such responsiveness is necessary for continuing needs and changing needs arising with development. Without the formal involvement of the user community at the highest levels of archive management, it is entirely possible and indeed probable that the archive will develop along the lines which are either superbly suited to the existing demands of the user community and terribly difficult to alter as the nature of the demand alters (due to developments in the field), or, as has happened in some cases, the archive may become so preoccupied with the technology of archival management itself that user needs are relegated to secondary importance. The skills and resources of the archival organization in this case, go into the concern for more and more exotic technology to facilitate archive operations without a balanced concern for users' needs.

Perhaps the most important function of an organization of users is to guarantee the legitimacy of any sanctions imposed on an archive user for violation of procedures generally agreed upon. Without such organizational framework, it is difficult for the archive to exert any sanctions other than simple refusal of further service to a user who violates some condition of use. With a user consortium, however, the possibilities of negative sanctions from peers begins to carry much more weight.

A common substantive focus is not absolutely essential to the development of user consortium since it is equally possible to develop one simply based upon propinquity. For example, all of the various users working within a region or at a single institution may band together to underwrite the continued operation of a facility to serve their common needs. It is perhaps even more important in this type of situation that a formal organizational framework be developed to include user representation at the policy and managerial levels since the struggle over priorities and resource allocation is exacerbated where there are diverse substantive interests. This is typically the case when an archive is organized along regional lines, as substantive interest may pull in many directions.

Whether an archive is organized along substantive lines or to serve the needs of scholars concentrated in a specific geographical area, there is still some question as to whether membership in a consortium should be open to individuals or institutions. The latter is preferable as the interests of institutions tend to be much more stable than those of individuals. Where services are provided to all affiliated with a member institution the problems of control over access to the data become a little complex. The question of an individual association with an institution in order to gain access to the data archive via the consortium becomes a little bit fuzzy in some cases. This is particularly so where the institution itself has many branches and parts and the nature of affiliations is not clearly stated. Thus in some instances it is the department of a university which may join a consortium. In others, it is a campus of a university. In still others, it may be a university with many campuses. Several local institutions may even join together and funnel their membership through only one institution in order to gain access to the consortium. This is a difficulty that must be solved by a consortium's member organization as providing services to many members with costs of only one membership reduces potential support for the archive considerably.

A second aspect in the development of consortia has to do with creating classes of membership related in some way to the type of usage that the members make of the archive. In this manner, big users of archive services may pay more, but they may have a class of membership permitting unlimited use of the archive facilities. As a consequence, they may get more services while still underwriting the interests of other members. Although reasonable, it appears that the larger the member institution, the less need it has for peripheral services by a consortium and there is a constant tendency to lose the larger members. A different class of membership may require only a small continuing payment to the consortium, in which case a large marginal charge is leveled for each of the rare occasions where some specific service is utilized.

The other major source for continued basic support for archive operations has come from governmental agencies and foundations. Where this has taken place, a case has usually been made for the intrinsic need for the kind of service provided. Nevertheless in order to continue obtaining basic support from external agencies that are not users of archive materials it is absolutely essential for archives to develop an extremely detailed system to account for the usage made of services. This accounting will inevitably be called for as continued funding is called into question which always happens where there is competition for the resources of the funding agency.

The problem of intrinsic need is normally solved by emphasizing one or more of the following three specific foci to the funding agency. The first is regional service, in which the archive provides services to users located in a geographical area who otherwise would be denied resources of this type. The second is disciplinary competence, where the archive concentrates into a single organization a set of scarce skills that otherwise cannot be mobilized for the solution of data users' problems. This mobilization involves not only substantive skills but technical and managerial skills as well. These must be brought together into that amalgam which characterizes the successful archive. Third is the problem centred focus where an archive's existence is justified by the importance of the problems upon which its resources are focused and presumably by the promise that the archive's existence will play a rôle in the solution of these problems.

The need for a special administrative structure is particularly acute where the sources of basic support are not strongly based within the user community. Great care must be taken to guarantee the responsiveness of the archive's management to the demands of users and particular care must be taken to anticipate changing needs of the user community. This is perhaps best accomplished by the creation of an advisory board constituted of potential, as well as present, users of the archive's services, able to meet directly with the funding agency in order to guarantee that the flow of funds to the archive will be a function of its responsiveness to user needs.

Regardless of the existence or function of any specific archive, a major problem is the need to create a facility to permit users to locate the sources of data and related material such as computer programmes, data processing facilities, or substantive experts that will help him pursue his research. This need can be served best by creation of a centralized international inventory, broad in the scope of its contents, efficient in its responsiveness, and accessible to users from the remotest regions. This inventory can contain several components. First, and perhaps most important, it should consist of no more than a directory of existing archives. Since this is a subject that changes relatively slowly, an archive directory can take the form of a conventional hard-copy publication for which regular supplements or updates are issued, and this directory can be made available through conventional channels of distribution, by advertising in scholarly journals and by making the publication available to scholarly bookstores, etc. Users of the archive directory might be encouraged to subscribe to a central service which notifies them of changes in the status of the entries within the directory. Directory entries should consist of at least seven bits of information including the title and location of the archive including addresses and telephone numbers. Where applicable, the special competence of the archive should be outlined, including a statement about the content or at least the emphasis of the archive in its content areas, the availability of analytic programmes at the archives and outlines of the procedures by which data are generated or acquired for the collection. The procedures used to gain access to the collection must be carefully outlined including, of course, an explicit delineation of all costs involved in procuring services of different types. The nature of the staff, not only the administrative but technical, should be included in this archive directory, as it will serve as a resource not only for users but for other archivists as well, and will permit the development of a broader and more rational division of labour in the archive process in general. Inclusion of this information will also provide the bare underpinnings of a professional directory for the archive movement. The location of skilled personnel for archive operations is a difficult task and to the extent that the directory can provide assistance in this area, it should do so. In this way, archive managers will have some idea of where to do recruiting as well as where to send candidates for additional training. In addition to the substantive description of the archive's holdings, some mention must be made within this directory of the units of analysis for every subject contained; that is, the level of aggregation. It does not help a user much to know that the emphasis of an archive is on political materials or voting studies when his interests focus on individual responses and the smallest unit of analysis available within the archive is a municipality. The format in which data may be made available must also be specified. This should include not only such statements that the punched cards or magnetic tapes are available,

but should specify in enough detail the conventions used. Examples of this are whether the tapes are available in seven or nine track forms, 800 or perhaps 1,600 bit per inch density, whether the cards are punched in an IBM compatible format or whether multiple punches have been used, and things of this nature.

A second type of inventory, one that changes somewhat more rapidly, is that organized by topics. Because the details of such an inventory will change rapidly although the general structure of it will not, it should be available in both hard and soft copy version. There should be both a substantially bound printed form and a machine readable form suitable for rapid and simple modification. This inventory should be organized by topics. Within areas of political science, for example, it might be organized by the problems of voting, of political instability, of governmental changes and the like. Under general topic headings there should be a notation of which studies are available and the appropriate parts of studies available. This would identify not only the populations studied including time index location, and the nature of the unit of analysis, but also make reference to other variables in the study. This topical inventory must, of course, identify archives in which materials are stored as well as provide some general statement as to the availability of the materials. It is important that materials not readily available are also inventoried in order to provide research scholars an overview of the kinds of work already done, the researchers responsible for it, and to place pressures upon the data sources to make their data more available. While the topic inventory may always be out of date, it will direct the potential user to those archives which contain the kind of materials in which he is interested and sensitize him to the kinds of specializations within archives that a more general description could not provide.

A third type of inventory that should be available would describe continuing data acquisition programmes and the nature of major data files within them. Because these programmes are slow to emerge and slow to disappear, this kind of inventory might also be in a printed and bound format. It would include such things as the topics of specialization, populations involved, the format in which the data is maintained, the location of the data, general rules about accessibility to it, and some comment on who is making use of this kind of data, not in terms of the specific individuals, but in terms of the results produced.

A fourth type of inventory which would be of immense use to the operators of data archives would focus upon the interests of users themselves. This inventory need only exist in machine readable form and would be queried in order to provide potential users, for example, with the names of other users of the same data sets, or to give archive managers some idea of who is making what kinds of inquiries about data sets. With this sort of information readily available in machine readable form it would be possible to enter into the selective dissemination of new information as it was obtained. In this way, the user community would be kept up to date as new data became available from one or another archive. At the same time, the exchange of the names of potential or actual users of the same data sets via this inventory might very well speed up the scientific information process by a tremendous amount. The short circuiting of this kind of information which often takes years to obtain via the publication of standard articles would be a great benefit to the scientific as well as policy making communities.

A third major area currently problematic for archive development and utilization might be resolved by the creation of appropriate programmes. The area in question is the shortage of both users and archive technical personnel. Training programmes should be established for both. Users must be trained to utilize the sources of data archives by giving them examples of resource utilization for scientific and policy purposes and providing them with surveys of available resources, instructing them how to use inventories and how to obtain data. Even with the data in hand, however, there is often some question as to how it might best be exploited. An introduction to analytic models and to causal modeling should be provided via a user training programme supplemented by an introduction to automated data processing techniques. This introduction would range from consideration of unit record technology through the most advanced computer technology, extending to aspects of microfilm and microfiche information retrieval and analysis.

A second training programme required is for the training of producers of data. It is necessary for researchers to develop the perspective that their own data may be used again by others, thereby encouraging more thorough utilization of existing data before generating new data. This also encourages considering in advance the problems involved in archiving data when they have finished with it. Thus, standards of documentation will be improved, documentation will become more thorough and more explicit. In addition, because of the potential comparative possibilities, it will become common practice to include standard comparative items, although of low utility for a specific study. Thus, a major thrust will be launched to articulate new data with existing data and provide an important basis for the cumulative work in the social sciences that is so desperately needed. Perhaps the first visible consequence of this move will be to see widespread implementation of the policy that requests for research support to include the funds necessary to archive the data upon completion of the initial research work. A concomitant statement that arrangements have been made with an existing archive to guarantee the acceptance of the data set within its collection would imply that minimum documentation and methodological standards

would have been met by the research scholar.

The third type of training programme advocated is one for the staffs of data archives themselves. This would cover the problems of dealing with users and developing competence in substantive areas so that data retrieval can be facilitated and in analysis techniques as well. Personnel familiar with the techniques related to computing and data processing are in very short supply indeed. In general most of the available personnel with data processing skills are ignorant of the analytic strategies of social science as well as the substantive concerns. Without this kind of knowledge, the work cannot be done in its most efficient fashion, nor will there be much creative development coming from the data processing component of the archive staff.

Perhaps the most obvious area in which training for archive staff is necessary is that related to the selective dissemination of information to users. This is not a common practice now in any of the major social science archives and before it could be, the skills associated with this service would have to be developed and refined within existing archive staff personnel. The ability to account for the costs in archive operations is another skill that is in very short supply and it is necessary to hold some training programmes to sensitize archive staff members to the needs for cost accounting as well as to introduce them to the details of specific cost accounting systems.

Cleaning and documenting of data to be included within the archive is, perhaps, the most difficult task of all. It requires a high degree of skill in data processing combined with a well developed substantive command of the materials to do an adequate job. It is not possible for someone who does not know about the substance of the materials with which he is working to do an adequate job of cleaning them. Knowledge of the substance alone is not enough, however, as data cleaning requires the skills of an expert data processor as well. Consequently, it is necessary to recruit people with substantive skills and train them to develop data processing skills in order for this work to be carried forward. Without question the one area of archive staffing most in demand and in shortest supply throughout the world is that of data cleaning. Finally there is the problem of training the archive staff in the acquisition process - giving them the skills to seek out and identify potential materials for inclusion, to convince the sources of these materials of the desirability for this kind of collaboration and to carry out the operations necessary for obtaining the materials. Doing this requires training people in the skills of diplomacy and salesmanship as well as those of packing and shipping, of computing related activities and, of course, a fine sense of the substantive importance of data and the methodological adequacy of any given data set.

A fourth area in which it is possible to move toward the development of the social science data archive community on an international scale has to do with publishing programmes. There is at the moment no readily identifiable source of publications based on the utilization of archive materials. There is no source which is a showplace for secondary analysis or for comparative analysis exploring the methodology of secondary analysis. There is no place where one can see, for example, how attempts have been made to determine the robustness of some association by examining it in different settings with different data sets, obtained by different scholars - a programme possible only with the use of data archives. Furthermore, there is no publication to which one can turn in which the utilization of existing data for policy purposes or for theory testing purposes is pointed out. Without such publications it is difficult to provide the models necessary to generate enthusiasm for this whole style of analysis. The creation of publications in these areas would go a long way towards eliminating the shortage of archive users by helping to generate more usage of archive materials.

A second publishing programme of vital importance is the creation of a newsletter or journal dealing with the problems of archive management itself. At the moment, there is no source to which archive personnel can turn to learn of new or developing data sources or uses; to learn about new information retrieval or analysis packages; to propose, debate or agree upon new technical standards for their operations or to exchange information about personnel desired or available for employment.

If training activities are to become more pronounced, there is also the need to publish curricular materials. This might begin with a user's guide to the locale and acquisition of existing data in the same way that historiography is taught. It is necessary to have materials telling how to utilize the kind of data inventory suggested earlier. Introductory curricular materials dealing with the fundamentals of data processing are needed and should be presented both from the unit record and the computer perspective as applied to the social sciences. Materials are necessary to teach potential users about the use of archived data for the development of indices and scales as well as considering measurement problems in general in the social sciences context. There is also very little material available to teach people how to handle (and why to use) more than two variables in analysis from the multiple cross tabular strategy, as well as with more complex multivariate statistical models such as regression, analysis of variance, factor analysis, and multiple classification analysis.

All of the above suggestions are of no avail unless it is possible to create a larger demand for the services of archives than currently exists. This can be done in part by demonstration projects utilizing archive resources. These projects may be held at archives to insure speedy turn-around in analysis and encourage the conversational format for teaching the analytical strategies of multiple variable analysis. They might also be held in appropriate settings such as ministries or universities where archives are not available, using local resources, if necessary, developing the technology of telecommunications to carry out the demonstration.

A second component for creating the necessary demand has to do with the availability of seminars for retraining professionals already established in their careers. For researchers trained prior to the computer revolution it is necessary to provide a structured opportunity in a non-threatening situation to learn the new technology. At present these are often the men of power and influence in the social science disciplines opposed to the utilization of data archives and computer methods for reasons based largely in the area of their own ignorance of them. By providing an opportunity to learn these skills and apply them to their own interests, the chances for influencing the development of the social and policy sciences in the direction of secondary analysis are increased considerably. Retraining seminars will help to legitimize secondary analysis as a scholarly enterprise. A real effort is necessary to utilize them.

The third component for creating demand for archive services derives from the training of consumers in the interpretation of social science results for policy purposes. Thus it is possible to train students in how data archives may be used for the study of historical processes, for the creation of new theories, and for the testing of social science models through simulation.

The final component in the effort to promote the development of social science archive movement is the most important. It is also the necessary first step before any other activities can succeed. A professional society for archive users and managers must be created. This would promote the flow of information through professional conferences, give professional identity to archivists and create a career line for them that does not exist now, thereby facilitating the recruitment of personnel to the archive profession. Such an association would provide the opportunity to attend the meetings of a professional society and give a degree of visibility to data archives that is currently lacking.

SUMMARY AND CONCLUSION

There are four basic principles which underly the conclusions of the report: (1) existing quantitative social science data can be used for purposes in addition to those for which they were initially collected, (2) scholars and planners should have ready and equal access to such materials, (3) potential users will be best served if they are informed regarding the characteristics of the material available to them, and (4) existing materials will be valuable resources to social scientists and historians of the future. It is appropriate and it is desirable for social science data archives to facilitate these goals. The technical requirements of a functioning social archive, however, are beyond the reach of most international organizations and it is not reasonable to expect the creation of an archive itself, to function within such a setting. Instead, it is recommended that a central co-ordinating federation be established within an international organization to facilitate co-operation among existing and yet to be created social science data archives - to aid in co-ordinating the data acquisitioning activities of these groups; to set standards for the processing, documenting, and storing of data; and, of central importance, to work toward the gathering and dissemination of information pertaining to the operation of archives and their contents.

The first step towards establishing such a federation would be to hold a conference to bring together the directors of existing social science data archives throughout the world, key individuals currently engaged in the planning and development of new archives, government officials and social scientists who constitute the body of archive users and governmental organizations and foundations which underwrite the financing of archive operations. The goal of this conference would be to establish the federation described in this synopsis in order to overcome the barriers to access to social science data described in the report itself. This federation, in addition to providing the focus for social science data archive developments throughout the world, would serve as the co-ordinating agency for the continuous gathering and disseminating of information regarding the contents of all archives.

Social science data archives of all kinds should be eligible for membership within the federation, although an emphasis should be placed at the beginning upon securing the membership of those offering a wide variety of machine readable data and services. These tend to be the archives whose contents change the most rapidly and it is for this reason that a special emphasis should be placed upon securing their membership in the proposed federation.

All members should be encouraged to try and meet the standards established by the federation in such matters as acquiring new materials, documenting materials and providing materials to other archives and their own users with appropriate information and assistance. The federation would work to establish appropriate standards through a committee structure. The major incentive for collaboration with the federation would be via the publication of guidelines and through the co-operation of agencies funding data archives that would insist that the guidelines be met in order for archives to achieve funding for their operations.

In general, the federation would promote the collective and articulated efforts of all archives in order to obtain an optimum division of labour in the acquisition and preparation of data for secondary and comparative analysis. The federation would by this means inhibit the development of exclusive arrangements between archives and data suppliers that act as an obstacle to the use of materials from these suppliers by other archives and their users.

The federation, recognizing that some data suppliers may wish to place limitations on the distribution of their material, will lend its support to all activities which minimize supplier limitations on rediffusion and will try to encourage maximum amounts of rediffusion of material called for by users throughout the world. At the same time, the federation would be devoted to the protection of archive data from improper uses including the invasion of the privacy of individual respondents and organizations involved in the original research.

The International Federation of Directors of Data Banks, as this association might be known, would work toward establishing simple standard statutes for promoting the continued relations between data banks and provide a linkage, currently missing for social scientists to the existing international bodies, such as UNISIST, the International Institute of Statistics, the International Federation of Documentalists, and the International Standards Institute and the International Labour Organisation. Through an annual meeting, this body would bring about a type of social science - academic - governmental data generating link that is currently not in existence and would facilitate the work of all groups involved. As many social scientists have discovered, many of the existing international organizations are not responsive to their particular needs because social scientists, other than economists, are not in any way represented upon them. The existence of an International Federation of Directors of Data Banks would provide this representation in the world of international scholarly bodies. It would not duplicate any of the existing functions but would complement them and permit a fuller and more fruitful utilization of the technical skills of existing information sciences and the substantive and analytic skills of the social scientist combined with the growing complex web of inter-organizational relations.

The International Federation of Directors of Data Banks could, as its first task, move toward the creation of a central inventory of archives and archive contents, building upon already existing regional and national efforts along this line. Training programmes in the utilization of existing social science data for secondary and comparative analysis could be developed at a later stage, and finally, it would be possible for this Federation to take the lead in developing standards for machine independent computing programmes essential to the proper utilization of social science data archives.

In order to accomplish these goals, an annual meeting convened by an executive officer should be held at which time work would be delegated to volunteer committees. Funding for the technical work of the committees would have to be sought outside of the organization itself, but under the Federation's aegis.

The benefits resulting from the development of such a Federation would be manifold. In particular, however, we can note the consequences for overcoming the series of barriers to the world-wide use of social science information. The Federation's existence would give to the archive movement greater visibility and a more concentrated focus. It would provide a central source for information about the contents and activities of archives throughout the world. Given the availability of knowledge about archive's contents and the means of gaining access to them, a much greater utilization and a much more rational utilization of existing resources can be expected. There is currently a continuing investment of scarce resources in the gathering anew and recompilation of information already extant, suitable for the solution of many problems. Thus, a paramount benefit of the creation of an International Federation of Directors of Data Banks would be the more rational utilization of scarce resources for the benefits of science and government planners. A second benefit would be for individual scientists in making available to them a broader and more comprehensive base of information with which to formulate

and test their theories. A marked and substantial growth in the rate of the development of the social sciences can be expected to result from the creation of this Federation. In a similar fashion, the structure of social science education will benefit due to the availability at low cost of materials useful to the social sciences which may be incorporated into more traditional curricula without bearing the extraordinary costs of initial data collection. With new technicians trained in the utilization of social science data and an infra-structure capable of providing relevant data on many pressing social science topics, it is to be expected that the planners in developing countries will be able to utilize already existing information with a relatively small expenditure of resources, where the pursuit of this information now is beyond their reach.

To accomplish these goals will require an expenditure of approximately $293,550 over the next six years distributed in the manner shown below.

BUDGET

Salaries and Wages	Year 1	2	3	4	5	6	Total
Senior Administrative personnel[1]	10,000	15,000	20,000	20,000	20,000	20,000	105,000
Clerical personnel[2][3]	8,000	11,000	15,000	15,000	15,000	15,000	79,000
Permanent Equipment[4]	700	300	200	-	-	-	1,200
Expendable Supplies and Equipment[5]	250	500	600	750	750	750	3,600
Space Rental[6]	2,500	2,500	3,000	3,500	3,500	3,500	18,500
Communications[7]	500	500	600	750	1,000	1,000	4,350
Publications[8]	250	500	750	1,500	1,500	1,500	6,000
Travel[9]	1,100	1,500	2,200	2,200	2,200	2,200	11,400
Data Processing[10]	500	1,000	1,500	2,000	2,000	2,000	9,000
Annual Meeting[11]	3,000	6,000	9,000	12,500	12,500	12,500	55,500
	26,800	38,800	52,850	58,200	58,450	58,450	293,550

NOTES

(1) Responsible for organization and conduct of annual meeting; recruiting members for executive and other committee work; and, most important, maintaining liaison with funding agencies to secure aid for the work of Federation committees and promote the acceptance of Federation standards and policies. Position initially filled by a one-half time appointment expanding to full-time in third year.

(2) Administrative assistant.

(3) Clerical workers, typist.

(4) Typewriter, files, office furniture, storage cabinet for magnetic tapes, storage cabinet for punched cards.

(5) Stationery, envelopes, file folders, etc.

(6) Administrative office plus storage for inventory-related data.

(7) Telephone, telegraph, postage and freight.

(8) Hard copy and magnetic tape versions of inventory.

(9) Visits by senior personnel to funding agencies, consultants and archive locations.

(10) Costs related to production of continuously updated inventory of archive holdings throughout the world.

(11) Based on providing an average of $250 support for each of 50 archive directors to facilitate their attendance at annual meeting, plus all costs of senior administrator.

REFERENCES

1. Brock, Clifton. "Political science." In Downs, Robert B., and Frances B. Jenkins. Bibliography: current state and future trends. Urbana: University of Illinois Press, 1967. p. 305.

2. Blau, Peter M., and Joan W. Moore. "Sociology." In Hoselitz, Bert F.,(ed.) A reader's guide to the social sciences. New York: Free Press, 1970. pp. 1-40.

3. Cf. Kiyoth, Jean Spealman,(ed.) Readings in nonbook librarianship. Metuchen, J. J.: Scarecrow Press, 1968. pp. 106-48.

4. Ferguson, Jack. Specialized social science information services in the United States. New York: Bureau of Applied Social Research, Columbia University, April 1965. ch. 7.

5. Pool, Ithiel de Sola. "Data archives and libraries." In Overhage, Carl F. J., and R. Joyce Harman,(eds.) INTREX: Report on a planning conference on information transfer experiments. Cambridge: M. I. T. Press, 1965. pp. 179-80.

6. Bisco, Ralph L. "The research library and data archives for social research." Speech prepared for the dedication of the Graduate Research Library, University of Florida, 1967.

7. National Research Council/Committee on Information in the Behavioral Sciences. Communication systems and resources in the behavioral sciences. Washington, D. C.: National Academy of Sciences, 1967. ch. 3. (Publication 1575).

8. Ibid., p. 37.

9. See, e.g., Conferences on Training Science Information Specialists. Proceedings, Oct. 12-13, 1961; April 12-13, 1962. Atlanta: Georgia Institute of Technology.

10. Swanson, Rowena W. "The entrepreneurs of technological change: the future development of information and technology transfer agents." In Aslib. Accelerating innovation: papers given at a symposium held at the University of Nottingham, March 1969. London: Aslib, 1970.

11. System Development Corporation. "Technology and libraries." In Knight, Douglas M., and E. Shepley Nourse. Libraries at large: tradition, innovation, and the national interest. New York: Bowker, 1969. p. 327.

12. Garfield, E. "Information retrieval." Science, 156: 3780. Quoted in Schur, H., and W. L. Saunders. Education and training for scientific and technological library and information work. London: HMSO, 1968. p. 50.

13. Lucci, York, and Stein Rokkan. A library center of survey research data. New York: School of Library Service, Columbia University, June 1957. pp. 93-96, 139-52. It should be noted that Lucci had an advisory committee that included librarians and received technical advice from Eric Meyerhoff of the Columbia Medical School Library.

14. Lewis, P. R. "Bibliographical co-operation between statisticians and librarians: suggestions for some projects." In Conference on Librarian-Statistician Relations in the field of Economic Statistics. Proceedings, July 5, 1965. ed. by K. A. Mallaber. London: Library Association, 1966. pp. 58-59.

15. Bisco, op. cit., p. 17.

16. Citro, Constance. "Data delivery on computer tape to libraries." In Conference of the Urban and Regional Information Systems Association. Papers from the 6th Annual Conference. Sept. 5-7, 1968. Urban and regional information systems: federal activities and specialized systems. ed. by John E. Rickert. p. 50.

17. A good one-volume introduction to U.S. programmes for foreign librarians is Bonn, George S. Library education and training in developing countries. Honolulu: East-West Center Press, 1966. It also had chapters on Asian and Latin American programmes. Another work with material on the training of foreign librarians is Tsien, Tsuen-Hsuin, and Howard W. Winger. Area studies and the library. Chicago, University of Chicago Press, 1966.

Appendix 1 - SAMPLE OPERATING BUDGET

	1-1-64 to 6-30-64 (6 mos.)	7-1-64 to 6-30-65 (12 mos.)	Total
Salaries			
Principal Investigator	–	–	–
Associate Research Sociologist (or Associate Research Political Scientist), Step III, one-half time[1]	3,225	6,450	9,675
Associate Research Analyst, Step III, one-half time[2]	3,225	6,450	9,675
Senior Typist Clerk, Step III, one-third time	1,520	1,600	3,120
Sub-total	7,970	14,500	22,470
Employee Benefits (10% of eligible salaries)			
Sub-total	797	1,450	2,247
Supplies			
Office supplies	200	300	500
Postage	100	100	200
Telephone	400	400	800
Sub-total	700	800	1,500
Travel			
Within the United States[3]	1,550	2,300	3,850
Other Direct Costs			
Data Processing[4]	1,000	3,000	4,000
University Overhead (25% of direct costs)			
	3,004	5,513	8,517
Total	15,021	27,563	42,584

---

1. To serve as staff secretary to co-ordinating committee, and to be responsible for supervision of project.
2. To serve as expert in information storage and retrieval systems.
3. Travel and per diem for two persons (a and b) to investigate major repositories and social science departments in the United States ($800 each time period. Also, travel for committee members to and from Ann Arbor and Berkeley).
4. IBM computer expenses in connexion with the development of information storage and retrieval systems.

Name of Data Library	Address	Director	Type of Data	Subject Matter
Archive on Political Elites in Eastern Europe	Dept. of Political Science 1028H Cathedral of Learning University of Pittsburgh Pittsburgh, Pa. 15213	Carl Beck	Biographical Information	Political elites in Eastern Europe
Archive on Comparative Political Elites	Dept. of Political Science University of Oregon Eugene, Oregon 97403	Lester Seligman		
Bureau of Applied Social Research	Columbia University 605 West 115th Street New York, New York 10025	Alan H. Barton	Sample Surveys	Health and Welfare, occupations and professions, mass communications, politics, education, organizations
*Bureau of Labor Statistics	United States Department of Labor			
Carleton University, Social Science Data Archive	Dept. of Political Science Carleton University Colonel By Drive Ottawa, 1, Canada	Roman R. March	Sample Surveys Biographies, Elections Statistics, Census Data	Politics and public opinion
Carlo Cattaneo Research Institute	Piazza dei Martiri Bologna, Italy			
Center for International Studies Data Bank	Mass. Inst. of Technology E53-365 Hermann Building Cambridge, Mass. 02139	Stuart McIntosh	Sample Surveys	Politics, social behaviour public opinion
Columbia University School of Public Health and Administrative Medicine Research Archives	630 West 168th Street New York, New York 10032	Jack Elinson Beatrice Mintz	Sample Surveys Operational data	Administrative medicine, public health
Council for Inter-Societal Studies	Northwestern University 1818 Sheridan Road Evanston, Illinois 60201	Richard D. Schwartz		
Data Archiv Scuola di Formazione in Sociologia	Via Daverio F Milano 20122, Italy	Guido Martinutti		
Département d'analyses Secondaire	Centre d'études Sociologique 82, Rue Cardinet Paris XVII, France	Raymond Boudon		
Department of Political Science	University of Oslo Blindern, Oslo 3, Norway	Steinar Witgil		
Graduate School of Industrial Administration	Carnegie Inst. of Technology Pittsburgh, Pennsylvania 15213	Howard Rosenthal	Ecological Statistics, Sample Surveys	French cantons : election and demographic statistics
Human Relations Area Files	Yale University P.O. Box 2054 Yale Station	Clellan S. Ford Frank W. Moore	Some machine-readable data; reports; bibliographies; texts	Social structure, organizations; diet practices; kinship
Institut Français d'Opinion Publique	20, Rue d'Aumale Paris IX, France	Jean Stoetzel Helene Riffault		

Name of Data Library	Address	Director	Type of Data	Subject Matter
Institut fur Demoskopie	Radcfzeller Strasse 8 Allensbach am Bodense Federal Republic of Germany	Elizabeth Noelle-Neumann		
*International Data Library	Survey Research Center 2220 Piedmont Ave. University of California Berkeley, California 94720	David Nasatir	Sample Surveys	Politics, communication, social behaviour Emphasis on Asia, Latin America
International Development Data Bank	Michigan State University 322 Union Building East Lansing, Michigan 48823			
*Inter-University Consortium for Political Research	University of Michigan P.O. Box 1248 Ann Arbor, Michigan 48106	Richard Hoffebert	Sample Surveys	Political behaviour Public opinion
Laboratory for Political Research	Dept. of Political Science University of Iowa Iowa City, Iowa 52240	George R. Boynton	Sample Surveys Voting studies	Politics; biography data on American and Argentine legislators
*Louis Harris Political Data Center	Dept. of Political Science University of North Carolina Cardwell Hall Chapel Hill, North Carolina 27514	James W. Prothro	Public opinion Surveys	Politics in individual states in U.S.
National Opinion Research Center	University of Chicago 6030 South Ellis Avenue Chicago, Illinois 60637	Norman Bradburn	Sample Surveys	Health and welfare, mass communication, community problems
Political Science Research Library and Political Data Program	Yale University 89 Trumbell Street New Haven, Connecticut 06520	Phyllis Stevens Bruce Russett	Sample Surveys science	Studies from Roper ICPR in political science
Public Opinion Survey Unit	Research Center, School of Business and Public Administ. University of Missouri Columbia, Missouri 65201	David C. Leege	Sample Surveys	Politics and public opinion in Missouri, U.S.
Project Talent Data Bank	132 N. Bellefield Avenue Pittsburgh, Pennsylvania 15213	William W. Cooley Lyle F. Schoenfeldt	Sample Surveys	High school student attitudes surveys, career plans, aptitude tests
*Roper Public Opinion Research Center	Williams College Williamstown, Massachusetts 02167	Philip K. Hastings	Sample Surveys	Politics, economics, business, education, public opinion
*Social Science Data and Program Library Service	Social Systems Research Inst. Rm. 4451, Social Science Bldg. University of Wisconsin Madison, Wisconsin 53703	Charles Holt Michael T. Aiken	Sample Surveys Data about social science computing programs	Economics, demography
*Social Science Research Council Data Bank	University of Essex Wivenhoe Park Colchester Essex, England	A.M. Pottey		
Steinmetz Institute	Herengracht 457 Amsterdam -C The Netherlands	Dr. Harm't Hart		
Survey Research Center	Department of Politics University of Strathclyde McCance Building Richmond Street Glasgow, C.I., Scotland	Richard Rose		
Survey Research Laboratory	437 David Kinley Hall University of Illinois Urbana, Illinois 61801	Robert Ferber Abraham Miller	Sample Surveys Statistics	Politics, economics, public opinion
U.C.L.A. Political Behaviour Archive	Dept. of Political Science University of California Los Angeles, California 90024	Dwaine Marvick		

Name of Data Library	Address	Director	Type of Data	Subject Matter
Yale Growth Center	Yale University 52 Hillhouse Avenue New Haven, Connecticut 06520	Gustav Ranis	National accounting	Country analysis of underdeveloped nations
Zentralarchiv Fuer Empirische Sozialforschung	Universtaet Zu Köln Bacghemer Strasse 40 Köln - Lindenthal Federal Republic of Germany	Erwin K. Scheuch		

Codebooks should contain the following information:

a) Study descriptions
1. Title
2. Author or Principal Investigator
3. Data Gathering Organization
4. Dates of Data Collection
5. Location of Sample
6. Sampling Criteria
7. Unit of Analysis
8. Method of Sampling
9. Intended Sample Size
10. Number of Actual Respondents
11. Method of Data Collection
12. Field Work Observations
13. Weighting Procedures Employed
14. Principal Variables
15. Personal Data
16. Derived Data
17. Types of Questions
18. Translator's Comments
19. List of Publications
20. Cleaning Comments
21. Explanation of Symbols used in Codebook
22. Abstract

b) Codebook
1. Variable Number
2. Unit Record Representation of Variable (card, column)
3. Question Wording - including instructions to interviewer
4. Response Categories and Corresponding punched card codes - including "Don't know"; "No Answer"; "Not Astred" and "Missing Data"
5. Frequency distributions for each response category
6. Identification of whether response alternative was:
    a) Chosen by interviewer
    b) Read to respondent
    c) Presented to respondent in the form of a list
    d) Chosen by codes
    e) Unknown who made coding decision

c) Conventions
1. When recoding - whether with multipunch data or not - recoded categories should go in a consistent direction; e.g., strongly agree to strongly disagree.
2. "Don't know", "No Answer", "Not Asked", and "Missing Data", responses should be distinguished and, when practicable, given a consistent coding from variable to variable.

Appendix 4 - MACHINE READABLE CODEBOOK

CODEBOOK FOR **IDLRS*20140090S   PAGE 001

CARD COLUMNS   MARGINAL   QUESTION AND CODE
ID   USED   COUNT

          INTERNATIONAL DATA LIBRARY AND REFERENCE SERVICE
                      SURVEY RESEARCH CENTER
                   UNIVERSITY OF CALIFORNIA, BERKELEY

          201-40-090S   STUDY DESCRIPTION

     1. TITLE OF STUDY
         MAINSPRINGS OF THE REBELLION-SPRING 1965 (TREND 2)
         STUDENTS INTERVIEWED IN NOVEMBER, 1964 AND
         RE-INTERVIEWED IN SPRING, 1965 HAVE NOT BEEN INCLUDED
         IN THIS SAMPLE. (SEE 201-40-090B PANEL INTERVIEW
         STARTING WITH QUESTION 68.)

     2. PROJECT DIRECTOR
         KATHLEEN E. GALES
         VISITING ASSISTANT PROFESSOR, DEPARTMENT OF SOCIOLOGY,
         U C BERKELEY
         SENIOR LECTURER, LONDON SCHOOL OF ECONOMICS

     3. ORGANIZATION WHICH COLLECTED +/OR PROCESSED DATA
         STUDENTS OF THE 105 COURSE, DEPARTMENT OF SOCIOLOGY,
         BERKELEY
         SURVEY RESEARCH CENTER, BERKELEY

     4. DATES OF DATA COLLECTION
         APRIL 1965

     5. LOCATION OF SAMPLE
         U C BERKELEY CAMPUS

     6. SAMPLING CRITERIA
         GRADUATE AND UNDERGRADUATE STUDENTS, REGISTERED AT
         SPROUL HALL.(THIS EXCLUDES LAW SCHOOL STUDENTS)

     7. PERSONS INQUIRED ABOUT
         RESPONDENT ONLY

     8. METHOD OF SAMPLING
         SYSTEMATIC SAMPLE FROM A RANDOM START
         A SYSTEMATIC SAMPLE OF 528 STUDENTS WAS SELECTED FROM
         THE ALPHABETICALLY ORDERED FILES OF THE REGISTRAR. NAMES
         WERE TAKEN AT AN EQUAL INTERVAL.

     9. INTENDED SAMPLE SIZE
         528

    10. ACTUAL RESPONDENTS
         443

CODEBOOK FOR **IDLRS*20140090S   PAGE 002

CARD COLUMNS   MARGINAL   QUESTION AND CODE
ID   USED   COUNT

    11. METHOD OF DATA COLLECTION
         PERSONAL INTERVIEW WITH SET QUESTIONNAIRE
         THE SURVEY WAS A CLASS PROJECT AND STUDENTS PARTICIPATED
         IN THE DESIGN OF THE INTERVIEW SCHEDULE AND ITS PILOTING

    12. FIELD WORK
         120 STUDENTS WERE TRAINED AS INTERVIEWERS WITHIN ONE
         WEEK. TEST INTERVIEWING AND DISCUSSIONS WERE HELD DURING
         CLASSES. FAILURE TO CONTACT IN THE SHORT PERIOD
         AVAILABLE FOR INTERVIEWING WAS THE MAIN REASON FOR THE
         NON-RESPONSE.

         SAMPLE AND POPULATION CHARACTERISTICS
                                          POPULATION   SAMPLE
                                          (26,448)   (443)
         SEX
         MALE   64   65
         FEMALE   36   35
                                             100   100

         YEAR IN SCHOOL
         FRESHMAN   13   13
         SOPHOMORE   12   14
         JUNIOR   19   21
         SENIOR   19   23
         GRADUATE AND OTHER   37   29
                                             100   100

         PLACE OF RESIDENCE
         SORORITY OR FRATERNITY   11   9
         RESIDENCE HALL   13   14
         ROOMING HOUSE   12   11
         PARENTAL HOUSE   8   8
         ROOM IN PRIVATE HOUSE   4   4
         APARTMENT ALONE OR WITH SPOUSE   18   18
         SHARED APARTMENT   20   23
         HOUSE   12   10
         OTHER OR UNKNOWN   2   3
                                             100   100

         THE ONLY CHARACTERISTIC ON WHICH THE SAMPLE DIFFERS
         SIGNIFICANTLY FROM THE POPULATION IS THE PERCENTAGE OF
         GRADUATES. MANY OF THE GRADUATES NOT CONTACTED WERE
         LIVING FAR FROM THE CAMPUS, AND IT IS LIKELY THAT
         BECAUSE OF THIS THEY HAD LESS THAN AVERAGE INTEREST
         IN THE FREE SPEECH MOVEMENT.
         THEIR OMMISSION HAS PROBABLY INTRODUCED A SLIGHT BIAS
         INTO THE RESULTS.
         THE INTERVIEW NORMALLY LASTED ABOUT HALF AN HOUR AND
         WAS CARRIED OUT, IN PRIVACY, USUALLY ON THE CAMPUS.

CODEBOOK FOR **IDLRS*201400905

CARD COLUMNS MARGINAL   QUESTION AND CODE
ID   USED   COUNT

A SPECIAL ANALYSIS WAS CARRIED OUT TO SEE WHETHER THE
THE INTERVIEWERS OWN ATTITUDES APPEARED TO HAVE
INFLUENCED THOSE OF THEIR RESPONDENTS. THIS WAS DONE BY
HAVING THE INTERVIEWERS THEMSELVES COMPLETE THE
QUESTIONNAIRE. ON CORRELATING THE ANSWERS OF
INTERVIEWERS AND RESPONDENTS ON ATTITUDINAL QUESTIONS,
NO ASSOCIATION WAS FOUND. THE RESULTS MAY THEREFORE BE
ASSUMED TO BE FREE OF INTERVIEWERS BIAS, ALTHOUGH THE
INTERVIEWERS HAD STRONG VIEWS ON THE MATTER BEING
INVESTIGATED.
PERCENTAGES BASED UPON THE WHOLE SAMPLE CAN BE ASSUMED
TO HAVE A SAMPLING ERROR OF AT MOST 5 PERCENT.

13. WEIGHTING PROCEDURES
    NONE

14. PRINCIPAL VARIABLES
    1. SUPPORT OF THE FREE SPEECH MOVEMENTS GOALS, TACTICS,
       LEADERS , AND ACHIEVEMENTS
    2. REACTIONS TO ORGANIZATIONS WHICH OPPOSED THE FSM
    3. ADVANTAGES AND DISADVANTAGES OF STUDYING AT BERKELEY
    4. CONTACTS WITH THE FACULTY
    5. THE ROLE OF THE FACULTY
    6. THE POLITICS OF THE ADMINISTRATION
    7. INTEREST IN POLITICS
    8. POLITICAL VIEWS
    9. CIVIL RIGHTS
   10. CIVIL DISOBEDIENCE
   11. RELATIONSHIP WITH PARENTS

15. PERSONAL DATA
    1. SEX
    2. AGE
    3. RACE
    4. MARITAL STATUS
    5. RELIGIOUS PREFERENCE
    6. PARTY PREFERENCE
    7. MAJOR FIELD OF STUDIES
    8. ACADEMIC STANDING
    9. POINT GRADE AVERAGE
   10. YEARS IN SCHOOL AT BERKELEY
   11. HOUSING
   12. FATHERS OCCUPATION
   13. PARENTS EDUCATION
   14. PARENTS POLITICAL AFFILIATION
   15. PARENTS RELIGIOUS PREFERENCE
   16. PARENTS INCOME

16. DERIVED DATA
    TYPOLOGY OF FRIENDS PARTICIPATION IN FSM

CODEBOOK FOR **IDLRS*201400905

CARD COLUMNS MARGINAL   QUESTION AND CODE
ID   USED   COUNT

17. TYPE OF QUESTIONS
    PRECODED - 43 QUESTIONS
    PRECODED ANSWER LIST - 4 QUESTIONS
    OPEN END - 11 QUESTIONS, 2 SUBQUESTIONS

18. TRANSLATION
    NONE

19. PUBLICATION AND REPORTS
    KATHLEEN E. GALES, A CAMPUS REVOLUTION, BRITISH JOURNAL
    OF SOCIOLOGY, XVII, 1, MARCH 1966

20. CLEANING COMMENTS
    THE MULTIPLE PUNCHED DATA DECKS HAVE BEEN TRANSFERRED
    ONTO MAGNETIC TAPE, RECODED AND CHECKED. THE FINAL CODE
    IS NUMERIC. THERE ARE TWO RECORDS PER CASE.

21. EXPLANATION OF IDL*RS CODEBOOKS
    THE CODEBOOK FOLLOWS THE FORMAT OF THE QUESTIONNAIRE.
    ABBREVATIONS
    Q.   QUESTION
    SQ. SUB-QUESTION
    P.   PERSONAL DATA
    I.   IDENTIFICATION FIELD
    V.   VARIABLE NAME, IF NOT A QUESTION
    CATEGORY EXPLANATION
    A.   ALTERNATIVE CATEGORY CHOSEN BY INTERVIEWER
    R.   ALTERNATIVE CATEGORY READ TO RESPONDENT
    L.   ALTERNATIVE CATEGORY PRESENTED TO RESPONDENT
         IN A LIST
    C.   ALTERNATIVE CATEGORY CHOSEN BY CODER
    U.   UNKNOWN WHETHER CODING DECISION MADE BY
         INTERVIEWER OR CODER
    R.   BLANK
    DK   DONT KNOW
    NA   NO ANSWER, NOT ASCERTAINED
    INAP. INAPPROPRIATE, QUESTION NOT ASKED
    NO CODE USED BY IDL*RS TO INDICATE MISSING INFORMATION

CODEBOOK FOR **IDLRS*201400905

| CARD COLUMNS | MARGINAL | QUESTION AND CODE |
| ID USED | COUNT | |

C O D E B O O K

1 1- 4		I1.	ID. FIELD
1 1- 3			CASE ID.
1 1- 4			1. FIRST LOGICAL RECORD (DECK)

(READ OR PARAPHRASE TO RESPONDENT) YOU HAVE BEEN CHOSEN
IN A SAMPLE OF STUDENTS AT THE BERKELEY CAMPUS WHO HAVE
BEEN CAREFULLY SELECTED TO GET AN ACCURATE PICTURE OF
STUDENT OPINION ABOUT THE RECENT STUDENT DEMONSTRATIONS.
A SIMILAR SURVEY WAS CARRIED OUT LAST NOVEMBER, IN
WHICH YOU MAY HAVE BEEN INTERVIEWED. THE INFORMATION
YOU GIVE US WILL BE TREATED AS CONFIDENTIAL, YOUR NAME
WILL NOT BE ATTACHED TO ANY OF YOUR ANSWERS. WE WILL USE
THESE ANSWERS TO SUMMARIZE HOW A SAMPLE OF BERKELEY
STUDENTS NOW SEES THE EVENTS OF LAST SEMESTER.

| 1 5-10 | | Q1. | THE FIRST QUESTIONS DEAL WITH YOUR OPINIONS ABOUT THIS UNIVERSITY, AND IN PARTICULAR, THE BERKELEY CAMPUS. WHAT DO YOU THINK ARE THE MAIN ADVANTAGES AND DISADVANTAGES OF BEING A STUDENT ON THIS CAMPUS. |

ADVANTAGES

| 1 5- 7 | | |

1 5	180	FIRST ANSWER
		C1. GOOD SCHOOL, HIGH LEVEL STUDENTS, EXCELLENT FACULTY, ETC.
	65	2. COURSES-VARIETY-GOOD COURSES OFFERED IN SPECIAL FIELD
	125	3. DIVERSITY, VARIETY OF ACTIVITIES, STUDENTS, ETC. STIMULATING ATMOSPHERE SIZE
	10	4. POLITICAL ACTIVITY LIBERAL VIEWS, ETC.
	18	5. GOOD FACILITIES
	15	6. NONE
	3	0. DK
	27	R. NA

1 6		SECOND ANSWER
	63	1. GOOD SCHOOL
	57	2. COURSES
	98	3. DIVERSITY
	23	4. POLITICAL ACTIVITY
	39	5. GOOD FACILITIES
	163	R. NO SECOND ANSWER

CODEBOOK FOR **IDLRS*201400905

| CARD COLUMNS | MARGINAL | QUESTION AND CODE |
| ID USED | COUNT | |

1 7		THIRD ANSWER
	18	1. GOOD SCHOOL
	11	2. COURSES
	32	3. DIVERSITY
	11	4. POLITICAL ACTIVITY
	21	5. GOOD FACILITIES
	350	R. NO THIRD ANSWER

DISADVANTAGES

| 1 8-10 | | |

1 8		FIRST ANSWER
	119	1. SIZE (UNQUALIFIED)
	77	2. SIZE OF CLASSES, SECTIONS, SEMINARS TEACHING ASSISTANT SYSTEM, ETC.
	70	3. IMPERSONALITY, INSUFFICIENT COMMUNICATION-EITHER NATURE UNSPECIFIED OR BETWEEN STUDENTS
	38	4. POOR CONTACT WITH FACULTY
	23	5. BUREAUCRACY, RED TAPE, ETC.
	6	6. OUTSIDE PRESSURE ON UNIVERSITY
	4	7. INADEQUATE FACILITIES
	16	8. NATURE OF STUDENT BODY-FREE SPEECH MOVEMENT ETC.
	61	9. NONE
	2	0. DK
	27	R. NA

1 9		SECOND ANSWER
	9	1. SIZE (UNQUALIFIED)
	21	2. SIZE OF CLASSES
	66	3. IMPERSONALITY
	50	4. POOR CONTACT WITH FACULTY
	8	5. BUREAUCRACY
	4	6. OUTSIDE PRESSURE ON UNIVERSITY
	7	7. INADEQUATE FACILITIES
	10	8. NATURE OF STUDENT BODY
	268	R. NO SECOND ANSWER

1 10		THIRD ANSWER
	3	1. SIZE (UNQUALIFIED)
	4	2. SIZE OF CLASSES
	8	3. IMPERSONALITY
	12	4. POOR CONTACT WITH FACULTY
	3	5. BUREAUCRACY
	3	6. OUTSIDE PRESSURE ON UNIVERSITY
	2	7. INADEQUATE FACILITIES
	5	8. NATURE OF STUDENT BODY
	403	R. NO THIRD ANSWER

CODEBOOK FOR **IDLRS*201400905   QUESTION ANC CODE

| CARD COLUMNS | MARGINAL | |
| ID | USED | COUNT |

1   11-12   Q2. WHICH OF THESE WOULD YOU SAY WAS YOUR MAIN REASON FOR
                   DECIDING TO BECOME A STUDENT AT BERKELEY. (SHOW CARD)

```
    23        L01. LOW TUITION
     7        02. SOCIAL LIFE
    23        03. CLOSE TO HOME
   231        04. HIGH ACADEMIC STANDING
    37        05. VOCATIONAL TRAINING
    11        06. CULTURAL OPPORTUNITIES
    43        07. ATMOSPHERE OF EXCHANGE CF IDEAS
    13        08. GEOGRAPHIC SETTING
     5        09. PRESSURE FROM HCME
    47        10. OTHER
     2        00. DK
     1        RR. NA
```

1   13-14   Q3. WHICH WOULD YOU SAY WAS THE NEXT MOST IMPORTANT.

```
    67        L01. LOW TUITION
    13        02. SOCIAL LIFE
    38        3. CLOSE TO HOME
    88        04. HIGH ACADEMIC STANDING
    36        05. VOCATIONAL TRAINING
    38        06. CULTURAL OPPORTUNITIES
    63        07. ATMOSPHERE OF EXCHANGE OF IDEAS
    55        08. GEOGRAPHIC SETTING
     6        09. PRESSURE FROM HCME
    19        10. OTHER
    10        00. DK
    10        RR. NA
```

1   15-27   Q4. COULD YOU TELL ME WHETHER YCU AGREE OR DISAGREE WITH THE
                   FOLLOWING STATEMENT.

1   15   GRADES AT THIS UNIVERSITY ARE AN ADEQUATE MEASURE OF
            ABILITY

```
    29        R1. STRONGLY AGREE
   195        2. MILDLY AGREE
   126        3. MILDLY DISAGREE
    83        4. STRONGLY DISAGREE
     8        0. DK
     2        R. NA
```

1   16   SCME OF MY CLASSES ARE SC LARGE THAT IT IS DIFFICULT
            FOR ME TO GET MUCH OUT CF THEM

```
    50        1. STRONGLY AGREE
   101        2. MILDLY AGREE
   130        3. MILDLY DISAGREE
   148        4. STRONGLY DISAGREE
    12        0. DK
     2        R. NA
```

CODEBOOK FOR **IDLRS*201400905   QUESTION AND CODE

| CARD COLUMNS | MARGINAL | |
| ID | USED | COUNT |

1   17   MOST OF THE STUDENTS AT CALIFORNIA SEEM TO BE
            UNFRIENDLY

```
     3        1. STRONGLY AGREE
    37        2. MILDLY AGREE
   180        3. MILDLY DISAGREE
   209        4. STRONGLY DISAGREE
    12        0. DK
     2        R. NA
```

1   18   I THINK THAT THE HONCR SYSTEM WOULD WORK AT CALIFORNIA

```
    45        1. STRONGLY AGREE
    96        2. MILDLY AGREE
   123        3. MILDLY DISAGREE
   125        4. STRONGLY DISAGREE
    52        0. DK
     2        R. NA
```

1   19   THE PROBLEM WITH CALIFORNIA (AT BERKELEY) IS THAT IT IS
            TOO BIG

```
    63        1. STRONGLY AGREE
   128        2. MILDLY AGREE
   119        3. MILDLY DISAGREE
   117        4. STRONGLY DISAGREE
    14        0. DK
     2        R. NA
```

1   20   I FEEL THAT MOST OF THE PROFESSORS ARE MORE INTERESTED
            IN THEIR RESEARCH THAN IN THEIR STUDENTS

```
    61        1. STRONGLY AGREE
   124        2. MILDLY AGREE
   155        3. MILDLY DISAGREE
    58        4. STRONGLY DISAGREE
     4        0. DK
     4        R. NA
```

1   21   THIS UNIVERSITY SOMETIMES SEEMS TO OPERATE AS A FACTORY

```
   144        1. STRONGLY AGREE
   198        2. MILDLY AGREE
    63        3. MILDLY DISAGREE
    24        4. STRONGLY DISAGREE
    13        0. DK
     1        R. NA
```

1   22   IN MY CONTACTS WITH ADMINISTRATIVE PERSONNEL I HAVE
            BEEN TREATED WITH THE CCNSIDERATION A HUMAN BEING
            DESERVES

```
   142        1. STRONGLY AGREE
   158        2. MILDLY AGREE
    57        3. MILDLY DISAGREE
    44        4. STRONGLY DISAGREE
    41        0. DK
     1        R. NA
```

CODEBOOK FOR **IDLRS*20140090S

| CARD COLUMNS | MARGINAL | QUESTION AND CODE |
| ID | USED | COUNT |

1   23   THE SYSTEM OF USING TEACHING ASSISTANTS WORKS WELL AT
              THIS UNIVERSITY
         75   1. STRONGLY AGREE
        175   2. MILDLY AGREE
        101   3. MILDLY DISAGREE
         46   4. STRONGLY DISAGREE
         43   0. DK
          1   R. NA

1   24   I OFTEN FEEL LONELY WALKING ON CAMPUS EVEN IF THERE ARE
              CROWDS OF PEOPLE AROUND
         42   1. STRONGLY AGREE
        104   2. MILDLY AGREE
         99   3. MILDLY DISAGREE
        186   4. STRONGLY DISAGREE
         10   0. DK
          2   R. NA

1   25   THIS UNIVERSITY IS AN IMPERSONAL INSTITUTION
         97   1. STRONGLY AGREE
        179   2. MILDLY AGREE
        100   3. MILDLY DISAGREE
         59   4. STRONGLY DISAGREE
          8   0. DK
          4   R. NA

1   26   STUDENTS SHOULD HAVE MORE CONTROL OVER EDUCATIONAL
              POLICIES ON THIS CAMPUS
         85   1. STRONGLY AGREE
        144   2. MILDLY AGREE
        117   3. MILDLY DISAGREE
         81   4. STRONGLY DISAGREE
         15   0. DK
          1   R. NA

1   27   STUDENT EVALUATIONS OF FACULTY SHOULD BE AN IMPORTANT
              FACTOR IN THE HIRING AND FIRING OF FACULTY
         91   1. STRONGLY AGREE
        158   2. MILDLY AGREE
        102   3. MILDLY DISAGREE
         76   4. STRONGLY DISAGREE
         15   0. DK
          1   R. NA

CODEBOOK FOR **IDLRS*20140090S

| CARD COLUMNS | MARGINAL | QUESTION AND CODE |
| ID | USED | COUNT |

1   28   Q5. WOULD YOU CONSIDER SUPPORTING A STUDENT STRIKE OR A
              SIT-IN TO PROTEST AGAINST SOME ASPECT OF EDUCATIONAL
              POLICY, SUCH AS A PARTICULAR FACULTY MEMBER OR
              PARTICULAR COURSES, TEC.
        199   A1. YES
        201   2. NO
         26   0. DK
         17   R. NA

              (IF YES) WHAT CIRCUMSTANCES MIGHT LEAD TO THIS. (NOT
              CODED)

1   29   Q6. HOW WELL SATISFIED ARE YOU WITH COURSES, EXAMINATIONS,
              PROFESSORS, AT THE UNIVERSITY.
         69   R1. VERY SATISFIED
        270   2. SATISFIED
         91   3. UNSATISFIED
          7   4. VERY UNSATISFIED
          6   R. NA

1   30   Q7. IS THE AMOUNT OF CONTACT BETWEEN FACULTY AND STUDENTS
              HERE ABOUT WHAT YOU EXPECTED, OR IS IT BETTER OR WORSE.
         96   R1. BETTER
        239   2. ABOUT WHAT EXPECTED
         97   3. WORSE
          4   0. DK
          7   R. NA

1   31   Q8. DO YOU THINK THAT YOUR PROFESSORS SPEND TOO LITTLE TIME
              WITH THEIR STUDENTS.
        202   A1. YES
        195   2. NO
         38   0. DK
          8   R. NA

1   32   Q9. DO YOU FEEL THAT THERE ARE IMPORTANT CHANGES THAT SHOULD
              BE MADE IN THE STRUCTURE OF THE UNIVERSITY.
        294   A1. YES
         83   2. NO
         61   0. DK
          5   R. NA

CODEBOOK FOR **IDLRS*201400909

CARD ID	COLUMNS USED	MARGINAL COUNT	QUESTION AND CODE

Q14. WHICH, IF ANY, OF THE FOLLOWING DO YOU THINK ARE EVER JUSTIFIABLE METHODS FOR THE EXPRESSION OF STUDENT GRIEVANCES.

1	37-41		Q14.
			PETITIONS
1	37	408	R1. YES
		35	R. NO
			ORGANIZING PUBLIC PROTEST MEETINGS
1	38	355	2. YES
		88	R. NO
			REFRAINING FROM GOING TO CLASS
1	39	240	3. YES
		203	R. NO
			PICKETING
1	40	289	4. YES
		154	R. NO
			SIT-INS
1	41	168	5. YES
		275	R. NO

Q15. HOW DID YOU REACT TOWARDS THE ORGANIZATIONS WHICH ACTIVELY OPPOSED THE FREE SPEECH MOVEMENT. (SHOW CARD)

1	42		Q15.
		3	L1. ACTIVE SUPPORTER (HANDING OUT LEAFLETS, ETC.)
		44	2. SUPPORTED, BUT NOT ACTIVELY
		24	3. SIGNED PETITION ONLY
		39	4. SUPPORTED, TOOK NO ACTION
		170	5. DISAPPROVED OF THEM
		9	6. WAS NOT AWARE OF THEM
		120	7. NEITHER APPROVED NOR DISAPPROVED
		21	8. NOT ON CAMPUS AT THE TIME
		3	9. OTHER
		3	0. DK
		7	R. NA

CODEBOOK FOR **IDLRS*201400909

CARD ID	COLUMNS USED	MARGINAL COUNT	QUESTION AND CODE

Q10. TAKING EVERYTHING INTO ACCOUNT, DO YOU THINK CALIFORNIA IS A GOOD PLACE TO GO TO SCHOOL.

1	33		Q10.
		403	A1. YES
		24	2. NO
		11	3. DK
		5	R. NA

Q11. NOW WE WOULD LIKE TO ASK YOU SOME QUESTIONS ABOUT THE EXTENT TO WHICH YOU PARTICIPATED IN THE DEMONSTRATIONS LAST FALL AND YOUR ATTITUDE TOWARD THEM. FOR EXAMPLE, TO WHAT EXTENT, IF ANY, DID YOU PARTICIPATE IN THE EVENTS OF OCTOBER 1 AND 2 INVOLVING THE POLICE CAR.

1	34		Q11.
		43	A1. SAT-IN AROUND CAR
		220	2. CAME TO WATCH
		61	3. IGNORED IT
		60	4. NOT ON CAMPUS
		9	5. ACTIVELY OPPOSED DEMONSTRATORS
		44	6. OTHER
		6	R. NA

Q12. REGARDING THE SIT-IN IN SPROUL HALL ON DECEMBER 2 AND 3, WHAT, IF ANY, WAS THE EXTENT OF YOUR PARTICIPATION.

1	35		Q12.
		9	A1. SAT-IN AND WAS ARRESTED
		29	2. SIT-IN, LEFT BEFORE ARRESTS BEGAN
		160	3. CAM TO WATCH
		77	4. IGNORED IT
		95	5. NOT ON CAMPUS AT TIME
		15	6. ACTIVELY OPPOSED DEMONSTRATION
		48	7. OTHER
		10	R. NA

Q13. AND IN REGARD TO THE STRIKE THAT TOOK PLACE ON CAMPUS AFTER THE SPROUL HALL ARRESTS.

1	36		Q13.
		78	A1. PICKETED AND STAYED AWAY FROM CLASS
		31	2. DID NOT PICKET BUT STAYED AWAY FROM ALL CLASSES
		60	3. DID NOT PICKET BUT STAYED AWAY FROM SOME CLASSES
		124	4. IGNORED THE STRIKE
		34	5. HAD NO CLASSES DURING STRIKE
		57	6. OPPOSED THE STRIKE
		28	7. NOT ON CAMPUS AT THE TIME
		25	8. OTHER
		6	R. NA

CODEBOOK FOR **IDLRS*2014009O5   QUESTION ANC CODE

CARD COLUMNS MARGINAL
ID USED   COUNT

1   43-44   Q16. HOW DID YOUR OVER-ALL REACTION TO THE FREE SPEECH
                     MOVEMENT CHANGE DURING THE FALL SEMESTER.

1   43   REACTION AT THE BEGINNING OF THE SEMESTER
         69   R1. STRONGLY APPROVE
        154   2. MILDLY APPROVE
        115   3. MILDLY DISAPPROVE
         64   4. STRONGLY DISAPPROVE
         41   0. DK

1   44   REACTION AT THE END OF THE SEMESTER
        141   1. STRONGLY APPROVE
        120   2. MILDLY APPROVE
         68   3. MILDLY DISAPPROVE
         88   4. STRONGLY DISAPPROVE
         25   C. DK

1   45-50   Q17. DID YOUR CLOSE FRIENDS DC THE FOLLOWING. (CHECK AS MANY
                     AS YOU WANT)

1   45   FIRST ANSWER
        138   R1. REMAIN NEUTRAL
        133   2. BECOME ACTIVE WITH FREE SPEECH MOVEMENT
        105   3. BECOME SYMPATHETIC WITH FREE SPEECH MOVEMENT
         28   4. BECOME SYMPATHETIC WITH STUDENTS FCR CALIFORNIA OR
                        UNIVERSITY STUDENTS FCR LAW AND ORDER BUT NOT A
                        PARTICIPANT IN THEIR ACTIONS
          3   5. BECOME ACTIVE IN STUDENTS FOR CALIFORNIA OR
                        UNIVERSITY STUDENTS FCR LAW AND ORDER
          6   6. BECOME HOSTILE TO ALL THESE GROUPS (I.E., FREE
                        SPEECH MOVEMENT, STUDENTS FOR CALIFORNIA,
                        UNIVERSITY STUDENTS FCR LAW AND ORDER)
         27   7. NO FRIENDS
          3   R. NA

1   46   SECOND ANSWER
         66   2. ACTIVE IN FREE SPEECH MOVEMENT
        113   3. SYMPATHETIC WITH FREE SPEECH MOVEMENT
         38   4. SYMPATHETIC WITH GROUPS OPPOSING FREE SPEECH
                        MOVEMENT
          6   5. ACTIVE IN GROUPS OPPCSING FREE SPEECH MOVEMENT
         11   6. HOSTILE TO ALL
        209   R. NO SECCND ANSWER

1   47   THIRD ANSWER
         50   3. SYMPATHETIC WITH FREE SPEECH MOVEMENT
         32   4. SYMPATHETIC WITH GROLPS OPPOSING FREE SPEECH
                        MOVEMENT
          9   5. ACTIVE IN GROUPS OPPCSING FREE SPEECH MOVEMENT
         20   6. HOSTILE TC ALL
        332   R. NO THIRD ANSWER

CODEBOOK FOR **IDLRS*201400905   QUESTION ANC CODE

CARD COLUMNS MARGINAL
ID USED   COUNT

1   48   FOURTH ANSWER
         17   4. SYMPATHETIC WITH GROLPS CPPOSING FREE SPEECH
                        MOVEMENT
          3   5. ACTIVE IN GROUPS OPPCSING FREE SPEECH MOVEMENT
         19   6. HOSTILE TO ALL
        404   R. NO FOURTH ANSWER

1   49   FIFTH ANSWER
          4   5. ACTIVE IN GROUPS OPPCSING FREE SPEECH MOVEMENT
          5   6. HOSTILE TO ALL
        434   R. NO FIFTH ANSWER

1   50   SIXTH ANSWER
          2   6. HOSTILE TC ALL
        441   R. NO SIXTH ANSWER

1   51-57   Q18. WOULD YOU AGREE OR DISAGREE WITH THE FOLLOWING
                     STATEMENTS.

1   51   CIVIL DISOBEDIENCE AS IT WAS BEING USED CN CAMPUS WAS
                     AN ACCEPTABLE TACTIC
        111   R1. STRONGLY AGREE
        107   2. MILDLY AGREE
         94   3. MILDLY DISAPPROVE
        119   4. STRONGLY DISAPPROVE
         11   0. DK
          1   R. NA

1   52   THE GOALS OF THE FREE SPEECH MOVEMENT WERE DESIRABLE
                     AND IMPORTANT
        252   1. STRONGLY AGREE
        113   2. MILDLY AGREE
         34   3. MILDLY DISAGREE
         25   4. STRONGLY DISAGREE
         15   0. DK
          4   R. NA

1   53   THE LEADERS OF THE FREE SPEECH MOVEMENT WERE POWER
                     SEEKERS WHO SEEMED TO HAVE NO LIMITS TO THEIR DEMANDS
         65   1. STRONGLY AGREE
        130   2. MILDLY AGREE
        113   3. MILDLY DISAGREE
        103   4. STRONGLY DISAGREE
         32   0. DK

CODEBOOK FOR **IDLRS*201400905

CARD ID	COLUMNS USED	MARGINAL COUNT	QUESTION AND CODE
1	58-63		Q19. WHAT WOULD YOU SAY WERE THE MAJOR GOALS OF THE FREE SPEECH MOVEMENT.
1	58-59		FIRST ANSWER
		153	01. RIGHT TO ADVOCATE POLITICAL ACTION
		40	02. RIGHT TO SOLICIT FUNDS, RECRUIT MEMBERS TO POLITICAL GROUPS
		68	03. MORE STUDENT INFLUENCE IN CAMPUS ADMINISTRATION
		16	04. SECURE GUARANTEES AGAINST DOUBLE JEOPARDY
		17	05. ELIMINATION OF RESTRICTIONS ON OFF-CAMPUS SPEAKERS
		39	06. SECURE CONSTITUTIONAL RIGHTS
		11	07. PERSONAL AGGRANDIZEMENT OR POWER-SEEKING ON PART OF LEADERS
		7	08. REVOLUTION ON CAMPUS
		10	09. EXPRESSION OF ALIENATION FROM MULTIVERSITY
		21	10. UNRESTRICTED FREEDOM
		33	00. NONE
		28	RR. NA
1	60-61		SECOND ANSWER
		33	01. RIGHT TO ADVOCATE POLITICAL ACTION
		44	02. RIGHT TO SOLICIT FUNDS
		49	03. MORE STUDENT INFLUENCE IN CAMPUS ADMINISTRATION
		16	04. SECURE GUARANTEES AGAINST DOUBLE JEOPARDY
		5	05. ELIMINATION OF RESTRICTIONS ON OFF-CAMPUS SPEAKERS
		22	06. SECURE CONSTITUTIONAL RIGHTS
		6	07. PERSONAL POWER-SEEKING
		5	08. REVOLUTION ON CAMPUS
		19	09. EXPRESSION OF ALIENATION
		13	10. UNRESTRICTED FREEDOM
		231	RR. NO SECOND ANSWER
1	62-63		THIRD ANSWER
		8	01. RIGHT TO ADVOCATE POLITICAL ACTION
		3	02. RIGHT TO SOLICIT FUNDS
		9	03. MORE STUDENT INFLUENCE IN CAMPUS ADMINISTRATION
		5	04. SECURE GUARANTEES AGAINST DOUBLE JEOPARDY
		5	05. ELIMINATION OF RESTRICTIONS ON OFF-CAMPUS SPEAKERS
		9	06. SECURE CONSTITUTIONAL RIGHTS
		2	07. PERSONAL AGGRANDIZEMENT
		3	08. REVOLUTION ON CAMPUS
		5	09. EXPRESSION OF ALIENATION
		6	10. UNRESTRICTED FREEDOM
		384	RR. NO THIRD ANSWER

CODEBOOK FOR **IDLRS*201400905

CARD ID	COLUMNS USED	MARGINAL COUNT	QUESTION AND CODE
1	54		THE UNIVERSITY ADMINISTRATION WAS LARGELY TO BLAME FOR THE WHOLE SITUATION
		137	1. STRONGLY AGREE
		181	2. MILDLY AGREE
		91	3. MILDLY DISAGREE
		19	4. STRONGLY DISAGREE
		14	0. DK
		1	R. NA
1	55		THE LEADERSHIP OF THE FREE SPEECH MOVEMENT WAS TAKEN OVER BY COMMUNISTS AND OTHER LEFT-WINGERS
		11	1. STRONGLY AGREE
		37	2. MILDLY AGREE
		64	3. MILDLY DISAGREE
		280	4. STRONGLY DISAGREE
		49	0. DK
		2	R. NA
1	56		IT WAS A MISTAKE TO CALL IN THE POLICE AND HAVE THE STUDENTS ARRESTED IN DECEMBER
		214	1. STRONGLY AGREE
		74	2. MILDLY AGREE
		66	3. MILDLY DISAGREE
		70	4. STRONGLY DISAGREE
		18	0. DK
		1	R. NA
1	57		THE FREE SPEECH MOVEMENT LEADERS WERE IDEALISTIC AND MOTIVATED BY MORAL VALUES
		142	1. STRONGLY AGREE
		180	2. MILDLY AGREE
		65	3. MILDLY DISAGREE
		21	4. STRONGLY DISAGREE
		33	0. DK
		2	R. NA

CODEBOOK FOR **ICLRS*201400909

CARD ID	COLUMNS USED	MARGINAL COUNT	QUESTION AND CODE
1	64		Q20. TO WHAT EXTENT WAS THE FREE SPEECH MOVEMENT SUCCESSFUL IN ACHIEVING ITS GOALS.
		57	A1. COMPLETELY SUCCESSFUL
		331	2. PARTLY SUCCESSFUL
		30	3. MOSTLY UNSUCCESSFUL
		1	4. ENTIRELY UNSUCCESSFUL
		21	0. DK
		3	R. NA
1	65		Q21. WHICH OF THE FOLLOWING STATEMENTS BEST DESCRIBES YOUR ATTITUDE TOWARD THE ROLE OF THE FACULTY IN CONTROVERSIES SIMILAR TO LAST SEMESTERS.
		123	R1. THEY SHOULD ACTIVELY SUPPORT ONE SIDE OR THE OTHER
		205	2. THEY SHOULD MEDIATE BETWEEN THE STUDENTS AND THE ADMINISTRATION
		20	3. THEY SHOULD STAY OUT OF THE CONTROVERSY
		84	4. OTHER
		2	0. DK
		9	R. NA
1	66-74		Q22. IT HAS BEEN SUGGESTED THAT THE DEMONSTRATIONS LAST FALL HAD VARIOUS EFFECTS ON THE CAMPUS COMMUNITY. DO YOU FEEL THAT ANY OF THE FOLLOWING RESULTED FROM THE FREE SPEECH MOVEMENT. (CHECK AS MANY AS APPLY)
1	66		BETTER STUDENT-FACULTY RELATIONS
		286	R1. YES
		157	R. NO
1	67		BETTER STUDENT-ADMINISTRATION RELATIONS
		103	2. YES
		340	R. NO
1	68		MORE INTEREST IN ASUC ELECTIONS
		251	3. YES
		192	R. NO
1	69		A MORE REPRESENTATIVE ASUC SENATE
		154	4. YES
		289	R. NO
1	70		MORE PARTICIPATION IN CAMPUS ORGANIZATIONS
		200	5. YES
		243	R. NO
1	71		MORE PARTICIPATION IN OFF-CAMPUS ACTIVITIES
		243	6. YES
		200	R. NO

CODEBOOK FOR **ICLRS*201400909

CARD ID	COLUMNS USED	MARGINAL COUNT	QUESTION AND CODE
1	72		BETTER REPRESENTATION OF THE INTERESTS OF GRADUATE STUDENTS ON-CAMPUS
		211	7. YES
		232	R. NO
1	73		RE-EXAMINATION OF EDUCATIONAL POLICIES
		352	8. YES
		91	R. NO
1	74		A GREATER SENSE OF COMMUNITY AMONG STUDENTS
		250	9. YES
		193	R. NO
1	75		Q23. DID YOU, PERSONALLY, EXPERIENCE ANY CHANGES SUCH AS THOSE JUST MENTIONED.
		239	A1. YES
		177	2. NO
		27	R. NA
1	76-79		SQ1. Q23.(IF YES) WHAT CHANGES.
1	76		FIRST ANSWER
		78	L1. BETTER STUDENT-FACULTY RELATIONS
		3	2. BETTER STUDENT ADMINISTRATION RELATIONS
		41	3. MORE INTEREST IN ASUC ELECTIONS
		14	4. A MORE REPRESENTATIVE ASUC SENATE
		11	5. MORE PARTICIPATION IN CAMPUS ORGANIZATIONS
		9	6. MORE PARTICIPATION IN OFF-CAMPUS ACTIVITIES
			7. BETTER REPRESENTATION OF THE INTERESTS OF GRADUATE STUDENTS ON-CAMPUS
		18	8. RE-EXAMINATION OF EDUCATION POLICIES
		31	9. A GREATER SENSE OF COMMUNITY AMONG STUDENTS
		33	0. OTHER
		204	R. INAP. (Q23. NOT CODED 1)
1	77		SECOND ANSWER
		11	1. BETTER STUDENT-FACULTY RELATIONS
		1	2. BETTER STUDENT ADMINISTRATION RELATIONS
		17	3. MORE INTEREST IN ASUC ELECTIONS
		9	4. A MORE REPRESENTATIVE ASUC SENATE
		13	5. MORE PARTICIPATION IN CAMPUS ORGANIZATIONS
		5	6. MORE PARTICIPATION IN OFF-CAMPUS ACTIVITIES
		26	7. BETTER REPRESENTATION OF THE INTERESTS
		27	8. RE-EXAMINATION OF EDUCATIONAL POLICIES
		41	0. OTHER
		292	R. NO SECOND ANSWER

CODEBOOK FOR **IDLRS*201400905   QUESTION AND CODE

CARD ID	COLUMNS USED	MARGINAL COUNT	QUESTION AND CODE
1	78		THIRD ANSWER
		4	1. BETTER STUDENT-FACULTY RELATIONS
		1	4. A MORE REPRESENTATIVE ASUC SENATE
		1	5. MORE PARTICIPATION IN CAMPUS ORGANIZATIONS
		4	6. MORE PARTICIPATION IN OFF-CAMPUS ACTIVITIES
		1	7. BETTER REPRESENTATION OF THE INTERESTS
		10	8. RE-EXAMINATION OF EDUCATIONAL POLICIES
		24	9. A GREATER SENSE OF COMMUNITY AMONG STUDENTS
		39	0. OTHER
		359	R. NO THIRD ANSWER
1	79		FOURTH ANSWER
		3	0. OTHER
		440	R. NO FOURTH ANSWER
2	1-4	I2.	ID. FIELD
2	1-3		CASE ID.
2	4		2. SECOND LOGICAL RECORD (DECK)
2	5-7	Q24.	ALL IN ALL, WHAT PERSONAL LESSONS, IF ANY, DID YOU LEARN FROM THE FREE SPEECH MOVEMENT LAST SEMESTER.
2	5		FIRST ANSWER
		28	C1. EFFECTIVENESS OF CIVIL DISOBEDIENCE
		35	2. BIAS OF MASS MEDIA
		9	3. POWER OF REGENTS
		5	4. LACK OF UNIVERSITY AUTONOMY
		48	5. EVALUATION OF IDEAS AND ATTITUDES
		60	6. RESPONSIBILITY FOR FORMING OPINIONS AND TAKING STANDS ON ISSUES
		8	7. POSSIBILITY OF UNDERESTIMATING OPPOSITION
		16	8. NEED FOR MORE COMMUNICATION
		47	9. ABILITY OF STUDENTS TO OBTAIN POWER BY MASS ACTION UNDERSTANDING OF HOW A MASS MOVEMENT DEVELOPS
		160	0. NONE
		27	R. NA
2	6		SECOND ANSWER
		6	1. EFFECTIVENESS OF CIVIL DISOBEDIENCE
		2	2. BIAS OF MASS MEDIA
		1	3. POWER OF REGENTS
		5	4. LACK OF UNIVERSITY AUTONOMY
		16	5. EVALUATION OF IDEAS AND ATTITUDES
		25	6. RESPONSIBILITY FOR FORMING OPINIONS
		6	7. POSSIBILITY OF UNDERESTIMATING OPPOSITION
		12	8. NEED FOR MORE COMMUNICATION
		22	9. ABILITY OF STUDENTS TO OBTAIN POWER
		348	R. NO SECOND ANSWER

CODEBOOK FOR **IDLRS*201400905   QUESTION AND CODE

CARD ID	COLUMNS USED	MARGINAL COUNT	QUESTION AND CODE
2	7		THIRD ANSWER
		1	1. EFFECTIVENESS OF CIVIL DISOBEDIENCE
		3	2. BIAS OF MASS MEDIA
		1	3. POWER OF REGENTS
		2	4. LACK OF UNIVERSITY AUTONOMY
		2	5. EVALUATION OF IDEAS AND ATTITUDES
		1	6. RESPONSIBILITY FOR FORMING OPINION
		2	7. POSSIBILITY OF UNDERESTIMATING OPPOSITION
		2	8. NEED FOR MORE COMMUNICATION
		4	9. ABILITY OF STUDENTS TO OBTAIN POWER
		425	R. NO THIRD ANSWER
2	8	Q25.	NOW WE HAVE SOME QUESTIONS ABOUT YOUR POLITICAL VIEWS. HOW INTERESTED WOULD YOU SAY YOU ARE IN NATIONAL POLITICS.
		205	A1. VERY INTERESTED
		184	2. MODERATELY INTERESTED
		42	3. SLIGHTLY INTERESTED
		10	4. NOT INTERESTED
		2	R. NA
2	9	P1.	HOW WOULD YOU CLASSIFY YOUR POLITICAL PARTY PREFERENCE.
		94	A1. REPUBLICAN
		78	2. INDEPENDENT
		228	3. DEMOCRAT
		13	4. SOCIALIST
		17	5. OTHER
		11	0. DK
		2	R. NA
2	10	P2.	WITHIN YOUR GENERAL PARTY PREFERENCE, WOULD YOU CONSIDER YOUR VIEWS LIBERAL, CONSERVATIVE, OR WHAT.
		55	R1. CONSERVATIVE
		108	2. MODERATE
		247	3. LIBERAL
		17	4. RADICAL
		13	0. DK
		3	R. NA
2	11	Q26.	DO YOU FEEL THAT THERE ARE IMPORTANT CHANGES THAT SHOULD BE MADE IN OUR SOCIETY.
		391	A1. YES
		36	2. NO
		16	0. DK

CODEBOOK FOR **IDLRS*201400909

CARD	COLUMNS USED	MARGINAL COUNT	QUESTION AND CODE

2 12-13 SQ1, Q26.(IF YES) WHICH DO YOU THINK IS THE MOST IMPORTANT.
```
192   C01. CIVIL RIGHTS, CIVIL LIBERTIES, EQUALITY
 20   02. EDUCATION
 20   03. REDUCE UNEMPLOYMENT OR POVERTY
  5   04. MAKE FOREIGN POLICY LESS MILITANT
  2   05. MAKE FOREIGN POLICY TOUGHER, MORE MILITANT
 15   06. MORE SOCIAL WELFARE
 11   07. LESS SOCIAL WELFARE
 44   08. CHANGE OF VALUES-LESS MATERIALISM
  2   09. OVER POPULATION
  5   10. AUTOMATION
 75   00. DK
 52   RR. INAP. (Q26. NOT CODED 1)
```

2 14-16 Q27. I WOULD NOW LIKE TO ASK YOU SOME QUESTIONS ON SPECIFIC ISSUES. COULD YOU TELL ME WHETHER YOU AGREE OR DISAGREE WITH THE FOLLOWING STATEMENTS.

2 14   RED CHINA SHOULD BE ADMITTED TO THE UNITED NATIONS
```
151   R1. STRONGLY AGREE
131    2. MILDLY AGREE
 61    3. MILDLY DISAGREE
 62    4. STRONGLY DISAGREE
 38    0. DK
```

2 15   I SUPPORT THE EFFORTS OF THE HOUSE ON UN-AMERICAN ACTIVITIES COMMITTEE
```
 21    1. STRONGLY AGREE
 77    2. MILDLY AGREE
 86    3. MILDLY DISAGREE
222    4. STRONGLY DISAGREE
 37    0. DK
```

2 16   FEDERAL AID AND INTERVENTION IS THE ONLY EFFECTIVE WAY TO SOLVE MANY OF OUR PRESENT-DAY SOCIAL PROBLEMS
```
120    1. STRONGLY AGREE
157    2. MILDLY AGREE
 91    3. MILDLY DISAGREE
 62    4. STRONGLY DISAGREE
 11    0. DK
  2    R. NA
```

2 17-23 P3. DO YOU READ ANY NEWSPAPERS, MAGAZINES OR PERIODICALS. (LIST ALL NAMES OF NEWSPAPERS AND MAGAZINES)

2 17   BERKELEY GAZETTE OR ANY OTHER EAST BAY LOCAL COMMUNITY PAPER
```
 40    C1. YES
376     2. NO
 27     0. NA ENTIRE QUESTION
```

CODEBOOK FOR **IDLRS*201400909

CARD	COLUMNS USED	MARGINAL COUNT	QUESTION AND CODE

2 18   SAN FRANCISCO CHRONICLE OR OTHER SAN FRANCISCO NEWSPAPERS
```
310    1. YES
106    2. NO
 27    0. NA
```

2 19   NATIONAL NEWSPAPERS
```
149    1. YES
267    2. NO
 27    0. NA
```

2 20-23 MAGAZINES

2 20   FIRST ANSWER
```
100    1. PICTORIAL NEWS (LOOK, LIFE, ETC.)
189    2. OTHER NEWS (TIME, NEWSWEEK, ETC.)
 31    3. LITERARY, ANALYTIC (SATURDAY REVIEW, HARPERS, ETC.)
  9    4. HUMOR, SATIRE (NEW YORKER, ETC.)
 18    5. POLITICAL AND SOCIAL OPINION (NATION, NATIONAL REVIEW, ETC.)
 10    6. PROFESSIONAL, SCIENTIFIC, TRADE OR TECHNICAL JOURNALS
 13    7. SPECIAL INTERESTS (WOMENS MAGAZINES, MENS MAGAZINES, SPORTS, ETC.)
 73    0. NONE
```

2 21   SECOND ANSWER
```
 22    1. PICTORIAL NEWS
 83    2. OTHER NEWS
 33    3. LITERARY
 21    4. HUMOR, SATIRE
 39    5. POLITICAL AND SOCIAL OPINION
 33    6. PROFESSIONAL
 27    7. SPECIAL INTERESTS
185    R. NO SECOND ANSWER
```

2 22   THIRD ANSWER
```
  2    1. PICTORIAL NEWS
  9    2. OTHER NEWS
 23    3. LITERARY
  8    4. HUMOR, SATIRE
 25    5. POLITICAL AND SOCIAL OPINION
 44    6. PROFESSIONAL
 34    7. SPECIAL INTERESTS
298    R. NO THIRD ANSWER
```

CODEBOOK FOR **IDLRS*201400905

CARD COLUMNS	MARGINAL	QUESTION AND CODE
ID USED	COUNT	

2 28

IT IS A GOOD THING FOR STUDENTS TO TAKE PART IN
PICKETING FOR CIVIL RIGHTS
1. STRONGLY AGREE   190
2. MILDLY AGREE   161
3. MILDLY DISAGREE   50
4. STRONGLY DISAGREE   20
0. DK   20
R. NA   2

2 29

CIVIL RIGHTS DEMONSTRATIONS OVER THE PAST FEW YEARS HAVE
HELPED THE NEGRO
1. STRONGLY AGREE   206
2. MILDLY AGREE   183
3. MILDLY DISAGREE   24
4. STRONGLY DISAGREE   11
0. DK   17
R. NA   2

2 30

MOST BUSINESS LEADERS IN THIS STATE ARE OPPOSED TO THE
CIVIL RIGHTS MOVEMENT
1. STRONGLY AGREE   48
2. MILDLY AGREE   115
3. MILDLY DISAGREE   111
4. STRONGLY DISAGREE   20
0. DK   146
R. NA   3

2 31

CIVIL DISOBEDIENCE IS WARRANTED IN CERTAIN CIRCUMSTANCES
1. STRONGLY AGREE   225
2. MILDLY AGREE   154
3. MILDLY DISAGREE   39
4. STRONGLY DISAGREE   21
0. DK   3
R. NA   1

2 32

THE METHODS OF CIVIL DISOBEDIENCE ARE EFFECTIVE AND
SHOULD BE USED INCREASINGLY TO HELP CORRECT SOCIAL
INJUSTICE
1. STRONGLY AGREE   70
2. MILDLY AGREE   138
3. MILDLY DISAGREE   129
4. STRONGLY DISAGREE   88
0. DK   16
R. NA   2

CODEBOOK FOR **IDLRS*201400905

CARD COLUMNS	MARGINAL	QUESTION AND CODE
ID USED	COUNT	

2 23

FOURTH ANSWER
1. PICTORIAL NEWS   7
2. OTHER NEWS   2
3. LITERARY   5
4. HUMOR, SATIRE   7
5. POLITICAL AND SOCIAL OPINION   12
6. PROFESSIONAL   5
7. SPECIAL INTERESTS   24
R. NO FOURTH ANSWER   381

2 24 Q28.

APPROXIMATELY HOW OFTEN HAVE YOU READ THE DAILY
CALIFORNIAN IN RECENT WEEKS.
A1. EVERY DAY   210
2. TWO TO FOUR TIMES A WEEK 166
3. ONCE A WEEK   32
4. RARELY OR NEVER   35

2 25-33 Q29.

WE WOULD LIKE TO KNOW HOW YOU FEEL ABOUT THE CURRENT
CIVIL RIGHTS CONTROVERSY. SPECIFICALLY, DO YOU AGREE
WITH THE FOLLOWING.

2 25

THE PROBLEMS OF SEGREGATION IN THE SOUTH ARE FOR
SOUTHERNERS TO SOLVE, NORTHERNERS HAVE NO RIGHT TO
INTERFERE
R1. STRONGLY AGREE   8
2. MILDLY AGREE   29
3. MILDLY DISAGREE   66
4. STRONGLY DISAGREE   337
0. DK   2
R. NA   1

2 26

CIVIL RIGHTS FOR NEGROES MAY BE AN ISSUE IN THE SOUTH,
BUT THERE ARE NO SERIOUS RACIAL PROBLEMS IN THE NORTH
1. STRONGLY AGREE   5
2. MILDLY AGREE   11
3. MILDLY DISAGREE   48
4. STRONGLY DISAGREE   375
0. DK   4

2 27

THE FEDERAL GOVERNMENT SHOULD BE MORE ACTIVE IN
ENSURING THE CIVIL RIGHTS OF NEGROES IN THE SOUTH
1. STRONGLY AGREE   263
2. MILDLY AGREE   118
3. MILDLY DISAGREE   45
4. STRONGLY DISAGREE   13
0. DK   2
R. NA   2

CODEBOOK FOR **IDLRS*201400905

CARD	COLUMNS USED	MARGINAL COUNT	QUESTION AND CODE
2	39-42		Q31. TO WHAT EXTENT DO YOU AGREE WITH YOUR PARENTS ON THE FOLLOWING IDEAS.
2	39		INTELLECTUAL BELIEFS
		113	R1. STRONGLY AGREE
		188	2. MILDLY AGREE
		61	3. MILDLY DISAGREE
		25	4. STRONGLY DISAGREE
		56	0. NA
2	40		RELIGIOUS BELIEFS
		113	1. STRONGLY AGREE
		140	2. MILDLY AGREE
		79	3. MILDLY DISAGREE
		54	4. STRONGLY DISAGREE
		57	0. NA
2	41		FUTURE GOALS
		173	1. STRONGLY AGREE
		152	2. MILDLY AGREE
		52	3. MILDLY DISAGREE
		19	4. STRONGLY DISAGREE
		47	0. NA
2	42		POLITICAL BELIEFS
		81	1. STRONGLY AGREE
		183	2. MILDLY AGREE
		90	3. MILDLY DISAGREE
		50	4. STRONGLY DISAGREE
		39	0. NA
2	43		P4. HOW LONG HAVE YOU BEEN RESIDENCE ON THE BERKELEY CAMPUS.
		31	A1. 1ST SEMESTER
		155	2. 2-3RD SEMESTER
		126	3. 4-5TH SEMESTER
		69	4. 6-7TH SEMESTER
		61	5. 8 OR MORE SEMESTERS
		1	0. NA

CODEBOOK FOR **IDLRS*201400905

CARD	COLUMNS USED	MARGINAL COUNT	QUESTION AND CODE
2	33		IF I BELIEVED THAT THE ENDS WERE MORALLY RIGHT I WOULD PARTICIPATE IN ACTIONS OF CIVIL DISOBEDIENCE
		125	1. STRONGLY AGREE
		128	2. MILDLY AGREE
		83	3. MILDLY DISAGREE
		70	4. STRONGLY DISAGREE
		35	C. DK
		2	R. NA
2	34-38		Q30. HOW FREQUENTLY DO YOU DISCUSS THE FOLLOWING IDEAS WITH YOUR PARENTS. (INCLUDING CORRESPONDENCE.)
2	34		INTELLECTUAL BELIEFS
		134	R1. FREQUENTLY
		163	2. OCCASIONALLY
		114	3. RARELY
		32	0. NA, NO PARENTS
2	35		RELIGIOUS BELIEFS
		86	1. FREQUENTLY
		119	2. OCCASIONALLY
		182	3. RARELY
		50	0. NA
2	36		PERSONAL PROBLEMS
		126	1. FREQUENTLY
		156	2. OCCASIONALLY
		132	3. RARELY
		29	0. NA
2	37		FUTURE GOALS
		213	1. FREQUENTLY
		154	2. OCCASIONALLY
		47	3. RARELY
		29	0. NA
2	38		POLITICAL BELIEFS
		157	1. FREQUENTLY
		151	2. OCCASIONALLY
		106	3. RARELY
		29	0. NA

CODEBOOK FOR **IDLRS*201400905   QUESTION AND CODE

CARD COLUMNS MARGINAL
ID   USED   COUNT

2   50   Q33. HOW DO YOU FEEL ABOUT KERRS DECISION TO RESCIND HIS RESIGNATION.
             323   A1. I AM GLAD HE DID IT
             38   2. I AM SORRY HE DID IT
             48   3. OTHER
             34   0. DK

2   51-54   Q34. WHY DO YOU FEEL THAT WAY.
2   51   GENERAL TONE OF RESPONSE
             156   C1. VERY FAVORABLE
             157   2. SOMEWHAT FAVORABLE
             54   3. NEUTRAL
             35   4. UNFAVORABLE
             41   R. NA

2   52-54   REASONS SPECIFIED
2   52   FIRST ANSWER
             60   1. PERSONAL ATTRIBUTES
             82   2. GOOD ADMINISTRATOR
             16   3. LIBERAL OR OTHER REFERENCE TO POLITICAL VIEWS
             88   4. FEAR OF REPLACEMENT
             63   5. RESIGNATION WAS A POLITICAL MOVE TO MAKE REGENTS COMPROMISE, A PERSONAL PROTEST, ETC.
             134   R. NA

2   53   SECOND ANSWER
             14   1. PERSONAL ATTRIBUTES
             38   2. GOOD ADMINISTRATOR
             21   3. LIBERAL
             25   4. FEAR OF REPLACEMENT
             10   5. POLITICAL MOVE
             335   R. NO SECOND ANSWER

2   54   THIRD ANSWER
             3   1. PERSONAL ATTRIBUTES
             3   2. GOOD ADMINISTRATOR
             4   3. LIBERAL
             6   4. FEAR OF REPLACEMENT
             6   5. POLITICAL MOVE
             421   R. NO THIRD ANSWER

2   55   Q35. AND HOW DO YOU FEEL ABOUT MEYERSONS DECISION TO RESCIND HIS RESIGNATION.
             316   A1. I AM GLAD HE DID IT
             17   2. I AM SORRY HE DID IT
             34   3. OTHER
             76   0. DK

CODEBOOK FOR **IDLRS*201400905   QUESTION AND CODE

CARD COLUMNS MARGINAL
ID   USED   COUNT

2   44-45   P5.   WHERE ARE YOU LIVING THIS SEMESTER.
             62   A01. RESIDENCE HALL
             23   C2. FRATERNITY
             17   C3. SORORITY
             23   04. U.C. APPROVED HOUSE
             13   05. OTHER ROOMING HOUSE
             18   C6. INTERNATIONAL HOUSE
             7   07. ROOM IN PRIVATE HOME
             28   08. APARTMENT ALONE
             52   09. APARTMENT WITH SPOUSE
             103   10. APARTMENT SHARED
             28   11. OWN OR RENT HOME
             15   12. UNIVERSITY VILLAGE
             34   13. AT HOME (WITH PARENTS)
             15   14. OTHER
             5   RR. NA

2   46-49   Q32. DO YOU AGREE OR DISAGREE WITH THE FOLLOWING STATEMENTS.
2   46   EACH PROFESSOR HAS THE RIGHT TO ESTABLISH RULES FOR STUDENT CONDUCT IN HIS CLASSES, FOR INSTANCE, NO SMOKING, NO READING NEWSPAPER, NO LATE ARRIVALS
             405   R1. AGREE
             34   2. DISAGREE
             4   0. DK

2   47   THE UNIVERSITY HAS THE RIGHT TO REGULATE ON-CAMPUS BEHAVIOR EVEN THOUGH THE BEHAVIOR MAY NOT BE ILLEGAL, FOR INSTANCE, RULES CONCERNING DRINKING, AND DRESS
             263   1. AGREE
             148   2. DISAGREE
             29   0. DK
             3   R. NA

2   48   THIS UNIVERSITY NECESSARILY IS REQUIRED TO ENFORCE OUR SOCIETYS LAWS, BUT BEYOND THIS IT HAS ALSO THE RIGHT TO IMPOSE PUNISHMENT FOR ON-CAMPUS INFRACTIONS OF THESE LAWS
             209   1. AGREE
             204   2. DISAGREE
             25   C. DK
             5   R. NA

2   49   THIS UNIVERSITY NECESSARILY IS REQUIRED TO ENFORCE OUR SOCIETYS LAWS BUT BEYOND THIS IT HAS ALSO THE RIGHT TO IMPOSE PUNISHMENT FOR OFF-CAMPUS INFRACTIONS OF THESE LAWS
             31   1. AGREE
             393   2. DISAGREE
             12   0. DK
             7   R. NA

CODEBOOK FOR **IDLRS*201400905   QUESTION AND CODE

CARD COLUMNS MARGINAL
ID   USED   COUNT

2   62   P7. WHAT IS YOUR CUMULATIVE GRADE POINT AVERAGE.
              68   C1. 1.6-2.4
             122   2. 2.5-2.9
             118   3. 3.0-3.4
              85   4. 3.5-4.0
              18   5. OTHER, UNCODABLE
              32   R. NA

2   63   P8. HOW OLD WERE YOU ON YOUR LAST BIRTHDAY.
              51   C1. 17-18
             120   2. 19-20
             108   3. 21-22
              70   4. 23-25
              27   5. 26-29
              36   6. 30 AND OLDER
              31   R. NA

2   64   P9. ARE YOU SINGLE, MARRIED OR ENGAGED.
             314   R1. SINGLE
              25   2. ENGAGED
              87   3. MARRIED
               9   4. DIVORCED OR WIDOWED
               8   R. NA

CODEBOOK FOR **IDLRS*201400905   QUESTION AND CODE

CARD COLUMNS MARGINAL
ID   USED   COUNT

2   56-59 Q36. WHY DO YOU FEEL THAT WAY.

2   56   GENERAL TONE OF RESPONSE
             197   C1. VERY FAVORABLE
             101   2. SOMEWHAT FAVORABLE
              62   3. NEUTRAL
              14   4. UNFAVORABLE
              69   R. NA

2   57-59 REASONS SPECIFIED

2   57   FIRST ANSWER
              86   C1. PERSONAL ATTRIBUTES
              80   2. GOOD ADMINISTRATOR
              17   3. LIBERAL OR OTHER REFERENCE TO POLITICAL VIEWS
              31   4. FEAR OF REPLACEMENT
              33   5. RESIGNATION WAS A POLITICAL MOVE
              17   6. SUPPORT FOR KERR
             179   R. NA

2   58   SECOND ANSWER
               9   1. PERSONAL ATTRIBUTES
              42   2. GOOD ADMINISTRATOR
               8   3. LIBERAL OR OTHER REFERENCE TO POLITICAL VIEWS
               5   4. FEAR OF REPLACEMENT
               8   5. RESIGNATION WAS A POLITICAL MOVE
               6   6. SUPPORT FOR KERR
             364   R. NO SECOND ANSWER

2   59   THIRD ANSWER
               2   1. PERSONAL ATTRIBUTES
               2   2. GOOD ADMINISTRATOR
               5   3. LIBERAL
               2   4. FEAR OF REPLACEMENT
               2   5. POLITICAL MOVE
               2   6. SUPPORT FOR KERR
             428   R. NO THIRD ANSWER

2   60-61 P6. IN WHAT FIELD ARE YOU MAJORING OR DO YOU PLAN TO MAJOR.
             101   C01. HUMANITIES
               7   C02. HOME ECONOMICS
              85   03. SOCIAL SCIENCE
              53   04. PHYSICAL SCIENCE
              39   05. LIFE SCIENCES
              21   06. BUSINESS ADMINISTRATION
              16   07. APPLIED SOCIAL SCIENCE
              64   08. ENGINEERING AND ARCHITECTURE
               1   09. AGRICULTURE AND FORESTRY
              18   10. OTHER OR GROUP MAJOR
              32   RR. NA

CODEBOOK FOR **IDLRS*201400905   QUESTION AND CODE

CARD COLUMNS   MARGINAL
ID   USED   COUNT

2   66   P11. WHAT WAS THE HIGHEST GRADE IN SCHOOL COMPLETED BY YOUR
                      FATHER.

                      12   A1. GRAMMAR SCHOOL INCOMPLETE
                      16   2.   GRADE 8
                      28   3.   HIGH SCHOOL INCOMPLETE
                      92   4.   HIGH SCHOOL GRADUATE
                      66   5.   COLLEGE INCOMPLETE
                      86   6.   COLLEGE GRADUATE
                      123   7.   ADDITIONAL EDUCATION BEYOND COLLEGE
                      11   0.   DK
                      9   R.   NA

2   67   P12. WHAT IS THE HIGHEST GRADE IN SCHOOL COMPLETED BY YOUR
                      MOTHER.

                      13   A1. GRAMMAR SCHOOL INCOMPLETE
                      9   2.   GRADE 8
                      24   3.   HIGH SCHOOL INCOMPLETE
                      129   4.   HIGH SCHOOL COMPLETE
                      111   5.   COLLEGE INCOMPLETE
                      81   6.   COLLEGE GRADUATE
                      56   7.   ADDITIONAL EDUCATION BEYOND COLLEGE
                      9   0.   DK
                      11   R.   NA

2   68   P13. WHAT IS THE POLITICAL PARTY AFFILIATION OF YOUR FATHER.

                      83   A1. CONSERVATIVE REPUBLICAN
                      68   2.   LIBERAL REPUBLICAN
                      76   3.   CONSERVATIVE DEMOCRAT
                      118   4.   LIBERAL DEMOCRAT
                      30   5.   INDEPENDENT
                      29   6.   OTHER
                      18   0.   DK
                      21   R.   NA

2   69   P14. WHAT IS THE POLITICAL PARTY AFFILIATION OF YOUR MOTHER.

                      71   A1. CONSERVATIVE REPUBLICAN
                      75   2.   LIBERAL REPUBLICAN
                      85   3.   CONSERVATIVE DEMOCRAT
                      121   4.   LIBERAL DEMOCRAT
                      25   5.   INDEPENDENT
                      32   6.   OTHER
                      20   0.   DK
                      14   R.   NA

CODEBOOK FOR **IDLRS*201400905   QUESTION AND CODE

CARD COLUMNS   MARGINAL
ID   USED   COUNT

2   65   P10. WHAT IS YOUR FATHERS OCCUPATION. (INTERVIEWER-IF
                      DECEASED OR RETIRED, OBTAIN FORMER OCCUPATION. IF NOT
                      KNOW OBTAIN OCCUPATION OF GUARDIAN OR MOTHER.)
                      SPECIFY
                      NOTE TO INTERVIEWER-TRY TO GET SOME PICTURE OF THE TYPE
                      OF WORK AND THE EMPLOYING ORGANIZATION. DETAILS.

               140   C1. PROFESSIONAL (ACTOR, ARCHITECT, ARTIST, CHEMIST,
                      DIRECTOR, DOCTOR, EDITOR, ENGINEER, GEOLOGIST,
                      INTERPRETER, JOURNALIST, LAWYER, MEDICAL DIRECTOR,
                      MUSICIAN, MILITARY OFFICER, MINISTER, MISSIONARY,
                      PRINCIPAL, PROFESSOR, PSYCHOLOGIST, SCHOOL OFFICIAL,
                      SOCIAL WORKER, WRITER, MATHEMATICIAN.)

               29   2.   SEMI-PROFESSIONAL (ACCOUNTANT, AUDITOR, CHIROPRACTOR,
                      COMMERCIAL ARTIST, DRAFTSMAN, DRUGGIST, FOREST
                      RANGER, MEDICAL TECHNICIAN, NURSE, OPTOMETRIST,
                      PHOTOGRAPHER, PHYSICAL THERAPIST, PILOT, SEA
                      CAPTAIN, SURVEYOR, VETERINARIAN, PHARMACIST, CLOTHES
                      DESIGNER, INTERIOR DECORATOR, LABORATORY TECHNICIAN,
                      PODIATRIST, 4-H DIRECTOR.)

               64   3.   SELF-EMPLOYED BUSINESSMAN (AUTO DEALER, CONTRACTOR,
                      EXPORT-IMPORT, MERCHANT, PUBLISHER OF NEWSPAPER,
                      OWNS PROPERTY, REAL ESTATE, UNDERTAKER)

               86   4.   HIGHER WHITE COLLAR AND/OR MANAGERIAL (APPRAISER,
                      BANKER, MAYOR, POLITICIAN, PRODUCER, PUBLIC
                      RELATION, PUBLISHING, PERSONNEL RELATIONS, RADIO
                      WORK, STOCKBROKER, COMPTROLLER, LABOR MEDIATOR,
                      SALESMAN (NOT CLERK), INSURANCE ADJUSTOR.)

               19   5.   LOWER WHITE COLLAR (AIRLINE STEWARDESS, BANK TELLER,
                      FURRIER, SHIPPING CLERK, RAILROAD CONDUCTOR,
                      MAILMAN, ARMED FORCES, FOREMAN.)

               27   6.   SKILLED WAGE WORKER (BAKER, CLOTHEIR, ELECTRICIAN,
                      MACHINIST, PAINTER (HOUSE AND SIGN), PLASTERER,
                      TOOL AND DIE MAKER, UPHOLSTERER, WELDER, PRINTER,
                      JEWELER, PATTERN MAKER, BARBER.)

               19   7.   SEMI-SKILLED AND UNSKILLED WAGE WORKER (BARTENDER,
                      BUS DRIVER, FACTORY WORKER, FISHERMAN (FOR SOMEONE
                      ELSE), GARDENER, RAILROAD WORKER, CONSTRUCTION
                      WORKER, ETC.)

               11   8.   SELF-EMPLOYED FARMER (SELF-EMPLOYED FISHERMAN,
                      RANCHER, ETC.)

               8   9.   OTHER OR UNCODABLE (WORKS FOR BORDENS, STUDENT, ETC.)
               40   R.   NA

CODEBOOK FOR **IDLRS**201400905

PAGE 033

CARD ID	COLUMNS USED	MARGINAL COUNT	QUESTION AND CODE

2 70 P15. WHAT IS THE RELIGIOUS PREFERENCE OF YOUR FATHER.

```
       158    A1. PROTESTANT
        77     2. CATHOLIC
        72     3. JEWISH
        40     4. OTHER
        81     5. NONE
        15     R. NA
```

2 71 P16. WHAT IS THE RELIGIOUS PREFERENCE OF YOUR MOTHER.

```
       189    A1. PROTESTANT
        90     2. CATHOLIC
        66     3. JEWISH
        35     4. OTHER
        53     5. NONE
        10     R. NA
```

2 72 P17. WHAT IS YOUR RELIGIOUS PREFERENCE.

```
       139    A1. PROTESTANT
        72     2. CATHOLIC
        50     3. JEWISH
       131     4. OTHER
         9     5. NONE
               R. NA
```

2 73 P18. HOW OFTEN DO YOU ATTEND CHURCH, TEMPLE, SYNAGOGUE.

```
       126    A1. NEVER
       161     2. ALMOST NEVER
        60     3. ONCE OR TWICE A MONTH
        90     4. ONCE A WEEK OR MORE
         6     0. NA
```

2 74 P19. APPROXIMATELY WHAT WAS THE TOTAL INCOME OF YOUR
           PARENTS OR GUARDIAN LAST YEAR, INCLUDING ALL SOURCES.

```
        50    A1. CLOSEST TO 5,000 OR UNDER
       133     2. CLOSEST TO 10,000
        74     3. CLOSEST TO 15,000
        41     4. CLOSEST TO 20,000
        68     5. CLOSEST TO 25,000 OR OVER
        42     0. DK
        35     R. NA
```

2 75 P20. SEX.

```
       286    A1. MALE
       154     2. FEMALE
         3     R. NA
```

CODEBOOK FOR **IDLRS**201400905

PAGE 034

CARD ID	COLUMNS USED	MARGINAL COUNT	QUESTION AND CODE

2 76 P21. RACE.

```
       365    C1. CAUCASIAN
        26     2. ORIENTAL
         3     3. NEGRO
         4     4. OTHER
        45     R. NA
```

2 77 P22. ACADEMIC STANDING. (NOTE FROM PUBLIC DIRECTORY CARD.
           IF YOU ARE UNCLEAR ON ANY OF THESE CATEGORIES, ASK THE
           RESPONDENT)

```
        54    A1. FRESHMAN
        62     2. SOPHOMORE
        94     3. JUNIOR
        99     4. SENIOR
       127     5. GRADUATE
         7     R. NA
```

2 78 V1. TYPOLOGY OF FRIENDS RESPONSES TO FREE SPEECH MOVEMENT
           FROM Q17.

```
        44     1. ALL CLOSE FRIENDS ACTIVE IN FREE SPEECH MOVEMENT
       103     2. ALL ACTIVE OR SYMPATHETIC
        35     3. ACTIVE AND MIXED REACTIONS
       196     4. NO ACTIVE FRIENDS
        17     5. FRIENDS ACTIVE ON BOTH SIDES
         9     6. ACTIVE ANTI-FREE SPEECH MOVEMENT AND MIXED REACTIONS
         3     7. ALL FRIENDS ANTI-FREE SPEECH MOVEMENT
         6     8. WITHDREW-HOSTILE BOTH SIDES
        30     0. NO FRIENDS
```

END

106

What business or profession would you <u>most</u> <u>like</u> to go into? (Occupation or kind of work)

3/66-67

88	C 01.	ARCHITECTURE 1¥
553	02.	ENGINEERING (BUILDING, CONSTRUCTION, INDUSTRIAL DESIGN) INCLUDING 2¥
317	03.	LAW 3¥
691	04.	MEDICINE (NURSING, VETERINARIAN, DENTIST, PHARMACY INCLUDING 4¥
400	05.	TEACHING (INCLUDING EXPERIMENTAL PSYCHOLOGY, EXTESION AGRICULTURE THERAPY) 5¥
70	06.	SOCIAL WORK (INCLUDING MINISTRY) 6¥
152	07.	GOVERNMENT SERVICE (INCLUDING MILITARY AND FOREIGN SERVICE) 7¥
70	08.	JOURNALISM (INCLUDING DRAMA) 8¥
193	09.	ART (INCLUDING MOVIE DIRECTOR PRODUCER, RADIO, TEXTILE, MUSICIAN, INTERIOR DESIGN) 9¥
41	10.	FOOD, RESTAURANT, HOTEL (INCLUDING FOOD TESTING 0¥
135	11.	SALES PROMOTION (INCLUDING MERCHANDISING) -¥
72	12.	ADVERTISING, PUBLIC RELATION +¥
134	13.	PERSONNEL (INCLUDING INDUSTRIAL MANAGEMENT, INDUSTRIAL PSYCHOLOGY) ¥1
108	14.	FARMING RANCHING ¥2
2	15.	SECRETARIAL ¥3
300	16.	NATURAL SCIENCE UNSPECIFIED (INCLUDING LAB. TECHNICIAN, CONSERVATION OF WILDLIFE, AGRONOMY, FLORICULTURE, MATHEMATICS, CHEMISTRY PETROLEUM GEOLOGIST) ¥4
23	17.	SOCIAL SCIENCE UNSPECIFIED (INCLUDING ECONOMICS) ¥5
453	18.	BUSINESS UNSPECIFIED (INCLUDING ACCOUNTING, TEXTILE INDUSTRY, DAIRY FACTORY, OIL BUSINESS) ¥6
105	19.	REAL ESTATE, FINANCE (INCLUDING BANKING, INSURANCE, INVESTMENT) ¥8
44	20.	OTHER (LABOR UNION, LIBRARIAN, PROFESSIONAL ATHLETICS) ¥9
607	21.	DK ¥-
27	22.	NA ¥0

DONE

★

SURVEY RESEARCH CENTER
DATA PROCESSING SERVICES FACILITY
UNIVERSITY OF CALIFORNIA, BERKELEY

APR. 26, 1967
PAGE 001

INTERNATIONAL DATA LIBRARY AND REFERENCE SERVICE
SRC KWIC INDEX OF STUDY TITLES

	TITLE	STUDY NO.
IN AMERICAN NATIONS	ACCORDING TO LATIN AMERICAN STUDENTS* P	900700003
IN AMERICAN NATIONS	ACCORDING TO LATIN AMERICAN STUDENTS* P	399700001
CKGROUND AND CAREER	ADJUSTMENT OF UNIVERSITY ALUMNI* BA	416400001
S IN CHRISTCHURCH*	ADJUSTMENT + RELIGION OF DUTCH IMMIGRANT	701700002
ATTITUDES RE	ADVERTISEMENT*	409690007
ITUDES RE DECEPTIVE	ADVERTISEMENT +GOVT RECORDS ON CITIZENS*	409690006
NORTH	AFRICAN STUDENTS IN FRANCE*	050500004
	AFRICAN STUDENTS IN GERMANY*	050520001
	AGRARIAN REFORM IN CHILE*	304610001
	AGRICULTURAL COOPERATIVES*	409690013
* ATTITUDES TOWARDS	AGRICULTURAL COOPERATIVES* FARMERS	409700001
VOCATIONAL	AGRICULTURE SCHOOL GRADUATES*	405400001
FARMERS* VIEWS ON	AGRICULTURE*	409690012
OLO, RECIFE + PORTO	ALEGRE* UNIVERSITY STUDENTS IN RIO, SAO	302590001
	ALL-INDIA POLITICAL POLL*	407500006
NROLLED STUDENTS AT	ALLAHABAD UNIVERSITY* NEWLY E	407400003
STUDENTS AT	ALLAHABAD UNIVERSITY*	407400004
JOSEPH* STUDENTS +	ALUMNI OF THE AMERICAN U OF BEIRUT + THE	508700001

SURVEY RESEARCH CENTER
DATA PROCESSING SERVICES FACILITY
UNIVERSITY OF CALIFORNIA, BERKELEY

APR. 26, 1967
PAGE 002

INTERNATIONAL DATA LIBRARY AND REFERENCE SERVICE
SRC KWIC INDEX OF STUDY TITLES

	TITLE	STUDY NO.
TMENT OF UNIVERSITY	ALUMNI* BACKGROUND AND CAREER ADJUS	416400001
ACCORDING TO LATIN	AMERICAN STUDENTS* PRESTIGE OF LATIN AM	900700003
NTS + ALUMNI OF THE	AMERICAN U OF BEIRUT + THE U OF ST JOSEP	508700001
TIFICATION IN LATIN	AMERICA* INTERNATIONAL STRA	900700004
ILITY IN FOUR LATIN	AMERICAN CITIES* STRATIFICATION + MOB	900780002
* PRESTIGE OF LATIN	AMERICAN NATIONS ACCORDING TO LATIN AMER	900700003
* PRESTIGE OF LATIN	AMERICAN NATIONS ACCORDING TO LATIN AMER	399700001
TIFICATION IN LATIN	AMERICA* INTERNATIONAL STRA	399700002
ACCORDING TO LATIN	AMERICAN STUDENTS* PRESTIGE OF LATIN AM	399700001
ILITY IN FOUR LATIN	AMERICAN CITIES* STRATIFICATION + MOB	302800001
ILITY IN FOUR LATIN	AMERICAN CITIES* STRATIFICATION + MOB	300700001
ILITY IN FOUR LATIN	AMERICAN CITIES* STRATIFICATION + MOB	304700001
POLITICAL	APATHY IN ROSARIO*	300710001
SE PANEL)* OUTCOMES	APPROACH TO PERSONAL DECISION-MAKING (2-	900400004
SE PANEL)* OUTCOMES	APPROACH TO PERSONAL DECISION-MAKING (2-	409400002
SE PANEL)* OUTCOMES	APPROACH TO PERSONAL DECISION-MAKING (2-	407400001
SE PANEL)* OUTCOMES	APPROACH TO PERSONAL DECISION-MAKING (2-	302400003
OUTCOMES	APPROACH TO PERSONAL DECISION-MAKING*	114400001

Appendix 7 – ANALYSIS REQUEST FORMS

SECCION DE ESTADISTICA BANCO DE DATOS SOLICITUD DE ANALISIS HOJA N-1A (DE CONTROL)

Nombre del investigador: _____

Fecha de la solicitud: _____

Comentarios: _____
_____
_____

DATOS: Proyecto: ☐☐☐   Estudio: ☐☐☐   Instrumento: ☐☐☐
Version: ☐☐   Numero de la cinta: ☐☐☐☐☐
Comentarios: _____
_____

FORMATO: Posiciones por registro: ☐☐☐☐   Registros por caso: ☐☐☐
Numero de casos: ☐☐☐☐☐☐
Comentarios: _____
_____

___ ESTADISTICAS BASICAS *(Hoja N-2)*

Numero de variables: ☐☐☐

___ RELACIONES BIVARIABLES. *(Hojas N-3 A y B)*

Numero de variables: ☐☐☐

Numero de dispersiogramas: ☐☐☐

___ REGRESION MULTIPLE *(Hojas N-4 A, B y C)*

Numero de variables de entrada: ☐☐☐

Numero de variables adicionales: ☐☐☐

Numero de ecuaciones: ☐☐☐

___ TABULACION SIMPLE *(Hoja N-5)*

Numero de variables: ☐☐☐

___ TABULACION CRUZADA *(Hoja N-6)*

Numero de cuadros: ☐☐☐

TITULO:

☐☐
☐☐

PARA USO INTERNO AL BANCO DE DATOS

Actividad	Fecha	Responsable	
Compormetido	----------	----------------	Tiempo invertido:
Dado al procesador	----------	----------------	
Procesado	----------	----------------	Consultas a la Seccion de Est. ___
Verificado	----------	----------------	Procesador ___
Regresado	----------	----------------	Computador ___

Comentarios: _____
_____

Seccion de estadistica
Banco de datos
Pedido de analisis
Hoja para tabulacion N-6

Investigador _____

Fecha _____

Cuadro numero ☐☐☐

TITULO PARA ☐☐☐☐☐☐☐☐☐☐☐☐☐☐☐☐☐☐☐☐☐☐☐☐☐☐☐☐
EL CUADRO ☐☐☐☐☐☐☐☐☐☐☐☐☐☐☐☐☐☐☐☐☐☐☐☐☐☐☐☐

Variable dependiente (filas)

___ igual a las (___ filas o ___ columnas) del cuadro numero ☐☐☐

___ segun:

NOMBRE	(*)NIVEL	CODIGOS

UBICACION DEL CAMPO

REGISTRO ☐☐☐

POSICION ☐☐☐☐

LARGO ☐☐

Variable independiente (columna)

___ igual a las (___ filas o ___ columnas) del cuadro numero ☐☐

___ segun:

NOMBRE	(*)NIVEL	CODIGOS

UBICACION DEL CAMPO

☐☐☐

☐☐☐☐

☐☐

Variables filtras (control)

___ no hay (usar todos los datos)

___ iguales a las vraibles filtras del cuadro numero ☐☐

___ segun:

NOMBRE	REGISTRO	POSICION	LARGO	CODIGOS

ENTERING STUDIES
IN THE DATA ARCHIVE

1620 TIME IN HRS. PER 1 DATA FILE

PROGRAMS USED	AVERAGE	LOWEST	HIGHEST
LOADING LOADING SEQUENCE CHECK *MARGINAL COUNTS	0.46	0.06	6.48
CLEANING PUNCH CLEANING CONTINGENCY CHECK UPDATE	1.06	0.18	3.37
CONVERTING PUNCH COUNT TRANSFER TO BCD MARGINAL COUNTS	0.50	0.10	5.30
MACHINE READABLE CODEBOOK CODE BOOK LISTING LOADING UPDATE PRINTING	0.31	0.10	0.76
TOTAL HRS. PER 1 STUDY	3.13	0.44	17.11

CSSDA B1080
RIM June 26, 1967

INVENTORY FORMAT

INSTRUCTION BOOKLET

COUNCIL OF SOCIAL SCIENCE DATA ARCHIVES

JUNE 1967

Contents: description of format fields
specifications to coders for
coding format

General Instructions

Each item will be coded on a separate IBM card or cards. Basically each item falls into one of three possible categories.

I.   Fixed format fields (Cols. 21-22) for items provided with pre-codes on the inventory format proper.

II. Fixed length variable format fields (Cols. 24-30) for items which do not exceed 7 Cols., e.g., archive ID #'s, sample size, organization code, county or state code.

III. Open field coding (Cols. 33-72) for alpha-numeric free form.

Summary of IBM control fields

Field #	Fixed fields	Description
1	Cols. 1-4	Archive ID #
2	Cols. 6-9	Study ID #
3	Cols. 11-13	Item #
4	Col. 15	Multiple response identification code
5	Cols. 17-19	Item continuation control
6	Cols. 21-22	Fixed format field
7	Cols. 24-30	Fixed length variable format field
	open field	
8	Cols. 33-72	For alpha-text, alpha-numeric and numeric

Description of IBM control fields

Field #	Fixed fields	Description
1	Cols. 1-4	Archive # of reporting institution (See list for 3 digit #).
2	Cols. 6-9	Serial number of this study for this reporting institution. (This number will be assigned by the reporting institution starting with #1 and continuing consecutively. A new number may or may not be assigned by the collating agency.)

Field #	Fixed fields	Description
3	Cols. 11-13	Item # from Inventory Format.
4	Col. 15	Subscript item sequence number for those situations where ordinarily only one response is expected for this item but in this exceptional case there are more than one, i.e., "Field work carried out by: NORC <u>and</u> SRC. There would then be two cards for item # 6: the first would have a "1" in Col. 15, and the second a "2". This Col. will be left blank in most instances.
5	Cols. 17-19	Card sequence # for this item. You are allowed up to 999 "continuation" cards for comments, descriptions and/or other alpha-text reportings.
6	Cols. 21-22	Response category for this item. (Where there is only one possible response indicating the presence or absence of an item, this Col. will always be punched "01" if the item is present. If this item is not present no card should be punched.

7	Cols. 24-30	This field is reserved for discreet numerical or alphabetically descriptions of items such as:
		  Number of cases in study
		  Number of cards per case
		  Internal study number or name, etc.
		This field (as should all) should be right justified

8	Cols. 33-72	Alpha-text descriptions, comments or qualifications for this item or further explanation of data in Cols. 24-30. Continuation cards when more than 40 spaces are needed should duplicate fields 1, 2, 3, 4, 6, 7. Field five should be augmented by 1 for each added card.
GENERAL NOTE:		'In some cases a search will be made for an 'item without success. Indication of a search 'can be made by using the field #8 option. 'Remember the format is sufficiently flexible 'so that it can be updated routinely.

Description of items

Item # 1. <u>Archive in which the study is stored:</u>

Each archive has been assigned a three digit identification code: Use codes below when filling out format.

KEY-PUNCHING
INSTRUCTIONS

' If the inventorying archive is key-punching the inventory '
' format, this number must appear in Cols. 1-4 (right '
' adjusted) on each IBM card used in the inventory. '

001 - The Roper Public Opinion Research Center

002 - Inter-University Consortium for Political Research

003 - Center of International Studies, M.I.T.

004 - International Data Library and Reference Service, Berkeley

005 - U C.L.A. Political Behavior Archive

006 - National Opinion Research Center

007 - Political Science Research Library and Political Data Program, Yale

008 - Bureau of Applied Social Research

009 - Project TALENT Data Bank

010 - Louis Harris Political Data Center

011 - School of Public Health and Administrative Medicine Research Archives

012 - Social Systems Research Institute

013 - Archive on Comparative Political Elites, Oregon

014 - Archive of Political Elites in Eastern Europe, Pittsburgh

015 - Political Science Data Archive, Carleton

016 - International Development Data Bank, Michigan State

017 - Survey Research Laboratory, Illinois

018 - Laboratory for Political Research, Iowa

019 - Public Opinion Survey Unit, Missouri

020 - Economic Growth Center, Yale

021 - Bureau of Labor Statistics

022 - Human Relations Area File

023 - Graduate School of Industrial Administration,
Carnegie Tech

024 - Latin American Social Science Data Archive

025 - Council for Inter-Societal Studies, Northwestern

Item # 2.   Archive Consecutive Serial Number:

A unique ID number for each study that is being inventoried:
This number may be the same as those appearing in items
3 and # 6, however it is recommended that a unique
number be assigned: (i.e., For purposes of identifying cards.

KEY-PUNCHING
INSTRUCTIONS

This number must appear in Cols. 6-9 (right adjusted)
on each IBM card used in the inventory.

Item # 3.   Archive Study Number:

This is the internal identification code assigned by the
archive to identify this study. This may or may not be the
same number appearing in Item # 2 and/or Item # 6.

KEY-PUNCHING
INSTRUCTIONS

The archive study number should be punched in Cols. 24-30
(right justified). This field may include alpha-text.
If archive numbers exceed the field size, then the number
should appear in Cols. 33-72. If for any reason there are
two or more ID numbers, use the field four (4) option.

Item # 4.   Title:

A given study may have several titles. Give all titles or
those most frequently used. Designate book title by (Book).
Give official archive title (for users) first. (If no title,
do not use this item.)
An example: Elmira Study,
             Voting (Book),
             Voting Study of 1948,
             Elmira Effectiveness Study.

KEY-PUNCHING
INSTRUCTIONS

Study titles should be punched in alpha-text in Cols. 33-72.
The inventory format provides space for 40 typewritter letters across each line. If the title(s) exceed this number,
indicate the use of a continuation card by punching the
sequence number of this card in Cols. 17-19 (right
adjusted). Generally, wherever alpha-text appears it will
be punched in Cols. 33-72. The first card of any alpha-text
description must have a one (1) punched in Cols. 17-19
(right adjusted).

Item # 5.   Write in name of originating organization. Codes will be provided by BASR. (Use field 8 if code is not provided in item # 1).

Item # 6.   Internal Identification Code assigned by the study's originating organization:

In some cases the original data supplier has assigned an ID number to the study. This number may be the same one used by the archive to identify this study.

In some cases the originating organization may have codes which exceed seven columns. If this is the case record ID number in field eight (8).

KEY-PUNCHING INSTRUCTIONS   See instructions for Item # 3.

Item # 7.   Sequence number of sub-survey:

This item allows the archive to identify different data sets within the same study while at the same time retaining the archive or organization identification number.

For example, if a study has separate samples, the "sequence number of sub-survey" would differ for each sample. If the samples or data sets differ greatly on the inventory format items, then a separate format should be filled out for each sub-survey. Not all items need be repeated for each sub-survey.

Considerable experimentation is needed to further clarify the functions of this item. It will probably apply to relatively few studies where several sub-sets of data appear. (For example, Project TALENT, some cross-national studies, panel studies, studies involving different levels of aggregate data, and studies interviewing different samples.)

For those archives reporting sub-surveys they should make clear to BASR which studies go together and which items are unique for each sub-survey.

Item # 8.   Questionnaire designed by:
and # 9.   Field work carried out by:

Code according to instructions provided on the code sheet: a pre-code will be developed for these items with the accumulation of responses; if archives participating in the inventory already have pre-codes for these items they may be used with accompanying explanations to the BASR staff, but they should be used in field eight only. Coders may use the code supplied for Item # 1.

Item # 10.   Starting field date of study: when the month or day are unknown code 00 00.

Item # 11.   Code the number of weeks. e.g. 04, 16, 24. (not three weeks)

Item # 12   The unweighted N refers to the sample size before any weighting procedures are used. The weighted N refers to the sample size after weighting of any segment of the collected sample (e.g., triple weighting late respondents by duplicating those cards and including them in the analysis deck.) If the study is a panel give maximum number obtained. If there is no weighting it is simply the number of cases.

Specifications and qualifications can be made using the field "8" option.

Item # 13.   The number of cases after weighting: weighting procedures may be described by using a field "8" card.

Item # 14.   If the identification of weighted cards is possible enter 1 in this field; if not leave blank.

Item # 15.   Number of cards per respondent. Number of IBM cards. Sometimes referred to as the number of decks.

Item # 16.   Expected sample size before losses. Further specification of sampling procedure can be made in item # 23.

Item # 17.   Each archive should describe their normal cleaning procedures. This will become part of the introduction to the inventory as recommended by the Inventory Committee.

Item # 18   If multiple punches or X Y and Blanks appear on the cards
and # 19.   for this study, indicate so by inserting a one in the blank space.

Item # 20.   Number of questions. A rough count is adequate here. In most cases the number of questions usually refers to the number of codes provided in the code book. For complex questions with several probes it may be necessary to use a comment card (field 8) e.g. cols. 24-30 code 19 and in Cols. 33-72. Indicate several probes etc.

Item # 21.   Same instructions as items # 18 and 19.

Item # 22.   Write in country or countries; if for a special state write in state. A code will be developed for this item.

Several pre-coded country lists exist with assigned numeric codes. If the volume of surveys now existing are already pre-coded in one format, then we recommend adopting that version to begin with. In the end, however, a general version must be agreed upon. So far I have seen an alphabetical list including all the countries and regions. This list was prepared for the OECD. The Yale Economic Growth Center was also a participant.

Item # 23.   Please write a short alpha-text description of the sample,
              including any special characteristics -- e.g., whether it
              is a universe of students in a particular field of study,
              etc. -- and the types of sampling procedures -- e.g.,
              "multistratum", "relational data," etc.

Item # 24.   Enter 1 if not available otherwise leave blank.

Item # 25.   Complete sampling description available from additional
              space for multiple sources if known.

Item # 26.   Sampling system. Code those which apply to this study.
              Enter appropriate number in blank space.

Item # 27.   See code sheet. Insert appropriate number in blank space.

Item # 28.   Insert the number of waves in the design. This should be
              elaborated upon in the sample description.

Item # 29.   Insert the number of studies which were conceived in the
              design stage to fit the general notion of a trend study:
              "Repeated interviews on the same content with different
              samples." This should be an explicit code and not an
              implicit one. For example all the studies in the American
              Soldier should not be listed. There are no doubt several
              studies in this series which were in fact designed as trend
              studies. Only these would be listed.

              If several studies seem very related this fact can be
              mentioned, along with a list of the studies in the abstract.
              (Item 121).

Item # 30.   If more than one data collection procedure used check
              those which apply.

Item # 31.   A list of languages will be developed. For the moment pre-
              code only English and English translations

                      0001 - English
                      0002 - English translation

              The format developed by the inventory committee calls for
              the language of the codebook (available at the archive) if
              this is an English translation code 0002. In most cases
              the language of the questionnaire can be ascertained by
              inspection of item 22 (country of survey or sub-survey).
              If however there is some ambiguity the coders can use
              field (8) for comments.

              The intent of the item is to tell the user in what language
              he can obtain the code book from the archive.

Items # 32-33   Indicate where publications are available, if not
       34-35.   with archive.

Item # 36.   If more than one principal publication use continuation
              cards. Please type if convenient.

Item # 37-   Face sheet items. Indicate with a "1" the presence of
      119.   any of the face sheet items. If an item is not present in
              the code book leave the format space blank.

Item # 120.   Write in alpha text. (Please type if convenient).

Item # 121.   INSTRUCTIONS FOR ABSTRACTS:

        The most time-consuming and therefore the most expensive task in
preparing inventory entries will be writing the descriptor list or abstract, in
response to the final question in the inventory format. Most of the previous
items in the format refer to the methodology of the study. This information
should not be repeated in the descriptor list or abstract. The descriptor list
or abstract should describe the study's substantive content.

        The Roper Center will use its own descriptor list for the studies
on deposit there--primarily the omnibus surveys of populations by commercial
and scholarly polling organizations. In the Roper Center's system, each question is tagged with a descriptor, and both the original question and the
descriptor appear in an index card in the files. For example, one question may
be tagged by the category "Political parties, Party preference"; another
"Military Affairs--Demobilization"; another "Government, Citizens' obligations";
another "cosmetics"; etc. Therefore, a list of descriptors for the inventory
entry of that study can be created simply by listing all the descriptors for
all the individual questions of that study. Following is an example of such
a study description constructed from the list of descriptors in the Roper
Center file for AIPO 411 (1948), by the Gallup organization:

        An omnibus survey containing questions on...
          --Taft-Hartley Law and legal restrictions on labor unions
          --Expectation of war
          --Marshall Plan and Foreign Economic Aid
          --Income taxes
          --Minimum wage
          --Political party preference, vote, and identification
          --Presidential candidate preferences
          --Kinsey study of sexual behavior
          --Vote recall

Another example, based on AIPO 560 (1956):

        An omnibus survey containing questions on...
          --Politics, national elections, USA, expectations, 1956 election
          --Politics, national elections, USA, candidate preference
          --Eisenhower, D D., attitude toward
          --Politics, non-voting
          --Taxation, burden
          --Taxation, income
          --Politics, party preference
          --Politics, primaries, desirability of
          --Politics, nominating conventions

                    --Education, federal aid to
                    --Minorities and ethnocentrism, education, segregation in
                    --Status, role, and prestige   --personal problems
                    --Government, U.S problems
                    --Government, state and local, leaders
                    --Truman, H.S., attitude toward
                    --Nixon, Richard, attitude toward
                    --Eisenhower, D.C., attitude toward
                    --Government, U.S., Cabinet
                    --Communications, postal
                    --Politics, level of information
                    --Numbers and measures, timepieces
                    --Food consumption, Italian foods
                    --Politics, national elections, USA, non-voting, 1952 election
                    --Politics, national elections, USA, vote recall, 1952 election

If a list seems too long, perhaps the less important descriptor tags might
be omitted.

        Since the Committee on Inventory and the Executive Committee recom-
mended that the Roper Center use its descriptor list for its own holdings, any
descriptor list used by other archives should use the Roper Center descriptor
list. When the time comes for actual work on the inventory, we shall supply
you with copies of the handbook Question Index: Coding Designations (Williamstown: The Roper Public Opinion Research Center, 1966). Other archives should
use this descriptor list to describe their omnibus surveys, if they have any.

                    * * * * * * * * *

        As we learned in the pretests, descriptor lists do not work well
for studies that concentrate on special topics in depth, such as those produced
by scholarly research centers for sociology, political science, education,
medical sociology, etc. Perhaps a brief descriptor list of your own invention
might be used. But we assume that all these studies will be described by a
terse abstract about the subject matter. The abstract would be a paragraph
in economical alphatext including information like the following:

1. Overall purpose of the study, as intended by its designers. Example of
    such a statement: "Description of the socialization process of students
    learning professional norms in two New York City Schools of Music."

2. Major conceptual variables. E.g.,: "Effects of peer group influence and
    college climates of opinion on student dishonesty." E.g., "Effects of
    industrial milieux on levels of information of workers, concerning plant
    management, trade union policy, relations between plant and community."

3. Possibly any particularly outstanding characteristics of the study from
    the standpoint of research method or substantive findings in the social
    sciences. E.g., "The People's Choice was the first panel study of the
    evolution of voting decisions in an election."

4. Avoid describing the methods and universe of the study, unless these have
    not been adequately described earlier in the inventory entry. But some
    unusual universes and samples might have to be described in the abstract.
    E.g., "All members of 172 Great Books discussion groups." E.g., "Compari-
    sons of attitudes of chiefs and citizens sampled from the same villages."

Following are some examples of good abstracts, which will be used as models:

A study of 963 secondary school students in the fifth form of Ghanaian public schools. The study is mainly concerned with the occupational and educational aspirations of the new generation of students, in relation to the background of their parents and their own realistic evaluations of their earning power and educational opportunities. Twenty-eight Ghanaian occupations were rated by the respondents according to prestige and probable salary. The students' feelings upon returning to the home village after the semester were examined. They were also asked to indicate the attitudes in their villages toward various ethnic groups of Ghana.

Processes of communication and decision involved in the application of 1,452 persons to a psychiatric clinic in Manhattan, New York City. The study is a reason analysis in that it tries to find out from people who applied to a clinic why they did so, who influenced them and how they came to acquire the necessary information. Based on responses to certain key items, a latent class model was constructed to find a circle of "Friends and Supporters of Psychotherapy" in order to show that personal influence was not exerted by single persons but by social circles.

Changes during the crucial three year period in which most male youth are socialized into the work force. The respondents are a nationwide sample of sophomore boys when the study begins, and these respondents are followed for a 36 month period. Basic questions:

1. What are the differential effects of three major patterns of education and socialization in late adolescence-- completion of high school, employment following high school dropout, and unemployment following dropout?
2. Against what basis of comparison can innovative developments in education and training be appraised?
3. What are the potent factors or dimensions in terms of which the effects of these several educational environments can be explained.

A study of the social backgrounds, perspectives on national issues, communications behavior, and activities in power roles of Venezuelan leaders aimed at deriving practical guidance for social policy and enlarging knowledge of elite functions in transitional societies.

Please do not write abstracts like the following, since they simply repeat a description of the research methods which have already been covered in the earlier parts of the inventory.

In May and June of 1954, two national polling agencies, the American Institute of Public Opinion (AIPO) and the National Opinion Research Center (NORC) conducted a nation-wide survey of public attitudes toward communism, conformity, and civil liberties under the auspices of the Fund for the Republic. The data was drawn from two samples:
(1) a national cross-section of the population (N = 4,933), and
(2) a special supplementary sample of local community leaders (N = 1,500).
The results of this study directed by the late Samuel A. Stouffer of Harvard University, were published in 1955 under the title, Communism, Conformity and Civil Liberties (Garden City, N.Y.: Doubleday and Company, Inc.)

Appendix 10 – SET-UP BUDGET

BUDGET
1/1/68 - 12/31/70

Salaries and Wages	1/1/68-12/31/69 Requested Support	University Contribution	Total	1/1/69 - 12/31/70 Requested Support	University Contribution	Total	1/1/68 - 12/31/70 Requested Support	University Contribution	Total
Principal Investigator Professor 10% academic year (19,100) (20,800)		1,910	1,910		2,080	2,080		3,990	3,990*
Director, Survey Research Center 5% (14,976)		749	749		749	749		1,498	1,498*
Asst. Research Sociologist IV[1] 50% (12,200)	6,100		6,100	6,100		6,100	12,200		12,200*
Post Grad Res. IV[2] 1st year	8,160		8,160				16,716		16,716*
2nd year				8,556		8,556			
Librarian II, 50%[3]	4,025		4,025	4,263		4,263	8,288		8,288
Research Assistant III[4] 50% - nine months	2,516		2,516	2,516		2,516			
10% - two months	1,118		1,118	1,118		1,118	7,268		7,268
Sr. Coder[5]	5,772		5,772	6,060		6,060	11,832		11,832*
Coder[6]	4,980		4,980	-		-	4,980		4,980*
Principal Clerk[7]	5,232		5,232	5,496		5,496	10,728		10,728*
Sr. Typist Clerk[8] - 50%	2,616		2,616	2,748		2,748	5,364		5,364*
Total Salaries and Wages	40,519	2,659	43,178	36,857	2,829	39,686	77,376	5,488	82,864
Employee Benefits									
10% of eligible* salaries	3,689	266	3,955	3,322	283	3,605	7,011	549	7,560
Expendable Supplies and Services									
Office Supplies 2,000 Postage and Freight 1,400 Telephone 1,000 Printing 1,000[9] Books 500[10] Computer Tapes 2,500[11] 8,400	4,450		4,450	3,950		3,950	8,400		8,400

BUDGET (continued)

	1/1/68 - 12/31/69 Requested Support	University Contribution	Total	1/1/69 - 12/31/70 Requested Support	University Contribution	Total	1/1/68 - 12/31/70 Requested Support	University Contribution	Total
Equipment									
2 storage cabinets for computer tapes[12]	200		200	200		200	400		400
2 bookshelves[13]	100		100	100		100	200		200
1 file cabinet[13]	100		100				100		100
Subtotal	400		400	300		300	700		700
Travel[14]									
Domestic	1,000		1,000	1,000		1,000	2,000		2,000
Foreign	1,000		1,000	5,400		5,400	6,400		6,400
Subtotal	2,000		2,000	6,400		6,400	8,400		8,400
Other Direct Costs									
Translations[15]	2,000		2,000	1,500		1,500	3,500		3,500
Acquisitions[16]--Surveys	6,000		6,000	4,000		4,000	10,000		10,000
Census Materials	400		400	100		100	500		500
Programming Development[17]	6,000		6,000	3,000		3,000	9,000		9,000
Data Processing[18] Key punch	15,000		15,000	8,000		8,000	23,000		23,000
Computer time	30,000		30,000	15,000		15,000	45,000		· 45,000
Subtotal	59,400		59,400	31,600		31,600	93,400		93,400
TOTAL DIRECT COSTS	110,458	2,925	113,383	82,429	3,112	85,541	195,287	6,037	201,324
Indirect Costs 42% of salaries and wages	17,018	1,117	18,135	15,480	1,188	16,668	32,498	2,305	34,803
TOTAL ESTIMATED COSTS	127,476	4,042	131,518	97,909	4,300	102,209	227,785	8,342	236,127

124

ITEM EXPLANATION

1) Assistant Research Sociologist will be responsible for the supervision of the project, for overseas travel, development of the information storage and retrieval system and other systems for internal operations and user services.

2) Post Graduate Research Sociologist will supervise all machine related activities including codebook production and the primary responsibility for study cleaning.

3) Librarian will catalog and manage the large volume of non-machine readable documentation collected by the International Data Library and Reference Service and establish and maintain a filing system for relating machine readable archive materials and non-machine readable documentation.

4) Research Assistant will be responsible for locating, establishing, and maintaining contact with actual and potential suppliers of studies. This includes maintaining a continuous review of the literature as well as extensive correspondence to secure new studies for the Archive.

5) Sr. Coder will be responsible for the production of machine readable codebooks and will aid in study cleaning operations.

6) Coder will aid in the production of the machine readable codebooks.

7) Principal Clerk will process user requests, aid in acquiring documentation for studies, respond to standard inquiries, and provide information about IDL and RS activities.

8) Sr. Typist Clerk will take dictation, write letters for other members of the staff, review monthly expenditures and control budget.

9) Printing costs include the production of inventory listings and materials descriptive of IDL and RS programs, activities and holdings.

10) Purchase of publications resulting from materials stored in the archive; technical information regarding archive activities; publications related to international and comparative research.

11) Acquisition of 166 computer tapes @ $15 a tape for the storage of individual studies.

12) Storage cabinets are necessary for the storage and preservation of archived data stored on magnetic tape.

13) Storage required for documentation related to archived studies.

14) Domestic: Travel and per diem each year for one person round trip to Washington, New York, Williamstown, Ann Arbor, Gainsville, and other centers within the United States which have overseas data.
Foreign: Travel and per diem for one to visit major research sites and sources of materials in Latin America and Asia, and to confer with archivists in Cologne, Amsterdam, and other European centers. The purpose of the trips is to secure materials for data archive; arrange for future studies to be mailed to the archive; gain information on

work in progress; and familiarize foreign scholars with the existence of the archive and techniques for its utilization.

Present figures are based on major stops (with consideration given to side trips to investigate field work and assess the adequacy of material obtained) in the major countries of Asia and Latin America, as well as European cities. Also included is travel and per diem within Asia for the Library's Asian representative affiliated with the Survey Research Center of the Chinese University of Hong Kong.

15) Translation costs of 100 studies are based on an average translation time of 22 hours per study.

16) Acquisition costs include approximately $1,000 for microfilm or Xerox copies of original instruments in the native languages, and purchase, duplication, and shipping costs of at least 200 high quality original studies.

Purchase of census materials and early attempts to create parameter files for each relevant study and country is estimated at $500.

17) As the Survey Research Center gains access to new computing facilities at the University's Computer Center, program development will have to be undertaken to utilize this new facility to its fullest. Programming work will be largely in the area of information retrieval in order to improve our current system of servicing user requests.

18) Data processing costs will include: codebook punching of 128 codebooks presently on hand, $19,000 (estimated at approximately 27 hours per unit or $148.50); and an additional 900 hours of key punching for record keeping and program development, $5,000. Computer use, $45,000. The computer is used extensively in the data "cleaning" process as well as for the production of specialized codebooks made from the general, machine readable codebooks. Included is the calculation of marginal frequency distributions and their merger with the rest of the study data, all of which can only be accomplished after the data has been reformatted in a manner suitable to manipulation by the computer and loading of the materials on magnetic tapes.

UNESCO PUBLICATIONS: NATIONAL DISTRIBUTORS

Argentina	Editorial Losada, S.A., Alsina 1131, BUENOS AIRES.
Australia	*Publications:* Educational Supplies Pty. Ltd., Box 33, Post Office, Brookvale 2100, N.S.W. *Periodicals:* Dominie Pty. Ltd., Box 33, Post Office, Brookvale 2100, N.S.W. *Sub-agent:* United Nations Association of Australia, Victorian Division, 4th Floor, Askew House, 364 Lonsdale St., MELBOURNE (Victoria) 3000.
Austria	Verlag Georg Fromme & Co., Arbeitergasse 1-7, 1051 WIEN.
Belgium	Jean De Lannoy, 112, rue du Trône, BRUXELLES 5.
Bolivia	Librería Universitaria, Universidad San Francisco Xavier, apartado 212, SUCRE.
Brazil	Fundação Getúlio Vargas, Serviço de Publicações, caixa postal 21120 Praia de Botafogo 188, RIO DE JANEIRO, G.B.
Bulgaria	Hemus, Kantora Literatura, bd. Rousky 6, SOFIJA.
Burma	Trade Corporation n.º (9), 550-552 Merchant Street, RANGOON.
Cameroon	Librairie Richard, B.P. 4017, YAOUNDÉ.
Canada	Information Canada, OTTAWA (Ont.).
Ceylon	Lake House Bookshop, Sir Chittampalam Gardiner Mawata, P.O. Box 244, COLOMBO 2.
Chile	Editorial Universitaria, S.A., casilla 10220, SANTIAGO.
Colombia	Librería Buccholz Galería, avenida Jiménez de Quesada 8-40, apartado aéreo 49-56, BOGOTÁ; Distrilibros Ltda., Pío Alfonso García, carrera 4ª, nºs 36-119 y 36-125, CARTAGENA; J. Germán Rodríguez N., Calle 17, 6-59, apartado nacional 83, GIRARDOT (Cundinamarca). Editorial Losada Ltda., Calle 18A, n.º 7-37, apartado aéreo 5820, apartado nacional 931, BOGOTÁ. *Sub-depots:* Edificio La Ceiba, Oficina 804, Medellín Calle 37, n.º 14-73 Oficina, 305, BUCARAMANGA; Edificio Zaccour, Oficina 736, CALI.
Congo (People's Republic of)	Librairie populaire, B.P. 577, BRAZZAVILLE.
Costa Rica	Librería Trejos S.A., apartado 1313, SAN JOSÉ. Teléfonos: 2285 y 3200.
Cuba	Distribuidora Nacional de Publicaciones, Neptuno 674, LA HABANA.
Cyprus	'MAM', Archbishop Makarios 3rd Avenue, P.O. Box 1722, NICOSIA.
Czechoslovakia	SNTL, Spalena 51, PRAHA 1 *(Permanent display)*; Zahranicni literatura, 11 Soukenicka, PRAHA 1. *For Slovakia only:* Nakladatelstvo Alfa, Hurbanovo nam 6 BRATISLAVA.
Dahomey	Librairie nationale, B.P. 294, PORTO NOVO.
Denmark	Ejnar Munksgaard Ltd., 6 Nørregade, 1165 KØBENHAVN K.
Arab Republic of Egypt	Librairie Kasr El Nil, 38, rue Kasr El Nil, LE CAIRE National Centre for Unesco Publications, 1 Tlaaat Harb Street, Tahrir Square, CAIRO.
Ethiopia	National Commission for Unesco, P.O. Box 2996, ADDIS ABABA.
Finland	Akateeminen Kirjakauppa, 2 Keskuskatu, HELSINKI.
France	Librairie de l'Unesco, place de Fontenoy, 75 PARIS-7e. CCP 12508-48.
French West Indies	Librairie Félix Conseil, 11 rue Perrinon, FORT-DE-FRANCE (Martinique).
Germany (Fed. Rep.)	Verlag Dokumentation, Postfach 148, Jaiserstrasse 13, 8023, MÜNCHEN-PULLACH. *'The Courier' (German edition only):* Bahrenfelder Chaussee 160, HAMBURG-BAHRENFELD. CCP 27 66 50.
Ghana	Presbyterian Bookshop Depot Ltd., P.O. Box 195, ACCRA; Ghana Book Suppliers Ltd., P.O. Box 7869, ACCRA; The University Bookshop of Ghana, ACCRA; The University Bookshop of Cape Coast; The University Bookshop of Legon, P.O. Box 1, LEGON.
Greece	Librairie H. Kauffmann, 28, rue du Stade, ATHENAI; Librairie Eleftheroudakis, Nikkis 4, ATHENAI.
Hong Kong	Swindon Book Co., 13-15 Lock Road, KOWLOON.
Hungary	Akadémiai Könyvesbolt Váci u 22, BUDAPEST V. A.K.V. Könyvtárosok Boltja, Népköztársaság utja 16, BUDAPEST VI.
Iceland	Snaebjörn Jonsson & Co. H. F., Hafnarstracti 9, REYKIAVIK.
India	Orient Longmans Ltd.; Nicol Road, Ballard Estate, BOMBAY 1; 17 Chittaranjan Avenue, CALCUTTA 13; 36a Mount Road, MADRAS 2; 3/5 Asaf Ali Road, NEW DELHI 1. *Sub-depots:* Oxford Book & Stationery Co., 17 Park Street, CALCUTTA 16; *and* Scindia House, NEW DELHI; Publications Section, Ministry of Education and Youth Services, 72 Theatre Communication Building, Connaught Place, NEW DELHI 1.
Indonesia	Indira P.T., Djl. Dr. Sam Ratulangic 37, DJAKARTA.
Iran	Commission nationale iranienne pour l'Unesco, 1/154, avenue Roosevelt, B.P. 1533, TÉHÉRAN.
Iraq	McKenzie's Bookshop, Al-Rashid Street, BAGHDAD; University Bookstore, University of Baghdad, P.O. Box 75, BAGHDAD.
Ireland	The National Press, 2 Wellington Road, Ballsbridge, DUBLIN 4.
Israel	Emanuel Brown, formerly Blumstein's Bookstores: 35 Allenby Road *and* 48 Nachlat Benjamin Street, TEL AVIV; 9 Shlomzion Hamalka Street, JERUSALEM.
Italy	LICOSA (Libreria Commissionaria Sansoni S.p.A.), via Lamarmora 45, casella postale 552, 50121 FIRENZE.
Jamaica	Sangster's Book Stores Ltd., P.O. Box 366, 101 Water Lane, KINGSTON.
Japan	Maruzen Co. Ltd., P.O. Box 5050, Tokyo International, TOKYO.
Kenya	The ESA Ltd., P.O. Box 30167, NAIROBI.
Khmer Republic	Librarie Albert Portail, 14, avenue Boulloche, PHNOM-PENH.
Korea	Korean National Commission for Unesco, P.O. Box Central 64, SEOUL.
Kuwait	The Kuwait Bookshop Co. Ltd., P.O. Box 2942, KUWAIT.
Liberia	Cole & Yancy Bookshops Ltd., P.O. Box 286, MONROVIA.
Libya	Agency for Development of Publication and Distribution, P.O. Box 34-35, TRIPOLI.
Luxembourg	Librairie Paul Bruck, 22 Grande-Rue, LUXEMBOURG.
Malaysia	Federal Publications Sdn. Bhd., Balai Berita, 31 Jalan Riong, KUALA LUMPUR.
Malta	Sapienza's Library, 26 Kingsway, VALLETTA.
Mauritius	Nalanda Co. Ltd, 30 Bourbon Street, PORT-LOUIS.
Mexico	CILA (Centro Interamericano de Libros Académicos), Sullivan 31 *bis*, MÉXICO 4, DF
Monaco	British Library, 30, boulevard des Moulins, MONTE-CARLO.
Netherlands	N.V. Martinus Nijhoff, Lange Voorhout 9, 's-GRAVENHAGE.
Netherlands Antilles	G. C. T. Van Dorp & Co. (Ned. Ant.) N.V., WILLEMSTAD (Curaçao, N.A.).
New Caledonia	Reprex S.A.R.L., B.P. 1572, NOUMÉA.
New Zealand	Government Printing Office, Government Bookshops: Rutland Street, P.O. Box 5344, AUCKLAND; 130 Oxford Terrace, P.O. Box 1721, CHRISTCHURCH; Alma Street, P.O. Box 857, HAMILTON; Princes Street, P.O. Box 1104, DUNEDIN; Mulgrave Street, Private Bag, WELLINGTON.
Niger	Librairie Manclert, B.P. 868, NIAMEY.
Nigeria	The University Bookshop of Ife; The University Bookshop of Ibadan, P.O. Box 286, IBADAN; The University of Nsukka; The University Bookshop of Lagos; The Ahmadu Bello University Bookshop of Zaria.
Norway	*All publications:* Johan Grundt Tanum (Booksellers), Karl Johansgate 43, OSLO 1. *'The Courier' only:* A/S Narvesens Litteraturjeneste, Box 6125, OSLO 6.
Pakistan	The West-Pak Publishing Co. Ltd., Unesco Publications House, P.O. Box 374, G.P.O., LAHORE. *Showrooms:* Urdu Bazaar, LAHORE, and 57-58 Muree Highway, G/6-1, ISLAMABAD. Pakistan Publications Bookshop Sarwar Road, RAWALPINDI; Paribagh, DACCA.
Peru	*'The Courier' only:* Editorial Losada Peruana, apartado 472, LIMA. *Other publications:* Distribuidora Inca S.A., Emilio Althaus 470, Lince, casilla 3115, LIMA.
Philippines	The Modern Book Co., 926 Rizal Avenue, P.O. Box 632, MANILA.
Poland	Osrodek Rozpowzechniania Wydawnictw Naukowych PAN, Palac Kultury i Nauki, WARSZAWA.
Portugal	Dias & Andrade Ltda., Libraria Portugal, rua o Carmo 70, LISBOA.
Southern Rhodesia	Textbook Sales (PVT) Ltd., 67 Union Avenue, SALISBURY.
Romania	I.C.E. LIBRI, Calea Victoriei, no. 126, P.O. Box 134-135, BUCUREŞTI.
Senegal	La Maison du Livre, 13, avenue Roume, B.P. 20-60, DAKAR; Librairie Clairafrique, B.P. 2005, DAKAR; Librairie 'Le Sénégal', B.P. 1594, DAKAR.
Singapore	Federal Publications Sdn Bhd., Times House, River Valley Road, SINGAPORE 9.
South Africa	Van Schaik's Bookstore (Pty.) Ltd., Libri Building, Church Street, P.O. Box 724, PRETORIA.